Hudson-Weems substantiates the **real** catalytic event that unleashed the long inhibited Black rebellion against the viciousness and brutality of White racism. It had preceded the much heralded Montgomery Bus Boycott by one hundred days ... the lynching of Till may no longer be denied as the genesis of the chronology of the Civil Rights Movement.

Talmadge Anderson, Editor-in-Chief
Western Journal of Black Studies

The Till case symbolized the sexual and racial dimensions of oppression which were part of the system of segregation. Her approach to the psychological dimensions of racism is illuminating.

Manning Marable, Ph.D., Professor of History & Director of
African American Studies, Columbia University

Many stories have been written about Bobo, none have told it like it was. The material I gave you was the experience I lived through and watched from the court trial in Sumner, Mississippi. I still have my press card. I am glad I found someone to tell it like I saw it.

Since I cannot find words to express my feelings of appreciation, I will just say thanks, thanks, thanks. [Excerpted from April 1988 telegram sent to author]

Rayfield Mooty (deceased)
Labor Union & Civil Rights Activist

Hudson-Weems has dug relentlessly in...
vealing the stench and ugliness ...
Emmett's death has provided a ...
were trapped in a web of hate.

Mamie Till-Mobley
Mother of Emmett Till

Emmett Till:

The Sacrificial Lamb of the Civil Rights Movement

Clenora Hudson-Weems, Ph.D.

Forewords by James B. Stewart, Ph.D. (2000)
Robert E. Weems. Jr., Ph.D. (1994)

Cover Design by Shirley Woodson

ISBN: 0-911557-20-2
Library of Congress Catalog Number: 94-070313
Third Revised Edition

BEDFORD PUBLISHERS, INC.,
TROY, MICHIGAN, USA 48098-4402

EMMETT TILL: THE SACRIFICIAL LAMB
OF THE CIVIL RIGHTS MOVEMENT
by Clenora Hudson-Weems, Ph.D.
Forewords by James B. Stewart, Ph.D. (2000)
Robert E. Weems. Jr., Ph.D. (1994)

Contributions to American History, African American History, African American Literature, Africana Studies
ISBN: 0-911557-20-2
Library of Congress Catalog Card Number: 94-070313
Third Revised Edition
Second Revised Edition 1995
First Published 1994

Bibliography: p.

History - American History, African American History & Culture,
American Literature
Africana Studies - Politics - Social Studies - Discrimination

1. Title

E. 185.61 H78 1994

Third Revised Edition
Bedford Publishers, Inc.
4198 Carson Drive
Troy, Michigan 48098-4402

Printed in the United States of America
10 9 8 7 6 5 4 3

Other works by author:

Toni Morrison, (co-authored with Wilfred Samuel)

Africana Womanism: Reclaiming Ourselves

Forthcoming:

Soul Mates (a novel)

In memory of

Strong Africana men in my life who have passed on:

My dear father, Matthew Pearson
(June 11, 1924–January 21, 2000)

My uncle, Sylvester Cohran (January 1972)

My uncle, King Cohran (1972)

My cousin, James McGlaun (March 1986)

My uncle, Jeremiah Cohran (1986)

Professor Jonathan Walton (July 1988)

My uncle, George Cohran (August 1989)

Professor Darwin Turner (February 1991)

Professor Richard K. Barksdale (October 1993)

My uncle, John Cohran (November 1993)

My oldest brother, Tommie Lee Hudson
(February 10, 1994)

My uncle, Dudley Cohran (July 1995)

and especially

Mr. Rayfield Mooty (January 1990)
who never gave up on the legacy of Emmett Till.
Without his involvement in the Till case, Emmett
would be just another dead, lynched Black male.

ACKNOWLEDGMENTS

I am eternally indebted to so many who contributed to my being able to complete this project. First, I am grateful to Mr. Rayfield Mooty, the second cousin by marriage of the subject of this project, Emmett "Bobo" Louis Till. Mr. Mooty's keen insights into the lynching of the youth, his undaunted quest for justice and his unyielding participation in the exposure of the murder case, guided me since the early stages of my research. I want to thank Mr. Mooty for having the vision even before I did; without him and his archival materials, this project could not have been realized. I would like to express my extreme gratitude to the inconceivably strong, heroic, dear mother of the "sacrificial lamb" for African-Americans, Mrs. Mamie Till Bradley-Mobley, who willingly and unselfishly gave to me her precious time, her true emotions, and her heartrending story. Mrs. Mobley's strength continues to inspire me; it helps me to truly accept Emmett's fate. I can only hope that my study can somehow shed more light on this case and help to keep Emmett's spirit alive for her and the rest of the world. I am extremely grateful to my Ph.D. committee at the University of Iowa for their expertise, which made possible my May 1988 dissertation, *Emmett Louis Till: The Impetus for the Modern Civil Rights Movement*. The dissertation was the seed for this book. Members of my committee were Dr. Jonathan Walton, Professor of History and my chair and mentor; Dr. Fredrick Woodard, present Chair of the African-American World Studies Program, my second reader and mentor; Dr. John Raeburn, Professor and then Chair of the Department of English; Dr. Linda Kerber, Professor of History and then Chair of the National American Studies Association; and Dr. Richard

Horwitz, Professor and Chair of the American Studies Program. Sincere gratitude goes to the Ford Foundation Doctoral Fellowship Program; the Ford fellowships made my work at the University of Iowa possible. The Foundation gave me the opportunity to present my thesis on Till in a plenary session of a Ford National Conference in Washington, DC in November 1987.

I am indebted to all of my informants for sharing their memories and feelings about the Till lynching as well as to my on- and off-campus colleagues and friends for listening and responding to my interpretation of the Till case, which officially commenced during my first year at the University of Iowa, 1985-86. Gratitude for technical computer expertise during my work on this project goes to Kevin Lemieux. Special gratitude goes to Fern McClanahan and Connie Reece for their invaluable clerical assistance, thereby making the final presentation of this project to my publisher possible. Finally, eternal gratitude goes to God for my family: my parents (Mary and Matthew); my siblings (Tommie, Juanita, Lee, McCray, and Tara), and their spouses and children; my parents-in-law (Robert and Delores); my sisters-in-law (Donna and Delores) and their children; my godson and nephew, Kahli; my daughter, Nima (Sharifa); and my husband, Robert.

Special thanks go to Rayfield Mooty, Mamie Till Mobley, and especially to the *Chicago Defender*, for captivating photographs which made this work come alive.

Contents

List of Photographs

FOREWORD

The year 1953 was notable, in part, because no lynchings were reported. In fact, two successive years had passed without incidences of mob violence directed at African Americans (Brundage, 1993). Such a year had not been experienced since before the end of the civil War. Thus, the Tuskegee Institute felt confident in proclaiming that "lynching as traditionally defined and as a barometer for measuring the status of race relations in the United States, and particularly in the South, seems no longer to be a valid index of such relationships." Unfortunately, this optimistic prediction was shattered by the lynching of Emmett Till in 1955.

As Dr. Clenora Hudson-Weems so forcefully demonstrates, the lynching of Emmett Till became a cornerstone of the modern civil rights movement. It galvanized national attention for at least three reasons. First, consistent with the perspective reflected in the Tuskegee Institute statement, a general belief existed that the sordid practice of lynchings was extinct. Second, Emmett Till's alleged transgressions were deemed insufficiently egregious to warrant such a grotesque execution, even in the eyes of many southern whites. Third, the activism of African American community leaders and the vigilance of the black press created a powerful connection between African Americans residing outside the South and their southern compatriots that could not be muted by the traditional means of intimidation.

The lynching of Emmett Till followed the "new" lynching protocol. Brundage (1993) notes that as the number of lynchings declined during the 1950s their character changed as well. There were fewer instances of barbaric public rituals viewed by large numbers of bystanders involving mutilation of corpses. Instead, small secretive mobs and law enforcement officials acting illegally became increasingly responsible for lynchings. Thus, public authorities assumed more of a direct role in using violence as a mechanism of social control to maintain the system of white supremacy. This changing protocol also blurred the distinction between the concept of "lynching," per se, and certain forms of murder, and contributed to reduced public awareness.

As the number of traditional lynchings declined, the memories of the gross barbarism practiced against African Americans faded. As Brundage (1993, p. 258) observes, "Perhaps nothing about the history of mob violence in the United States is more surprising than how quickly an understanding of the full horror of lynchings was receded from the nation's collective historical memory."

Recent events suggest the need to revisit the sordid history of lynchings to assist in creating a better understanding of, and new strategies to combat, contemporary patterns of public violence directed at people of African descent. The brutal murder/lynching of James Byrd on June 9, 1998 in Jasper, Texas has served as a wake-up call for those who would today, like the Tuskegee Institute did in 1953, assume that mob violence is no longer a valid indicator of the state of race relations. Mr. Byrd was chained to the back of a pickup truck by three white men and dragged to his death. His head, neck, and one arm were found a mile away from his body. He was so horribly mangled that fingerprints were the only means of identification. Two of the perpetrators had white supremacist tattoos on their bodies, and had known ties to the Ku Klux Klan and the Aryan Nation.

Mr. Byrd was apparently a random victim accused of no specific transgressions by his attackers. While there were some cases of random lynchings in the first half of the 20th century, the majority involved charges of various types of disrespect of white women (including reckless eyeballing) or some criminal act. One lynching that bears some similarities to the Byrd case occurred on February 25, 1913 in Marshall, Texas. According to a report that appeared in the February 27, 1913 issue of the *Birmingham News* "two Negroes" were lynched that night and "a Negro named Anderson was hanged by one mob for reasons unknown" (Ginzburg, 1962, pp. 80-81).

Like the case of Emmett Till, the lynching of James Byrd galvanized widespread public reaction. As an example, the NAACP called for a national day of mourning to be held on Sunday, June 14, 1998. In a speech to a large gathering of Baptists, NAACP President and CEO, Kwesi Mfume, declared that the slaying "is reminiscent of the lynchings that took place regularly in this country decades ago. Unfortunately, many Americans have been lulled into the belief that these incidents of hate no longer take place, when in fact, we have seen a steady increase in hate crimes." The NAACP appealed to Attorney General Janet Reno to bring federal charges against the perpetrators under the Hate Crimes Act of 1998 and urged the Congress to pass amendments to strengthen the Hate Crimes Act.

The Byrd case received widespread national attention, in part, because it was perpetrated by a secretive mob and involved elements of the old protocol, i.e., physical mutilation. However, slayings by police authorities, which are more prevalent, have generally provoked regional rather than national responses. The visibility of such slayings is muted by the practice of lumping them into the general category of incidents of policy brutality. One recent case that has received significant media attention is that of Tyisha Miller in Riverside, California. Ms. Miller, who was 19 years old, was shot to death by four policemen while sitting in her locked, disabled car on December 28, 1998. The mortal wounds were two shots to the head and one to the chest.

Similar incidents have occurred across the country. As an example, on March 19, 1998 a former white Detroit police officer was found guilty of beating a black motorist, Malice Green, to death in 1992 with a flashlight. The original guilty verdict was overturned because the jury had viewed the movie *Malcolm X* during a break in deliberations. The fact that the movie begins with a videotape of the beating of Rodney king was deemed to be prejudicial. The King beating occurred approximately 20 months prior to the killing of Green.

As a final example, Johnny Gammage was stopped by police outside of Pittsburgh on October 12, 1995. He was driving a Jaguar sedan owned by his cousin and business partner, professional football defensive lineman Ray Seals. When Gammage stepped out of the car he was carrying a cellular phone that police claim they thought was a gun. A struggle ensued between Gammage and five police officers with the end result that Mr. Gammage died of suffocation caused by pressure on his back and neck. The officers were acquitted of charges of involuntary manslaughter.

Another case involved twenty-two-year-old Amadou Diallo of West Africa. On February 3, 1999 while returning home to his apartment, four white New York police officers shot the unarmed Guinean native to death. On that fateful morning, at least forty-one shots were fired. The case was tried in Albany, New York and the jury comprised of eight whites and four blacks returned a unanimous not-guilty verdict.

Interestingly, none of the cases described directly involved one of the key dynamics of traditional lynching—

outrage at the possibility that an interracial sexual encounter occurred. As noted by Messerschmidt (1998, p. 149):

> *The collective struggle for supremacy over African American men was a means with which to gain recognition and reward for one's masculinity, and a means with which to solve the gender and race problems of accountability. Mob violence was a situational resource for surmounting a perceived threat by reasserting the social dominance of white men. Lynching the 'bestial black rapist' reconstructed masculinities in hierarchial terms of essential, biological inequality. In short, these white-supremacist men gained status, reputation, and self-respect through participation in mob lynchings that symbolically—especially through the ritual of castration—disclaimed any African American male rights to citizenry.*

In many respects, the O.J. Simpson case epitomized the worst fears of white supremacists. Here was a case where an "uppity" black male was married to a white woman, whom he abused and allegedly murdered. Simpson's acquittal has clearly contributed to a mindset whereby civil authorities are seen by white supremacists as no longer being capable of controlling black males. This mindset has the potential to engender more acts of mob violence. This possibility is enhanced by the proliferation of hate groups whose ideology, in part, focuses on the loss of white male privilege and status. Many of these groups have strategic plans to perpetrate acts of mob violence against outsiders. This phenomenon is much more ominous than the old lynching protocols operative during the first half of the 20th century, which generally reflected some degree of spontaneity.

How are people committed to violence reduction and positive patterns of inter-group intercourse to respond to these developments? A useful starting point is the re-examination of the history of racially-motivated lynchings. Thus, Professor Hudson-Weems' reconsideration of the impact of the lynching of Emmett Till on the modern Civil Rights Movement is an important foundation upon which to build. There are, in fact, the early stirrings of a new movement to counter the emergent pattern of violence directed at people of African descent. This new movement can learn valuable lessons from strategies used to make the Till case a linchpin of efforts to reduce the use of physical violence as a means of social control.

This new movement is taking a variety of forms. One of particular significance to the perspective presented above involves efforts to uncover the details of earlier incidents of mob violence directed at peoples of African descent. The film, *Rosewood,* is an example of the effective use of the visual media to pursue this goal. It explores the Rosewood Massacre, which took place in the northern Florida town of Rosewood over a period of a week, beginning the night of December 31, 1922, and lasting into the first days of 1923. On the political front, in 1997 the Tulsa Race Riot Commission was formed to investigate the circumstances surrounding a riot that occurred in 1921, one of the worst race riots in U.S. history, which may have claimed several hundred black lives. The riot was sparked by false charges that an African-American male had assaulted a white woman in an elevator. In the wake of the riot some 1,400 homes and businesses in Tulsa's Greenwood district, a prosperous area known as "Black Wall Street," were destroyed. As a final example, Councilman Lawrence Johnson of Waco, Texas is seeking an official statement denouncing the 1916 lynching of Jesse Washington, a 17-year-old black man, known as the "Waco Horror."

Washington was hanged over a bonfire and mutilated on the City Hall lawn after being convicted of the murder of a white woman. In addition to the denunciation of the incident, Councilman Johnson seeks a public commitment from the city's leaders to pursue racial harmony.

Such a public acknowledgment of the horrific history of lynching and its ongoing impact on contemporary race relations on a national scale is a necessary starting point for excising the forces that encourage public violence in general, and lynchings in particular, from the body politic. If such a movement is not initiated, the country runs the risk, in the words of James Baldwin, of facing "the fire next time." Professor Hudson-Weems' masterful treatment of the Emmett Till case can serve as an important starting point for undertaking an authentic process of racial reconciliation.

James B. Stewart, Ph.D
Professor of Labor Studies and Industrial Relations
and African and African American Studies
Pennsylvania State University
President, National Council for Black Studies
Spring 2000

REFERENCES

Brundage, W. Fitzhugh. *Lynching in the New South, Georgia and Virginia, 1880–1930*. Urbana, IL: University of Illinois Press, 1993.

Ginzburg, Ralph. *100 Years of Lynchings*. Baltimore, MD: Black Classic Press, 1962.

Messerschmidt, James. *Men Victimizing Men: The Case of Lynching, 1865-1900*. In *Masculinities and Violence* (pp. 125-151), edited by Lee Bowker. Thousand Oaks, CA: Sage Publications, 1998.

FOREWORD

If Emmett Till's resurrection to historical prominence does nothing else, it should stimulate reflection upon the unpalatable, yet significant, role of lynchings in the African-American historical experience. Notwithstanding Supreme Court Justice Clarence Thomas' reference to his confirmation hearings as a "high-tech lynching," in contemporary America, lynchings are phenomena that many persons, especially those under forty years of age, have difficulty visualizing. Just as many young Americans literally cannot imagine a time when African-Americans were denied the vote and forced to sit on the back of buses, many, likewise, cannot imagine the fear that lynchings generated among southern blacks during the Jim Crow era. Unfortunately, as we observe a growing entrenchment of conservative forces in present-day American society, African-Americans, especially, need to be reminded of the maxim: "those who don't know their past are doomed to repeat it."

Perceptive individuals, for several years, have recognized distinct parallels between the first Reconstruction period, which followed the Civil War and the second Reconstruction period, which is often referred to as the modern-day Civil Rights Movement. During the late nineteenth century, European-Americans ultimately decided that the issue of African-American rights should be placed on the "back burner" of national priorities. Likewise, European-Americans during the late twentieth century expressed a similar sentiment by electing arch-conservative Ronald Reagan to two terms as President and catapulting Reagan's Vice-President, George Bush, into the White House.

The parallels between the late nineteenth and twentieth centuries do not stop there. African-Americans, in response to growing white hostility during the late nineteenth century, became increasingly concerned with self-help programs centered around economic development and cooperation. Similarly, in recent years, the call for increased business activity and racial self-sufficiency has accelerated in African-American enclaves.

The contemporary increase of violent attacks against African-Americans represents the most chilling parallel between the African-American experience of the late nineteenth and twentieth centuries. For example, the National Institute Against Prejudice and Violence report on "Campus Ethnoviolence" cited instances of racial harassment and violence taking place on more than 250 college and university campuses between 1986 and 1988. This is especially disturbing on two counts. First, it appears that a hardening of racial attitudes is occurring among young white Americans. Moreover, and this is frightening, the collective position of late-twentieth-century African-Americans could be devastated by a dramatic resurgence of overt anti-black sentiment.

Unlike the black community of the late nineteenth century, the labor of contemporary African-Americans is no longer needed in the United States. Although the years immediately following slavery witnessed attempts to recruit Europeans to replace African-American workers, these efforts proved unsuccessful. Consequently, southern landowners and industrialists had to continue their historic reliance upon African-American labor.

In recent decades, however, automation, along with the relocation of American industries in low-waged Third World countries, has resulted in a marked decrease in the number of unskilled and semi-skilled jobs historically held by African-Americans. In addition, the United States Supreme Court now seems bent upon dismantling Affirmative Action guidelines. Consequently, even the job security of skilled and educated African-Americans appears threatened.

Considering that Africans were initially brought to this country to labor for Europeans, if that labor is no longer needed, what does America have in store for its increasingly "obsolete" African-American population? David Duke's recent rise to national prominence, as unthinkable as it seems, may provide insight as to how the United States will deal with this vital question.

Although this former Klansman and Nazi claims to have repudiated his past, his 1991 campaign for Governor of Louisiana featured carefully worded denunciations of Louisiana's unemployed African-American community. Although structural considerations appear to be the primary reasons for widespread African-American unemployment in contemporary America, Duke portrayed blacks as lazy drug addicts whose idleness is being rewarded by welfare payments. Moreover, Duke contended that this transfer of funds to "undeserving" African-Americans threatened the economic security of European-Americans.

When David Duke and his ilk create scenarios claiming that African-Americans are the cause of European-Americans' economic problems (either through welfare or Affirmative Action) he, and others like him, create a situation that tends to promote and excuse violent attacks against blacks. For instance, none of us has to be reminded of Rodney King's beating by Los Angeles police and their subsequent acquittal (of police brutality charges) by an all-white jury in Simi Valley, California.

Clenora Hudson-Weems' multi-faceted study of the lynching of Emmett Louis Till comes at an important time in American history. Perhaps, this thorough and moving depiction of America's "ugly" past may sensitize enough of us to actively work toward avoiding a potentially "ugly" American future.

Robert E. Weems, Jr., Ph.D.
University of Missouri-Columbia
Department of History
Fall 1994

Preface

September 1955: Conversation between Mary and Matthew Pearson, parents of Clenora Hudson, and her response.

> *"Lord have mercy. Pitiful. Matthew, did you hear about that child? Those folks killed that poor, little boy 'cause he whistled at a white woman, they say."*
>
> *"That black kid? Emmett. I think that's what they say his name was. Yea, Mary, they been talking about that all day on the job, especially the black porters. They say that's all they're talking about from Chicago to New Orleans. And they did him worst than they would do a dog, just 'cause he whistled at a white woman."*

I shall never forget it as long as I live. I was ten, just four years Emmett's junior. I can't explain how I felt. It was a horrific incident. All I wanted to do was sleep. If I could just sleep, I could escape, at least for the moment, only to awaken again to the harsh reality of it. I felt so empty, void, so very insignificant.

A child's murder can be so disarming. Devastating. How can another kid, or anyone explain it? How can one react, respond, or take a position? Some cried, some cursed, and many said, "No more." Others frowned, recoiled and again took the stand, "No more." Indeed, it is no surprise that an atrocity such as Emmett's death could and did move a nation to the point of no return. There was no going back. No matter the cost—life or death—this sort of thing must never happen again.

Like many Americans, I thought I had buried Till in 1955. But the anger, fear, and emptiness I felt as a child looking at Emmett's mutilated face in a *Jet* magazine photograph was conjured up again, some thirty years later, when, for a brief moment in October 1984, I thought my child, too, had been kidnapped.

I had been living in Delaware since 1980, working as director of Black Studies and professor of English at Delaware State College. My daughter, Sharifa, then nearly five years old, was playing as usual on a Saturday morning in the back of our place with two little neighborhood friends, Megan and Brent. I was upstairs, lying on my bed, talking on the telephone with a colleague when Sharifa ran into the room to give me that occasional kiss and say, "I love you, Mommy," before returning, I assumed, to her playmates.

After about fifteen minutes, I realized some time had passed since I had checked on her, so I abruptly ended the conversation with my friend. When I got outside, I saw that the kids had left, and I assumed that without permission Sharifa had gone into their house with them.

Annoyed, because I thought she'd disobeyed my orders of never leaving home without permission, I went to their door and asked the babysitter to tell her to come out. To my surprise, the babysitter responded that Sharifa had never come in and had returned home earlier. Realizing that she had not been seen for some time, I ran around the block looking for her, thinking this was most unusual.

After returning in a blue funk to my neighbor's house to make absolutely sure that they had not overlooked Sharifa, I ran back home, kicked open the front door, and I struck it with my fist, crying out, "Damn, they got her!" Calling her name, I frantically searched the house from basement to upstairs, checking closets and looking under the furniture.

Finally, feeling defeated, I returned to my room and collapsed on the bed, thinking how I should call both my parents and the police. And just at that moment, I noticed the small mound on the far side of my king-size bed and hastily pulled back the covers; there was Sharifa. Apparently, she had climbed into bed and fallen asleep without my noticing it, while I was talking on the phone.

Many things ran through my mind during those brief minutes of terror, imagining what she might be going through in the hands of abductors. It was then that—out of the blue—Emmett flashed back in my mind. What his mother must have gone through when she first heard he was missing! Unlike mine, her fears had become reality. In my elation over Sharifa's safety, I once again put Till's memory to rest.

Nine months later, in the fall of 1985, I went to the University of Iowa; since the time of the scare with my daughter, I had been seriously considering Till as a case study. But the actual probing of the incident did not commence until I was back home in Memphis during the Christmas vacation from late December 1985 to mid-January 1986.

I took a trip to the courthouse in Sumner, Mississippi, where the murder and kidnapping trials, or mockeries of trials, had been held in 1955. There I purchased all the surviving papers of the proceedings, which were few in number since the court transcripts had been destroyed. I was told by the clerk that they were not required to keep them.

At that time, I also discussed the case with people both in Mississippi and in Memphis, and I was led to search out Till's second cousin Rayfield Mooty for an interview. Mooty, then a retired labor-union leader who is now deceased (January 12, 1990), was the one primarily responsible for calling the case to the public's attention, along with Emmett's mother, Mamie Bradley-Mobley. Both Mamie, an attractive sixty-six-year-old former public school teacher, and the vibrant eighty-year-old Mooty lived in Chicago.

I first interviewed Mooty in Chicago in April 1986, and as our day-long conversation extended well into a Saturday night, he reiterated how Emmett's case was bigger than anyone had ever acknowledged. He forewarned me that the chapter of dissertation I intended to devote to Till would soon become insufficient.

The conversations I had then with Mr. Mooty—and a couple of other former labor-union workers, Ola Kennedy, Curtis Strong, and Edward Young—along with the materials and photographs Mr. Mooty shared with me persuaded me that Till's lynching was an extremely significant factor in the Civil Rights Movement, in spite of the popularized consensus that it was the Montgomery bus boycott that set the stage for the movement. The Till incident graphically portrays the ugliness of racism—its violence and victimization. It has been lastingly imprinted on the collective American consciousness, but this horror has been seriously underplayed as a stimulus for the movement.

Due to the nature of cultural taboos, Till's behavior toward Carolyn Bryant often drew ambiguous reactions from people. After all, Till was an outsider, a black northerner, who had failed to conduct himself properly according to the rules of southern etiquette. These factors made the Till case somewhat embarrassing for civil rights' leaders, especially for liberal whites and the black bourgeoisie. Whites have feared what might be brought about by full exposure of such a vicious example of institutionalized racism in America. Even the well-intentioned have felt more comfortable venerating a mature woman who refused to surrender her seat on a bus to a white man rather than a young black man who was murdered for whistling at a white woman. Black leaders have feared that the sexual overtones of the case might jeopardize the standing they did have with the dominant culture.

Historians, too, have shoveled earth over Emmett Till. They invariably focus on Rosa Parks, morally the less troubling of the two. Unlike Till, Parks was not the victim of a brutal racist act. Her deliberate and courageous stand has simply proven more palatable than the horrible image of a mutilated Till.

In an interview with Mamie, a day-long session at her Chicago home on January 6, 1988, she confirmed what I had concluded to be the legacy of Till. Till has been permanently etched in the mind of American society, and he did, as he continues to do even in his death, ignite rage against and intolerance for racial atrocities.

Who knows better than the people what ushered them into the Civil Rights Movement? Seeing how futile it was to rely on the traditional resources of the historian, my approach has been both personal and grassroots: I interviewed the "secondary victims," Till's relatives, his close friends, and members of that vast portion of the general public who were able to empathize with Emmett. The impromptu testimonies of individual African-Americans and some whites that inform my book echo the importance of Till's murder in the formation of their personal commitment to civil rights.

The impetus that Till's murder gave to African-American activists clearly places him, with others, at the head of the Civil Rights Movement, not in the background, as is the case of the only existing monument to him, which is located in Denver, Colorado. There Till yet stands in the shadow of Dr. Martin Luther King, Jr. A movement obviously needs its dynamic leaders, its courageous individuals, but the people also need the searing memories branded into their consciousness by suffering victims like Emmett Till.[1]

[1] Much of this narration comes from my 1988 article entitled "The Unearthing of Emmett Till: A Compelling Process." Permission to use this source was granted by the *Iowa Alumni Review*.

Introduction

Emmett Till died [in 1955] six years before the first "freedom riders" arrived in Mississippi to fight for integration, seven years before James Meredith became the first black man to enroll at the University of Mississippi, eight years before state NAACP Field Secretary Medgar Evers was shot to death in Jackson and nine years before three civil rights workers died during the "freedom summer" of 1964.

—Joe Atkins[1]

The Modern Civil Rights Movement

The modern Civil Rights Movement of the fifties and sixties was characterized not only by individual rebellion and spontaneous unorganized riots, but also by organized protest, including march-in and sit-in demonstrations. During this fervent era, African-Americans were still the victims of many forms of oppression: social and economic discrimination, inferior education and housing, and political disenfranchisement. African-Americans continued to struggle against racism, as they had struggled against the institution of slavery. The struggle for civil rights, however, differed from earlier forms of black resistance in that

[1] Joe Atkins, "Slain Chicago Youth was a 'Sacrificial Lamb'" in *The Clarion-Ledger Daily News* (Jackson MS, 25 Aug. 1985), p. 1.

there were more organized protests with coordinated efforts and communication from state to state. A large scale resistance occurred in the North and in the South simultaneously. For the first time in history, the struggle received national and even international attention in media coverage. "By his death, Emmett Till took racism out of the textbooks and editorials and showed it to the world in its true dimensions."[2] The struggle of the fifties and the sixties was different from earlier periods of protest and created a distinct period in the history of American culture.

Most traditional historians mark the beginning of the modern Civil Rights Movement with the 1956 Montgomery bus boycott, sparked by the refusal of Rosa Parks, a seamstress and Montgomery secretary for the National Association for the Advancement of Colored People (NAACP), to relinquish her bus seat to a white man on December 1, 1955. This simple act and its repercussions led to organized demonstrations spearheaded by Rev. Dr. Martin Luther King, Jr., whose name became synonymous with the bus boycott and the Civil Rights Movement. Other historians go further back about a year and a half to May 17, 1954, and mark the start of the movement with the 1954 U.S. Supreme Court decision *Brown versus Topeka, Kansas Board of Education*, which ruled unconstitutional the "separate but equal" public school system, thereby officially ordering desegregation.

Remarkably, however, no historian has ever fully gauged the impact on the American conscience of the widely publicized lynching, on August 28, 1955, of a fourteen-year-old black Chicago youth, Emmett (BoBo) Louis Till, and the subsequent "trial" of Till's assailants. The incident shocked and stunned some; it instilled terror in

---

[2] *The Commonweal* magazine editorial, Sept. 23, 1955, quoted in Joe Atkins, *The Clarion-Ledger*, August 25, 1985.

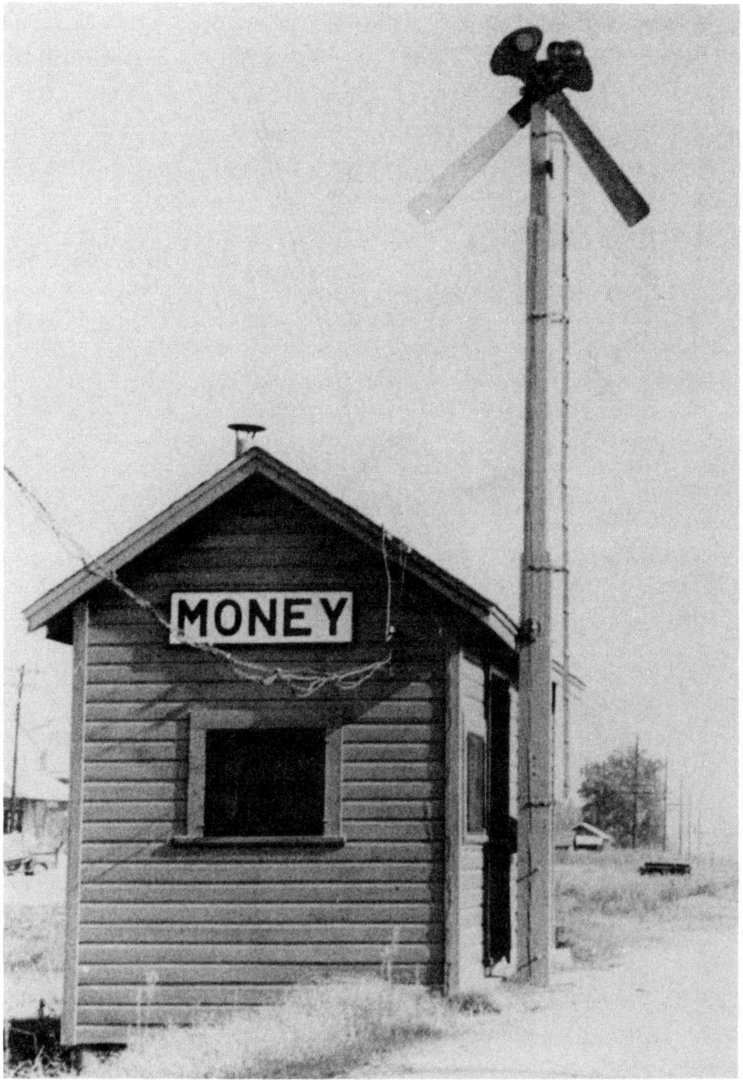

Photograph 1. **Train station, town of Till incident—Money, Mississippi.** [*Chicago Defender*]

Photograph 2. **Grocery store, scene of "crime".** [*Chicago Defender*]

countless others. Widely covered by national and international news, the incident and its aftermath culminated in widespread national social upheaval in black communities across the nation (demonstrated in Chicago during the display of Till's body) and fermented demands for justice and equality.

As we reevaluate the modern Civil Rights Movement, we must consider the countless unsung heroes as well as the sung heroes, whose ideas offer strategies for lessening the ills, demands, and concerns within the African-American community. We cannot adequately reflect on Rev. Dr. Martin Luther King, Jr., the symbol of the Civil Rights Movement, without reflecting on the established mother of the movement, Mrs. Rosa Parks. She heroically refused to relinquish her bus seat to a white man on December 1, 1955, which was the seed for the year-long 1956 Montgomery bus boycott. And likewise, we cannot adequately reflect on the Montgomery bus boycott without reflecting on and remembering the infamous lynching of Till, just three months and three days before Mrs. Parks's personal demonstration. Till's brutal lynching in Mississippi, on August 28, 1955, was undoubtedly impressed on the minds of the Alabamians, giving them strength to carry the boycott through. Indeed, the image of Till, permanently etched in American consciousness, could not die, thereby setting the stage for the boycott. Because Till's bloated face was the embodiment of the ugliness of American racism, America found the need and desire to attach itself to a more palatable incident.

Many organizations rallied to support the black community. Numerous speaking engagements of Till's mother, Mamie Bradley, and Rayfield Mooty, a second cousin of the victim, were sponsored by the labor unions, the NAACP, black churches, and other organizations. The exposure of the public to this information about the incident significantly impacted on society. There was a definite increase in the activities of national organizations, as demonstrated in the successful campaign launched by the NAACP in particular, which reportedly "collected $3,001.50 from the attendants [at the Baltimore NAACP rally protesting Till's lynching alone] and gained hundreds of new memberships."[3] This collective financial support could help to weld a broad collective front to combat racial injustices.

It became clear to blacks that they needed to participate in and to contribute financially to the movement to secure their civil rights. For the first time since its formative period, membership and financial support for the NAACP sky-rocketed. (Prior to this incident, it had been on a downhill turn.) The response of the black community, in particular the organized mobilization of organizations to combat racism, points to the Till outrage as having contributed significantly to the rise of the Civil Rights Movement. Although histories of the Civil Rights Movement skip over the importance of the Till case, the event did much to dramatize a new era of demands from black people in the United States.

Background and World War I

African-Americans had since slavery gathered in secret to rebel against atrocities of the slave system. They had consciously orchestrated the slave revolts led by Gabriel Prosser and Nat Turner in the early nineteenth century. In more recent times, specifically the periods be-

---

[3] "100,000 Across Nation Protest Till Lynching," The *New York Times,* October 1, 1955, p. 40.

fore and after World War I, forces created an inevitable racial clash. Those included the great migration of blacks from the South to the North during the World War I period, the expectations of the black soldiers who had fought for this country and had received better treatment in foreign lands, the anxiety during the Depression over unemployment and labor-management conflicts, and the threat of black political power.

In *From Plantation to Ghetto,* August Meier and Elliott Rudwick survey some of the crucial features in African-American history that laid down the foundation for the modern Civil Rights Movement. They focus on what the blacks themselves were doing to improve their conditions, a key stimulus for the Great Migration just before World War I. They bring out the aspirations of black Americans, which have become an important part of the fabric of American life. They conduct an analysis of the movement of blacks from rural to urban and from South to North. Identifying the migration as a major watershed in African-American history, they conclude: "It appears that the peaks of black movement were during periods of acute economic crisis—toward the close of the depression of the 1870's, at the height of the Populist-agitation around 1890, and perhaps again during the minor depression that hit the United States on the eve of the First World War."[4]

The number of black migrants in the North was startling, about one half million, during the World War I period, and this radically changed urban life. Racial hostility toward blacks ensued, and the problems of adjustment for black southern immigrants were inevitable. There was the growing problem of housing and job competition, which intensified the tensions between the races. More important

---

[4] August Meier and Elliott Rudwick, *From Plantation to Ghetto* (New York: Hill and Wang, 1966), p. 214.

according to Meier and Rudwick, "In addition to these external pressures from whites, there were also internal forces among blacks that contributed to the increasing ghettoization of Negro life. Motivated by pride, habit, and the need for mutual protection from rejection, Negroes found a refuge within their own community."[5] They concluded that the Great Migration had indelibly impacted on black life in both a negative and a positive way. Hence, that mass of blacks in the North had created a foundation for a political base for blacks. "Though no one realized it at the time, and though other factors were also essential in bringing about the events that were to follow, by mid-century the vote of the black ghetto in the North had reached the proportions that made possible the civil rights revolution."[6] This is of importance to this study, as the distinction between northern and southern blacks is fundamental to the Till case.

William Tuttle also examines and discusses the economic, political, and social milieu in his book *Race Riot: Chicago and the Red Summer of 1919*. He places his subject, which is the incident of the drowning of a black Chicago youth on the white section of the Chicago beach, in the context of the history of the city. He concludes that both blacks (who were no longer going to accept second-class citizenship) and whites (who were not willing to surrender their superior stance in this society) had reached the end of their toleration level. The beach incident became a catalyst for expressing their hostility: "Fundamental to an explanation of the Chicago riot, and thus an essential beginning point, is the World War I migration—that influx of Southern black people which doubled the city's black

[5] Meier and Rudwick, p. 218.
[6] Meier and Rudwick, p. 250.

population in less than three years, thereby bringing to a climax racial tensions and animosities in labor, housing, and politics that had threatened to erupt for years."[7] Like Meier and Rudwick, Tuttle places the Great Migration at the center of the racial conflicts and changes in the Northern city.

Garveyism

During the early stages of this disillusionment of blacks after World War I, a black nationalist from Jamaica who reached the peak of his career in the twenties, Marcus Garvey, offered black nationalism and national independence as an alternative to Booker T. Washington's accommodationist policy. According to Tony Martin's *Race First*, "He [Garvey] had succeeded as no one else had in gathering up the worldwide feelings of dismay at the loss of independence and defiance against colonialism and oppression, which characterized the 'New Negro' spirit of the age."[8] Martin portrays Garvey as a symbol of black pride and resistance against unjust practices toward black Americans. He asserts that the new breed of militant blacks, most of whom were members of the working class, were disillusioned with Washington and, thus, were receptive to Garveyism. In *Philosophy and Opinions of Marcus Garvey*, a collection of his orations and writings that outline his oftentimes misunderstood philosophy, Garvey proposes the solution to the central issue for black people, the so-called Negro problem:

---

[7] William Tuttle, *Race Riot: Chicago and the Red Summer of 1919* (New York: Atheneum Publisher, 1970), p. 156.

[8] Tony Martin, *Race First* (Dover, Mass.: The Majority Press, 1976), p. 13.

> *As far as Negroes are concerned, in America we have the problem of lynching, peonage and disenfranchisement ... We are determined to solve our own problem, by redeeming our Motherland Africa from the hands of alien exploiters and found there a government, a nation of our own, strong enough to lend protection to the members of our race scattered all over the world, and to compel the respect of the nations and races of the earth.*[9]

The Great Depression and World War II

After Garvey's heyday came the Great Depression, a critical period for blacks who were accurately described as "the last hired and the first fired." *The Negro in Depression and War: Prelude to Revolution 1930-1945*, a collection of articles edited by Bernard Sternsher, examines how the Great Depression and World War II indelibly shaped African-American life, particularly as the foundation for the modern Civil Rights Movement. The essays shed light on the historical struggles and gains of blacks during critical periods, emphasizing protests and the participation of blacks in the labor movement. Paving the way for today's black Americans and demonstrating the importance of creating strategies for blacks for upward mobility, Mary McLeod Bethune's essay, "My Secret Talks with FDR," illustrates the strategic precision of President Franklin D. Roosevelt. Although I cannot condone Roosevelt's failure to sign the Anti-Lynching Bill, just as I cannot overlook his

---

[9] Amy Jacques-Garvey, ed., *Philosophy and Opinions of Marcus Garvey* (San Francisco, CA: Julian Richardson Associates, Publishers, 1967), p. 52.

refusal to save refugees from fascist Germany, I do recognize Roosevelt's attempt to explain how and why he proceeds, in general, to effect improvements for the black populace and how his procedure works out better in the long run: "Mrs. Bethune, if we do that now, we'll hurt our program over there. We must do this thing stride by stride, but leaving no stone unturned."[10] She realizes that during these particularly trying times for blacks, not to mention the financial crunch for whites, gradual progress was the most that could be expected. Indeed, it was not until World War II that economic relief came in sight.

In spite of the financial relief resulting from World War II, blacks were still experiencing extreme job discrimination. Finally, A. Philip Randolph, a prominent labor-union leader, threatened a March on Washington, which was scheduled to take place on July 1, 1941. This was a movement to protest the unfair treatment of blacks in matters of employment. When President Franklin D. Roosevelt was advised of this planned demonstration, he issued Executive Order #8802, which banned discrimination against blacks in employment, particularly concerning government contracts. He appointed an outfit to oversee it, the first Fair Employment Practices Committee ensuring fair employment. But "it was not until the threat of the March grew to major proportions, the date of its scheduled demonstration drawing closer and attracting increasing attention in the 'race' press, that Negro leaders were again given personal access to President Roosevelt."[11] This points to the power of mass movements and the significance of

---

[10] Mary McLeod Bethune, "My Secret Talks with FDR" in Bernard Sternsher's *The Negro in Depression and War* (Chicago: Quadrangle Books, 1969), p. 56.

[11] Herbert Garfinkel, *When Negroes March* (New York: Atheneum, 1973), p. 38.

an interaction between the black masses and the federal government to effect changes, a feature that has continued to be a key issue in successful modern social movements.

The war economy improved conditions for blacks. Before the forties were over, the Armed Forces were desegregated, thereby further reinforcing a sense of hope for black Americans; however, the struggle was not over. Black Americans were determined to realize their rightful place in American society as full-fledged citizens, "endowed with certain inalienable rights."

The Effect of the Till Case

The struggles in the twenties, thirties, and forties created a militant attitude within the African-American community that prepared blacks for future combat against white racism. They foreshadowed what was to come in the fifties and the sixties. The Great Migration, World War I, Garveyism, the March on Washington, and World War II dramatically demonstrated blacks uniting for social change. Before the fifties, however, the masses of black Americans had never united in a concerted effort to gain racial parity as they did during the modern Civil Rights Movement.

Like earlier events that unified the black movement, the Till case was a unifying cause around which countless Americans rallied to challenge the assault on humanity. The case evoked strong empathy, particularly because of the victimization of a child, whom the murderers had reduced to "nigger," making the murder a matter of color alone, with no demonstration of age consciousness. The violation of the rights of blacks, and more important, the threat to the security of childhood were at the heart of the matter.

Two issues surface in this reexamination. First, the case was unique in publicizing the degradation of the lives of blacks in the South. Second, the Till case undermined black northerners' false sense of security, their illusion that a relatively better social status and better education in the North insulated them against Jim Crow terrorism. The brutal racism of the Till case raised the consciousness of the black masses and their sympathizers, North and South, underlining the political and social powerlessness of blacks within the American system. It pointed once again to the need for the enfranchisement of blacks as full-fledged American citizens, a crucial concern of the Civil Rights Movement.

The Till case galvanized people in the North (such as Congressman Charles Diggs of Detroit, Michigan), to go South in order to participate in exposing the case and prosecuting the murderers. After going through the traditional channels of the court system, African-Americans involved in the attempt to bring to justice the malefactors and those who sympathized with their aims were disillusioned by the acquittal of the alleged murderers by the jury. The need for alternative strategies was made clear. The Montgomery bus boycott, which began a brief three months after the trial, illustrates this phenomenon. Because the influential Brotherhood of Sleeping Car Porters had focused national and international attention on the Till lynching (organizing rallies and speaking engagements with Mamie Bradley and Rayfield Mooty), the black masses, in particular, followed the case closely. Blacks everywhere felt intense sympathy for Mrs. Bradley and realized the need for remedies other than through the courts and the legal system to create changes in race relations. All over the United States, blacks in record numbers joined mass demonstrations and national organizations, old and new, to demonstrate their allegiance to the evolving Civil Rights Movement.

The activities associated with the new Civil Rights Movement bore a direct relationship to the effect the Till case had on the American people. The media documented the upheaval. In a comparison of the newspaper handling of the Till murder trial, Warren Breed studied eleven newspapers, Negro and white. He found that qualitative analysis showed North-South and Negro-white differences to some degree. For example, he found that:

> *Southern papers almost never mentioned the existence of caste-like race relations. Northern papers did ... Southern papers apparently taboo 'think pieces' about southern race relations, relying entirely on immediate 'news' ...*
>
> *Much of the southern press omits the "Mr." and "Mrs." before names of Negroes. Mrs. Bradley was referred to as Mamie Bradley, Mamie, Mayme, the Bradley woman, the Chicago woman, and the woman. In the North she was Mrs. Bradley ...*
>
> *The Negro weeklies dramatized the story by investing its characters with emotions ... Finally, the case was employed as a wedge to step up the appeal for Negroes to register and vote, all over the country, and to join the NAACP; and the Negro press much more frequently than the white referred to the three other killings of Negroes in Mississippi during 1955.*[12]

Television was especially effective. This new media source brought the Till case, the Montgomery bus boycott, and

---

[12] Warren Breed, "Comparative Newspaper Handling of the Emmett Till Case," *Journalism Quarterly* (Summer 1958): 295, 296.

civil rights demonstrations into the homes of countless Americans of all colors and ethnic groups. The growing outrage and impatience with American racism encouraged violent and nonviolent confrontation with institutional and cultural discrimination. The momentum established the mind-set of blacks around the nation. People recognized the atrocity as something they would not tolerate. The Till case was a catalyst for the explosion, given the timing of the events, the swelling tension (such as the critical voter registration drives throughout the South and particularly in Mississippi), and the social rage and political upheaval (such as resistance to poll taxes and testing requirements at city, county, and state levels). The Till case exemplified one of the most dynamic forces of its time.

> *In nineteen hundred and fifty-five, Emmett Till was found dead in Tallahatchie River, and they had newspapers from all over the continent North America, some from India, and it was the best advertised lynching that I had ever heard. Personally, I think this was the beginning of the Civil Rights Movement in Mississippi in the twentieth century ... From that point on, Mississippi began to move.*[13]

Unfortunately, however, this observation has not been incorporated into the traditional annals of American history. There is a compelling need to rediscover this appalling episode and to bring to the forefront this chapter in American and African-American history.

---

[13] Amzie Moore, quoted in Howell Raines, *My Soul Is Rested*, pp. 234-35.

The Purpose of This Study

Conventional interpretations of the Till murder case before Juan Williams's *Eyes on the Prize* do not recognize the significance of the episode. It has not been given its proper place in history, and its true significance to the Civil Rights Movement has yet to be established. Williams's work makes a positive effort in introducing Till and his historical significance. *Eyes on the Prize* presents the Till case as a major focus of the first episode, called "The Beginnings," and this is indeed significant because of the lack of historical attention by traditional historians. This is a beginning.

This research, however, elaborates on the significance of Till and serves as a comprehensive written commemoration in honor of a sacrificial lamb. This memorial is long overdue considering the dearth of attention to the Till case in traditional documentation. Till receives only one reference in John Hope Franklin's *From Slavery to Freedom* in a catalogue of black victims during that era. Nowhere is Till mentioned in Kenneth G. Goode's *From Africa to the United States and Then: A Concise Afro-American History*. Peter M. Bergman's *The Chronological History of the Negro in America* lists Till with two other victims of lynchings in Mississippi in 1955. Likewise, Albert Blaustein's and Robert Zangrando's *Civil Rights and the American Negro* makes only one passing reference to Till as an example of white intimidation. No reference is made to Till in Benjamin Quarles's *The Negro in the Making of America*. One sentence on the case appears in Mary Berry and John Blassingame's *Long Memory: The Black Experience in America*, an allusion to the American taboo against the black man and the white woman. Vincent Harding's *The Other American Revolution* makes no reference to Till. Given the consciousness-raising impact of this case on American society and the world in general, and the subsequent mass resistance to the denial of the civil rights of African-Americans, the Till case proves to be seminal. The omission of this data, whether consciously orchestrated or not, prevents standard histories from accurately presenting essential fundamental material. A fuller knowledge of the Till case is required for an accurate perception of the Civil Rights Movement. Such a suppression subverts American cultural history. In other words, in ignoring African-American history, American history is necessarily distorted.

This study is conducted from the "bottom up," relying upon the testimonies of the victims. This is a broader framework than that used by most established historians. The perspective of the members of this group is vital to an alternative interpretation of the movement. Because the views of marginal people, who are politically and economically disenfranchised in relation to this case, have not yet been given their due in traditional histories, the analysis of the Till case and American history is incomplete. The contention is that the perspective of the oppressed, unlike that of the oppressors, will not be dictated by a need to maintain the status quo, and their input may be a more reliable account of the case, thereby making it possible for its true impact to be discovered. While the victims cannot be summarily exempted from prejudices, they would be less inclined to support an established tradition of institutionalized racism that systematically perpetuates rationalized injustice.

This study utilizes a variety of sources, such as unpublished interviews with people of various walks of life, newspaper and magazine articles, letters, legal documents, still photography, and literature, all to augment traditional historical documents. This type of evidence renders a more holistic and vivid presentation and allows an analytical and detailed account of the impact of the Till case.

A key issue is the analysis of the underdevelopment of the Till case by traditional historians who, in their accounts of the modern Civil Rights Movement, have ignored those varieties of source materials that make a broader perspective possible. To achieve this broader perspective, this study investigates, analyzes, and reassesses a variety of the events surrounding the Till case—the murder, the sentiment of the public, the trials, and the consequences.

It is the desire that this study will reveal the interlocking destiny of all Americans, which is a prerequisite for an in-depth understanding of the fifties and the sixties. Challenging traditional interpretations, this study has analyzed the dynamics of the conflict between the black and white cultures through an analytical study of the Till murder case (which demonstrates the results of that clash) and the modern Civil Rights Movement (which is the manifestation of the confrontation between the opposing forces).

Part 1

The Case

1
Night of Horror

You may not realize it but you are making history. Bobo is not the only Negro that was lynched in Mississippi, but this is the first trial of its kind that has ever been held in Mississippi. The kind of death your son died is responsible for this trial.

—Rayfield Mooty to Mamie Bradley
(from the unpublished biography of Mooty)

In Chicago

Actually, we were planning a vacation, Emmett and I. And when Papa Mose came and Emmett found out that the other boys were going to be with Papa Mose, then he switched his plans. And that really shook me up a lot because I was getting ready as fast as I could to take off for Detroit. Then we were going to go to Omaha, Nebraska. My first vacation. The first one!

(Mamie Bradley-Mobley)[1]

---

[1] Tape-recorded interview with Mamie Bradley-Mobley, Chicago, IL, 6 January,1988.

It seemed that Emmett's plans to vacation with his mother were all set, until relatives from the South came to Chicago and persuaded him otherwise. In mid-August 1955, Mose Wright, a sixty-five-year-old cotton sharecropper from Money, Mississippi, went to Chicago, Illinois, for a funeral. He took with him his twelve-year-old son, Simeon. While there, Simeon visited with two of his Chicago cousins, Emmett Louis Till, affectionately called Bobo, who had turned fourteen less than a month before, and Wheeler Parker, Jr., aged sixteen. They planned a way to extend their good time: the two Chicago youths would join the Wrights in their journey back home so they could enjoy a Mississippian vacation.

Photograph 3 (p. 29) of Till was taken in his living room at his Chicago home during his last Christmas holiday (December 1954). It exudes a sense of pride in his dress, a sense of security and self-assurance in his expression, and even a degree of arrogance in his demeanor. An African-American male of these attributes would undoubtedly pose a threat to traditional southern life with its prescribed, subservient lifestyle for African-Americans. A proud African-American male like Till could be conceived of by southern whites as an unwelcome, antagonistic force in a southern environment by his mere presence and, thus, could be regarded and treated both as an intruder and, more important, as a danger to the established, unnatural harmony between the unequal races.

Till stands in his comfortable Chicago home, amid material affluence, carpeting and a very recent media invention, the television, which ironically became the very medium for spreading his story to the mass. He is stylishly attired, a real dapper, white shirt and dark tie, dress trousers and dress shoes and socks, all of which poverty has deprived the average African-American Mississippian and more important, which the typical southern racist would

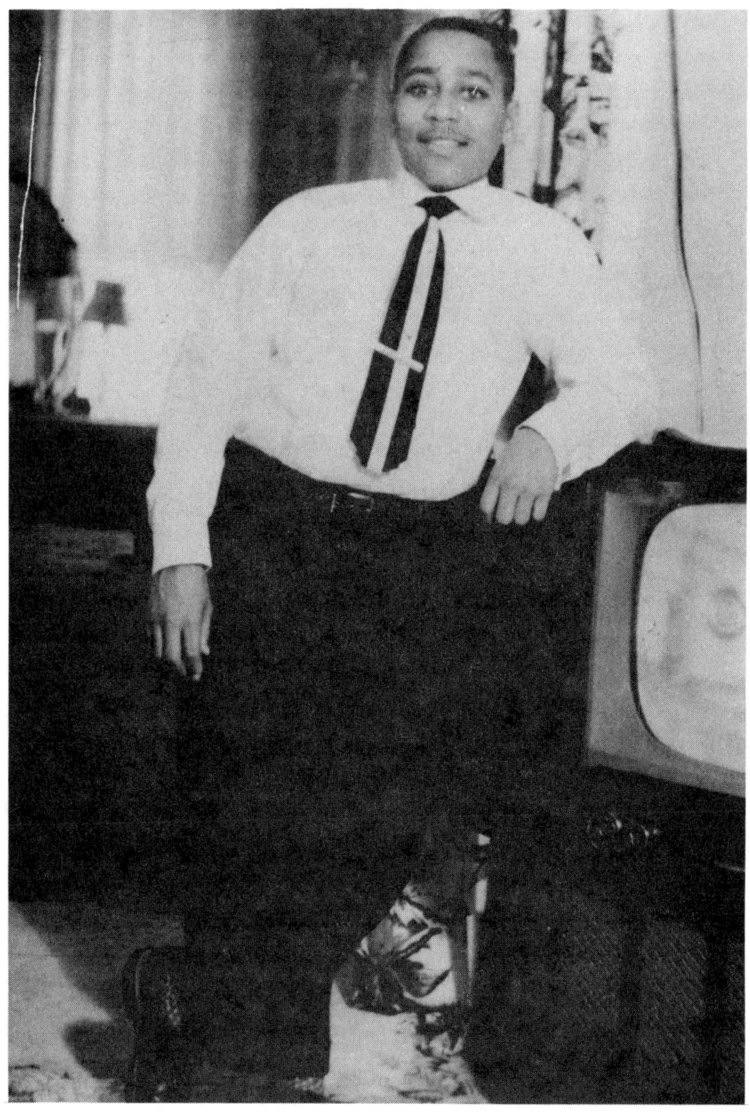

Photograph 3. **Last photo of Till (Christmas '54) before lynching.** [Mamie Till Mobley]

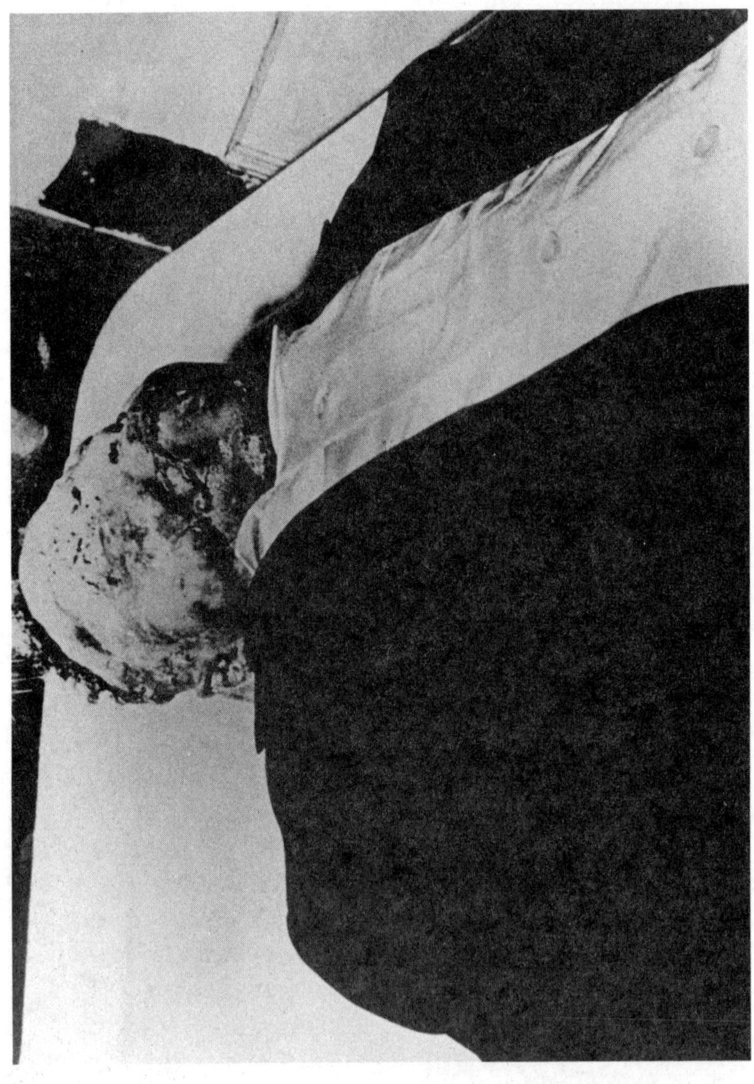

Photograph 4. **Till in casket after lynching.** [*Chicago Defender*]

regard as unbefitting to a person of that race. He seems to be comfortable with these luxuries, which seem commonplace for him, as his facial expression and pose, leaning on the television with a sense of casualness, suggest confidence. In transferring all of these qualities, and the African-American youth, to a rural southern environment, which is hostile both to the notion of an "uppity nigger" and an outsider, the outcome would be predictable.

The difference between the political, economic, and social milieu of the large Chicago metropolis and the rural Mississippi Delta in 1955 was vast, even though the two had strong connections. Chicago got more than its share of southern blacks, as it became the mecca for Mississippi blacks seeking a northern refuge. It was a city crowded with Deep South black immigrants who had relocated to the North in search of better living conditions. The industrial northern city offered many more jobs than were available in the South, particularly in its numerous large stockyards. While relations between blacks and whites were not exactly great, rigid Jim-Crowism (legal separation, that is) was not the case up North. In Chicago, there was *de facto* (by practice) segregation, whereas in Mississippi, there was *de jure* (by law) segregation. In Chicago, there were predominantly black and white neighborhoods, schools, and churches, but there were also exceptions. Public facilities on the whole were integrated. Emmett lived in a predominantly black middle-class neighborhood and attended a predominantly black school, but there were a few white classmates, friends, and teachers. There were also some interracial marriages, which demonstrated the intermingling of black and white. Clearly, the "veil" or the curtain of separation between the two races, as DuBois metaphorically presents it, was not as clearly drawn in Chicago as it was in the Deep South.

Emmett, born and raised in Chicago, was accustomed to more relaxed relations between the two races. His train ride to Mississippi, then, became the first for him in two ways—it was his first trip to Mississippi and it was his first meeting with the real Jim Crow. Given his age and inexperience, his lack of awareness of southern customs (as demonstrated in the so-called wolf-whistling scenario) is both understandable and to be expected.

Race relations in Mississippi in 1955 were another story. Nothing redeeming has ever been said about Mississippi in this context. It was the cornerstone and the definition of Jim Crowism for black folk. Segregation on all fronts was absolute law. Blacks and whites lived in different neighborhoods, attended separate schools, worked in different capacities or on different levels when working together, and there were no instances of interracial social intermingling or interracial marriages. The subservient attitude and mannerism of the Mississippi blacks mirrored their Jim Crow conditions. When Emmett arrived in the small town of a population of 350, he must have observed the inferior conditions of blacks there—their humble huts, their meager clothing, and their oppressed speech and mannerisms. His great-uncle's tiny sharecropper's home, for example, was much like those of the majority of blacks in that area—small, crowded, and tattered. The clothing worn by the hardworking black sharecroppers, many of whom were relatives whom he met while there, and children who greeted him upon his arrival and with whom he spent his time playing, left much to be desired. The "Ya sir" and "Naw sir" place of blacks in that society was, indeed, oppressive. Even the adults feared the whites, including whites who were many years their juniors. The subservient position and mannerisms of his Great-Uncle Mose and Great-Aunt Elizabeth in relation to all whites, for example, reflected that of most blacks there. But the concerns of Emmett, the child, were naturally not those of an adult. And so promised camaraderie was the preoccupation of Emmett. There was his Mississippi cousin, Simeon, and the other kids in the area who were anxious to show him the fun and excitement of the tiny Deep South town of Money—a town that was to be the site of the wolf-whistle, the infamous Till abduction, and the brutal lynching. This was followed by the subsequent five-day mock trial in the nearby Sunflower County Courthouse, whose capacity was 158, in the town of Sumner, whose motto was ironically "A Good Place to Raise a Boy." To be sure, Emmett's focus was more on the fun that awaited him as a child, than on the oppressive conditions of blacks.

As the story goes, Emmett and his Chicago cousin Wheeler were seduced into going back to Mississippi with the Wright family. Wheeler experienced no difficulty in convincing his parents to let him go to Mississippi. Emmett, on the other hand, needed some help persuading his family. He was an only child who stuttered from having had infantile paralysis as a child, and his mother and grandmother had been accused of overprotecting him. He was a city boy from the North whose behavior and mannerisms might not easily mesh with the rural racist southern environment. And he was asking not only to go South, but to go to Mississippi, a place described by Endesha Ida Mae Holland in her play "From the Mississippi Delta" as "a testament to African-American inferiority."[2] These factors no doubt played a significant role in the mother's and grandmother's hesitancy. It was clear there were odds stacked up against Emmett and his desires, so both Simeon and Wheeler accompanied him. They first approached Emmett's mother, Mamie Bradley. They pleaded

---

[2] Endesha Ida Mae Holland, "From the Mississippi Delta," 1987, p.1.

with her and then with his grandmother, Alma Spearman (Moses Wright's sister-in-law), whose approval was just as important and critical as the mother's.

"Please cousin Mamie, Aunt Alma, can Bobo go with us?" pleaded Wheeler.

"Yea, it'll be fun," added Simeon.

Emmett's mother and grandmother agreed reluctantly. Mrs. Bradley's reluctance was enhanced by the fact that she, along with her fiancé, Mr. Gene Mobley, had planned to take a trip with Emmett to Detroit to visit his maternal grandfather, John Carthan, and then to Omaha. Mrs. Bradley was excited about this trip because it was to be her first vacation from her job with the federal government, where she was a voucher examiner in charge of secret and confidential information. Emmett, too, was enthusiastic because Mr. Mobley had promised to let him drive the new car, a 1955 Plymouth, on the expressway. He was thrilled, that was, until something more exciting came along.

In preparation for Emmett's newly directed vacation plans, Mrs. Bradley advised him that he was to conduct himself properly, both as a child and as a black man. Born in Mississippi herself, although she left at the age of three, she knew all too well the folk wisdom about the appropriate conduct expected of the black male, man or child. Emmett, she thought, needed to be reminded that he would be in a different environment.

> *I did warn him that he had a place down there, that it was a little bit different from Chicago. I told him that if anything happened, even though you think you're perfectly within your right, for goodness sake, take low, if necessary get on your knees and beg apology. Don't cross anybody down there because Mississippi is not like Chicago. What you can get away with here*

> *you might not be able to do it there. No matter how much it seems that you have the right, just forget your rights while you're in Mississippi ... But I didn't really think all of these things ... If I exaggerated a little bit, maybe I would make Emmett conscious that he was going to a different place and to be reasonably careful.*[3]

Mamie, however, never imagined that her only son would become the victim of the much feared overt racial violence characteristic of the South.

To Mississippi

She purchased Emmett's round-trip train ticket to Mississippi and in no time, he, his two cousins, and his great-uncle Moses were jubilantly on their way. They arrived there in the heat of the summer, on August 20, and things went on uneventfully for the first few days. Then that Wednesday evening, August 24, in Money, only a few days after they arrived, the boys and some other friends went to the community grocery store owned by Roy Bryant, to buy some candy. Bryant's twenty-one-year-old wife, Carolyn, waited on the youths; her husband was out of town at the time (he returned two days later).

According to Simeon, "After he [Emmett] came out of the store and she was going towards her car, then he whistled. He did whistle and after that, we all became afraid. We ran and jumped in the car, went down Dalfair

---

[3] Tape-recorded speech of Mamie Bradley, South Bend, IN, 1955.

Road; I think we lived about three miles from Money."[4] They all knew, Carolyn Bryant included, that Till's gesture was inappropriate. However, without further incident, they left the area and, according to Wheeler, "Till begged us not tell my grandfather, so we didn't tell. And there was a girl there; her name was Ruth Crawford. She's a black girl, a little younger than me. She's still there I understand. And she told us 'you all gonna hear some more from this.'"[5] It was said that when Bryant returned, his wife told him about the incident. Obviously she was still enraged, so much so that three days were not enough to cool her desire for revenge. She must have known that her husband's reaction would be to some extent a threat to the youth's safety.

Somewhat leery about what could come out of the incident, Emmett's fear led him to ask his great-aunt Elizabeth Wright for his return ticket home. He wanted to go back home where he thought he would be safe. His fear was incessant, and finally, he had to tell her himself what had happened. Even though she had spent her entire life in Mississippi and knew the limitations imposed on blacks (in relation to keeping in their place with whites), for some reason she thought that Emmett did not have anything to fear, at least to the point of fleeing back home. Obviously Emmett did, and it was reported that on at least three occasions, he futilely begged her for his return ticket. Moreover, the kids had begun to tease him, telling him that he could be killed for whistling at a white woman in Mississippi. By this time, Emmett knew he had committed a

---

[4] Tape-recorded interview with Simeon Wright, Chicago, IL, 19 July 1986.

[5] Tape-recorded interview with Wheeler Parker, Chicago, IL, 19 July 1986.

crime that was unpardonable according to the law of the land, and he feared for his life.

Three days passed without incident. However, about 2:30 a.m. that hot Sunday morning of the fourth day, August 28, Emmett experienced the ultimate terror. Twenty-four-year-old Roy Bryant and his thirty-six-year-old stepbrother, J. W. Milam, intruded the home of sixty-five-year-old Moses Wright, the black sharecropper, in Money, Mississippi. Bullying and threatening Wright's family with a flashlight and a gun, they came and abducted the youth. Wheeler remembers that one of the two white men advised his grandfather, Mr. Wright, that they "wanted the fat boy from Chicago"[6] who had violated Carolyn Bryant's honor. They came in search of revenge for what was considered America's greatest taboo: an attack by a black man on the sanctity of white womanhood.

As they stormed through the house, Mrs. Wright pleaded with them to let her take care of him. After they ignored her plea, she then begged them not to kill him. Till's second cousin Rayfield Mooty remembers being told that one of them angrily told her to "get back in that bed and let me hear that mattress squeak."[7] Determined not to let anything interfere with their plans, they forced her into silence. They had come prepared with a gun and a cotton gin fan, which seemed to indicate that Till's fate was premeditated by the murderers, notwithstanding their later confession to William Bradford Huie.

First they reached the room where Wheeler was sleeping. Discovering that he was not the one, they then went to Simeon's room where he and Emmett were sleeping. Wheeler recounts the loud and angry conversation:

---

[6] Parker

[7] Tape-recorded interview with Rayfield Mooty, Chicago, IL, May 1986.

"They were over there talking to 'em [Emmett] and he was saying 'yes' and 'naw,' you know, like that. So they didn't like it; they started cursing. They didn't appreciate it so they were cursing."[8] They told Emmett to get up, get dressed, and come with them. Emmett followed their instructions, overtly displaying no fear, which inflamed the men even more.

Given the particulars, it is not surprising that Till's verbal expressions, too, would not be permissible in the southern context. In fact, when the assassins came for him and questioned if he were the boy from up North, Till simply responded, "yes," rather than "yassar." Indeed, this further ignited indignation on the part of the white men, who were totally unprepared and unaccustomed to African-Americans, even among the senior citizens, not addressing them with "sir." According to Rayfield Mooty, it was said that they threatened to kill him right there if he addressed them again in that manner.[9] Even Till's sixty-five-year-old great uncle, Moses Wright, whose home the murderers had invaded, knew better than that. Till's then thirteen-year-old cousin, whose bedroom he was sharing, attested to Till's lack of adaptability to southern black subservience, for according to him, Till demonstrated no fear of the white men when they awakened him at gun-point, instructing him to get dressed and come with them. According to Simeon, Till just got up and dressed, with not a hint of fear, not a word of plea.[10] Perturbed by Till's behavior, they were used to African-Americans crying, begging for mercy and apologizing for any wrong that they

---

[8] Parker.

[9] Videotape-recorded interview with Rayfield Mooty, Chicago, IL, April 1986.

[10] Tape-recorded interview with Simeon Wright, Chicago, IL, 19 July 1986.

might have done. Not so with Till, the northerner who obviously could not imagine his ensuing fate. Obviously, proper southern etiquette had not been instilled in him. He was naive.

Simeon, too, recalls vividly that night of terror: "I think they struck Emmett one time. He got up and put his clothes on and after that, he didn't say anything else. He just put his clothes on and took on out. During this time, my mother offered them money. They hesitated for a little bit and then they just took him on out." According to members of his family, Emmett was described as a brave, proud leader, who was not accustomed to displaying fear. According to Parker, as the two abductors left with Till, who displayed an air of nonchalance, they told the Wrights that if he was not the one, they would bring him back. They knew when they left they would not be bringing him back, as they had confirmed his identity with a black man, LeRoy "Too Tight" Collins, who had accompanied them there.

"He's the one," he confirmed.

Till's color, too, did not help him, for it was a reminder to the irrational southerner of improper miscegenation. The youth was light-skinned with light eyes. His mother had even expressed her concern about his appearance when he was a baby: "He was blonde and blue-eyed and this bothered me until Mama told me not to worry, that he would change."[11] Unfortunately Till had all of the ingredients for meeting a tragic death, particularly if placed in a hostile southern environment. He did not look nor act the part of an acceptable African-American youth in a southern context. Hence, his appearance and his man-

---

[11] Mamie Bradley, "Mamie Bradley's Untold Story," *The Chicago Daily Defender*, Wednesday, 29 February 1956, p. 5.

nerisms, too, contributed to his ultimate tragic doom and destiny.

For a teenage indiscretion—characteristic behavior of teenagers going through the *rites de passage*—Emmett was taken away, flogged, mutilated, and lynched. His executioners then shot him through the head before using barbed wire to tie a seventy-pound cotton gin fan around his neck and casting him into the Tallahatchie River.

Terror

The reign of terror, of horror, for blacks under extreme southern racism was awesome. It was such that the family could do nothing initially, having been forewarned by the white abductors to keep their mouths shut. All they could do was hope that the whites would not kill Emmett. All they could do was wait and so they did. It was not until late that morning that they succumbed to their fear of the inevitable for Emmett.

Mrs. Wright was particularly devastated. She left her home within an hour after the men left with Till, never to return. In fact, her fear was such that her thirteen-year-old son had to go back, with his father, to collect some clothing necessities for her. She spent the first day or two hiding in fear at the home of her brother and sister-in-law, Crosby and Lula Smith. Shortly thereafter, she escaped to Chicago where she died years later. Her husband and children later joined her.

According to Paul Burton of *The New York Times*, "Mose Wright gave away his three dogs Sunday, sold his chickens and furniture and prepared to leave forever the land of his birth."[12] However, he returned to testify. His heroism overpowered the threats to his life and his fear for it, for he identified Emmett's abductors, heroically pointing his finger at the two in court: "Thar he."

Emmett Till Returns to Chicago

The perpetrators must have expected Emmett Till to remain on the floor of the muddy river for all eternity; however, as fate would have it, three days later he arose, and with his resurrection arose the consciousness of a significant portion of American society.

Till's nude body was not found until Wednesday, August 31, three days after Mrs. Wright's brother, Crosby Smith, had reported the kidnapping (at 12 noon on Sunday, September 28) to the Leflore County sheriff's department and to Till's family in Chicago. Crosby Smith began an exhausting search for the youth. The local sheriff, Bill Smith (a white man unrelated to Crosby), who eventually led the murder investigation, joined the youth's uncle in combing the nearby countryside. But it was an unsuspecting white teenager, seventeen-year-old Robert Hodges, who accidentally discovered the body while fishing the Tallahatchie.

The grotesque image was hauntingly morbid and shockingly mutilated. Emmett's face was disfigured beyond recognition.

> *"It was a sad thing. I happened to be down there fishin'," recalls 65-year-old Roosevelt Sutton of Webb, a black man who saw Till's body pulled from the* river.

---

[12] Paul Burton, "Mose Wright Prepares to Leave Home," *New York Times*, 1 Oct. 1955, p. 2.

> *"All I know is the body. It was ruined. He had a graduation ring on his finger."*
>
> *On the day the boy's body was found, Smith accompanied a deputy sheriff to a black graveyard near Wright's cabin.*
>
> *"They had got the body out to the cemetery and dug the grave," Smith says. "I got there and had the deputy sheriff with me. He told them that whatever I said, went. Everybody was standing around with a look on their face. I said, "No, the body ain't going in the ground."*[13]

It was such an ugly sight that some Mississippi officials, anxious to prevent outsiders from witnessing this evidence of racist brutality, were about to carry out a speedy funeral when Crosby Smith and the sheriff arrived with a court order for the return of the corpse to Chicago. At the grave side were members of the Wright family and friends who were timidly awaiting the immediate Mississippi family members, Mr. and Mrs. Mose Wright and Mr. and Mrs. Crosby Smith. The child's body would have been buried without the mother had it not been for Curtis Jones. According to Simeon, "The only someone stopped them was Curtis. He called back to Chicago and said they fixing to bury him."[14] Mooty, then, contacted the governor.

Giving in to legal pressure, Mississippi authorities finally relinquished Till's body, but only after issuing strict orders that the sealed box not be opened. Crosby Smith secretly escorted the box back North, where he delivered Emmett to his mother, Mamie Bradley, in an emotional scene at Chicago's Twelfth Street Train Station.

---

[13] Quoted in Joe Atkins, *The Clarion-Ledger*, August 25, 1985.
[14] Wright.

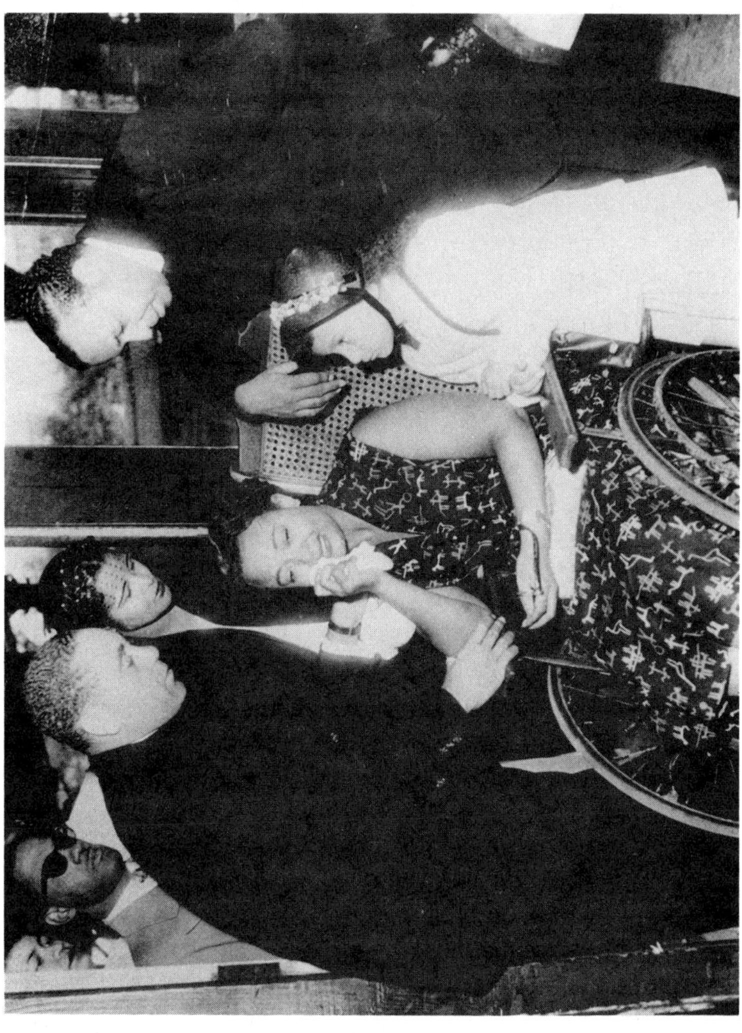

Photograph 5. **Mamie sobs on return of Till to Chicago (12th Street Train Station).** [*Chicago Defender*]

Photograph 6. **Mamie at funeral (sympathizers supporting her).** [*Chicago Defender*]

Photograph 5 (p. 43) documents the occasion of the return of Till's body from Mississippi to his home, Chicago. All the spectators are distraught, having come to the train station to share Mamie Bradley's tragic loss and appear to be themselves lost for words or direction as they wait for the body to be delivered. Centered is Till's grief-stricken mother, who is surrounded by supportive empathizing family and friends. She is captured as perhaps at the height of her emotional collapse; she appears to be literally unable to withstand this ordeal. So crushed and distraught by this ordeal, she is literally transported into the receiving room in a wheelchair. Not photographed here but whose presence at the station cannot go unmentioned is Mamie's father, John Carthan, her Uncle Crosby Smith, who escorted and delivered the body from the land of the murder, and her cousin by marriage, Rayfield Mooty. Among the supporters photographed here are the ministers, Bishop Isaiah Roberts and the Rev. Louis Henry Ford respectively, on either sides of Mamie. Her aunt Lily Smith stands just behind her, lending her moral support. An unidentified little girl stands attentively next to Mamie, a reminder of childhood innocence.

When the box arrived at the station, Mr. Mooty held that the mother would have to see what was inside. According to him, "She was insisting on seeing the box because she had just paid $750 to bring that box here, and she wanted to see what was in it ... After we saw what was in the box, she decided she wanted to leave the box open."[15]

The fact that Mr. Mooty (himself a relative of the young victim and a long-standing civil rights activist whose life in the United Steelworkers of America-CIO had

[15] Tape-recorded interview with Rayfield Mooty, Chicago, IL, 19 July 1986.

been a constant struggle for equality) took control of the matter and demonstrated critical distance by responding quickly and politically during this crucial period, says a lot about his strong character. Perhaps the explanation to his unusual response to the tragedy lies in his previous activities as a labor-union leader who had become accustomed to the need to act quickly. Mrs. Bradley too, though only thirty-three years old and distraught, was heroic. She, like Mooty, insisted that the box be opened; and it was. Demonstrating immense strength, she examined her child's body from head to toe confirming that it was, in fact, the body of her son, a critical issue which was later introduced during the murder trial.

The Funeral

The display of the body and the funeral during the three-day Labor Day weekend were strategically planned by Mamie and Rayfield who recognized the need to let the public witness this atrocity. Photograph 4 (p. 30), the grotesque shot of Till in the casket, represents the embodiment of brutal racism and death. We see one of his eyes gouged out, perhaps ironically symbolizing the destruction of "ocular rape" of which he has been accused. Photograph 6 (p. 44) captures Mamie at the utter peak of despair and grief during the funeral.

One of the owners of Rayner's Funeral Parlor, A. A. Rayner, Jr., who was in charge of funeral arrangements for Till's body once it arrived in Chicago, recounts the anger of the crowd and the hostile reaction to authority and order during the display of Till's body:

> *They sent one policeman and he stood in the door, the little side door. We had them come in the side door and go out the back. Before long, they were throwing rocks at the buses that went by; the buses had to detour and go around on Drexel. Then someone came out there and started passing out Communist literature, and before long we had a couple of sergeants, policemen, a couple of lieutenants, everybody was down there then. But this poor policeman was down there by himself for a long time, and they literally tore his clothes off getting into that one little door. They tore his uniform off him.*[16]

Indeed, the crowd was impatient and enraged because of this cruel and senseless murder of a child. Maria K. Mootry, a black educator in her mid-forties, remembers,

> *The first thing I remember was standing in line, and the line snaked for blocks just like with Harold Washington's funeral. We stood in line for at least two hours, everybody waiting, patient, to see the body of Emmett Till with their own eyes ... I remember his face; it was greenish. White people were saying that this was not an eleven-year-old kid; he looked like an old man ... I'll never forget it—all those people brought together by the death of a child.*[17]

Photograph 7 (p. 49), taken outside Roberts Temple at 41st and State Streets just before Till's funeral, depicts the multitude of people who came to witness the funeral. It is a striking testimony of our emotional autonomy that dates

---

[16] Tape-recorded interview with A. A. Rayner, Jr., Chicago, IL, 19 July 1986.

[17] Quoted in full in Appendix 2.

back to American slavery. Obviously, so many people could not have been friends, acquaintances, or relations. They are, after all, attending the funeral of a child, and the huge turn-out, then, indicates the horror and outrage that blacks felt collectively regarding his slaughter. The huge crowd of over 6,000 demonstrates the collective strength of the masses, which carries them into the genesis of a distinct Movement to end the reign of racial terrorism in America during the fifties.

Photograph 8 (p. 50) is taken of the crowd inside the temple as people come to view the body. Their sad gaze at the face of the battered body share the same general expressions as the crowd: a sense of despair. Collectively their faces suggest that they have had enough.

However, according to the minister who presided at the funeral, Bishop Isaiah Roberts, anger had somewhat subsided by the time of the burial: "There was a lot of crying. I don't think there was any display of anger at the cemetery. It was mostly all sadness."[18] (See Photographs 9 (p. 51) and 10 (p. 52)).

Demonstrations

After the murder, there were rallies, demonstrations, almost every type of protest imaginable. Labor unions, the NAACP, and politicians joined unaffiliated Americans in casting in their ballots of protest against the atrocity. Riots, mass demonstrations, and rallies organized nationally (and local ones organized by national groups) ensued as Americans took a stand against racism. Arkela Revels, a black storyteller and community activist, remembers:

---

[18] Tape-recorded interview with Bishop Isaiah Roberts, Chicago, IL, 20 July 1986.

Photograph 7. **Outside Roberts Temple just before funeral.** [*Chicago Defender*]

Photograph 8. **Inside Roberts Temple during funeral.** [*Chicago Defender*]

Photograph 9. Mamie, her mother Mrs. Spearman, grief-stricken at graveside. [*Chicago Defender*]

Photograph 10. **Mamie, ministers, family and friends at graveside as body is finally committed to ground.** [*Chicago Defender*]

> *Within a few weeks, we were getting messages from our black newspapers and black churches that they were going to hold rallies so that people could get the true story about what had happened ... I heard about the rally at New Bethel Baptist Church, headed by Rev. C. L. Franklin (Aretha Franklin's father). He had been announcing the rally, the purpose and was providing leadership at a very crucial time. At the rally they had speakers; the mother of Emmett Till was there and people had the opportunity to meet her, which gave people a more realistic identification with this case. People wanted to contribute either time or money to draw attention and awareness, creating enough friction that the whole city of Detroit was very much riled up to the point that masses of people that had never formally been really active (they had been passive protesters) protested.* [19]

Indicating how a neighboring state (New Orleans, Louisiana) publicized the incident and its impact, a staff writer for *The Pittsburgh Courier*, George Pitts, reports incidents of national violent unrest following the Till lynching: "Bitter race violence, festering throughout the nation like a malignant wound, sounded a grim aftermath to the Emmett Louis Till lynch-murder in Money, Miss. ... As the eyes of the country focused on the upcoming Till trial other outbreaks were reported."[20]

David Jordan, a teacher and city councilman in Greenwood, Mississippi, later muses as he recounts the tension in Mississippi during that time, "It was shocking to learn that somebody in our midst, this close to Green-

---

[19] Quoted in full in Appendix 2.

[20] George Pitts, "Violence Continues to Fester," *The Pittsburgh Courier* (New Orleans, LA, 24 Sept. 1955), p. 4.

wood, could kill a 14-year-old child. After that happened, we were ready to do whatever was necessary to change the social conditions which had made this possible."[21]

This straightforward narration is a reconstruction of the sequence of events leading up to Till's death. Demonstrating the power of oral history, affording the reader the bare facts as related by those who were there, this narration reveals what motivated Till to visit Mississippi and what awaited him there. It presents the ingredients of southern racial terrorism, the explosion of horror, and the effect this horror had upon the black community, demonstrating the impact of the Till incident, in particular, on the modern Civil Rights Movement.

[21] David Jordan, "Land of the Till Murder Revisited," *Ebony* by Clotye Murdock Larsson (March 1986), p. 58.

2
The Trials

Till was kidnapped and slain on August 28, 1955, for whistling at a twenty-one-year-old white woman. Joe Atkins in *The Clarion-Ledger* gives a chronology of the events that followed:

> *Aug. 29—J. W. Milam, 36, and Roy Bryant, 24, are arrested on kidnapping charges in Leflore County in connection with Till's disappearance. They are jailed in Greenwood and held without bond.*
>
> *Aug. 31—Till's body is pulled from the Tallahatchie River ...*
>
> *Sept. 6—A Tallahatchie County grand jury indicts Milam and Bryant on murder and kidnapping charges.*
>
> *Sept. 19—The murder trial begins in Sumner.*
>
> *Sept. 23—An all-white, all-male jury acquits Milam and Bryant on the murder charges. The kidnapping charges in Tallahatchie County were dropped after testimony showed the abduction occurred in Leflore County.*

Nov. 9—A Leflore County grand jury in Greenwood refuses to indict Milam or Bryant for kidnapping.[1]

Two photographs show Emmett Till's relatives together as three of them are preparing to leave for the murder trial in Sumner, Mississippi. From left to right in Photograph 11 (p. 57) are Rayfield Mooty, John Carthan, Mamie Bradley, Alma Spearman (grandmother of Till), and Henry Spearman (step-grandfather of Till). Each seems to focus inwardly on the tragic circumstance that has called them together.

Photograph 12 (p. 58) gives a close view of the facial expressions and emotions of the three subjects as they board the plane for their departure. Their lips are sealed. But their eyes are open. Again Mamie Bradley is in the middle, with her father at her left and her cousin at her right, which reinforces her position as the mother of the victim around whom all else revolves. They suggest a sense of uncertainty regarding both the situation that awaits them and its outcome. They seem to be asking "what next?" with no indication that they are optimistic about any aspect of the whole ordeal. Notwithstanding their sense of uncertainty, they bravely forge on, with a determination, the life force of the Civil Rights Movement, to somehow bring justice to the wronged.

Only Bryant and Milam were tried for the kidnapping and murder, and, after a five-day-long trial, on September 23, 1955, an all-white all-male jury took one hour and seven minutes of deliberation to find them not guilty on both counts. Although they admitted to having taken Till from Wright's home, they claimed they had talked with him, found that he was not the one they were looking for,

---

1 "A Chronology," Joe Atkins, *The Clarion-Ledger*, August 25, 1985.

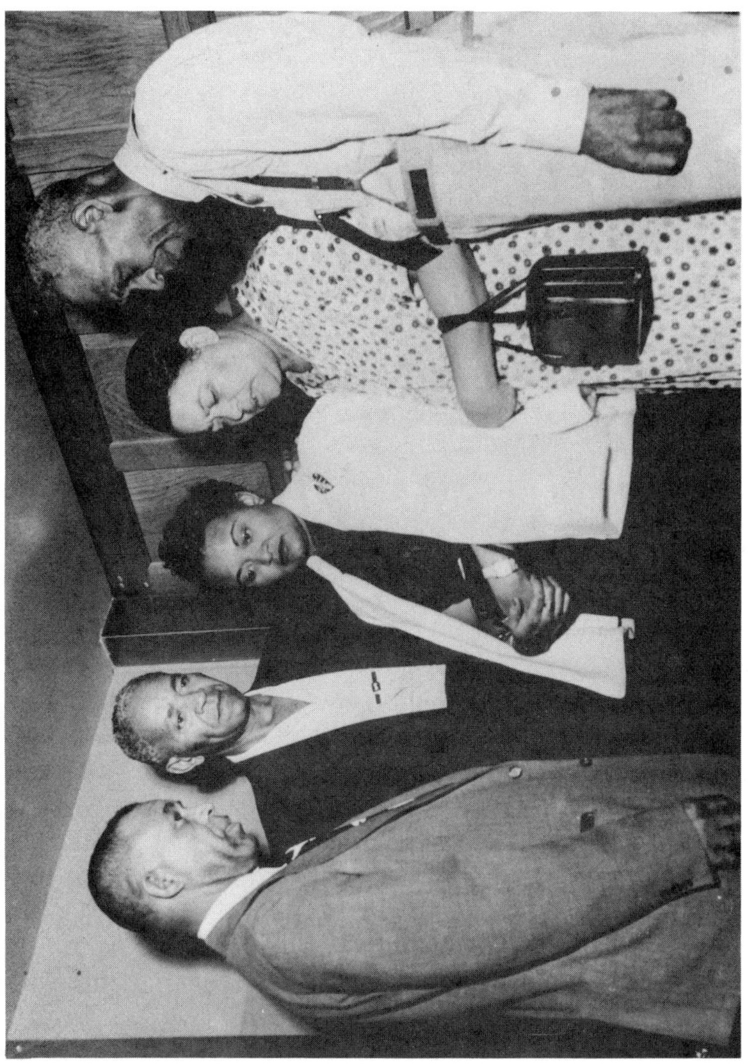

Photograph 11. **The Midway Airport in Chicago before departure for trial (September 19, 1955).** [Rayfield Mooty]

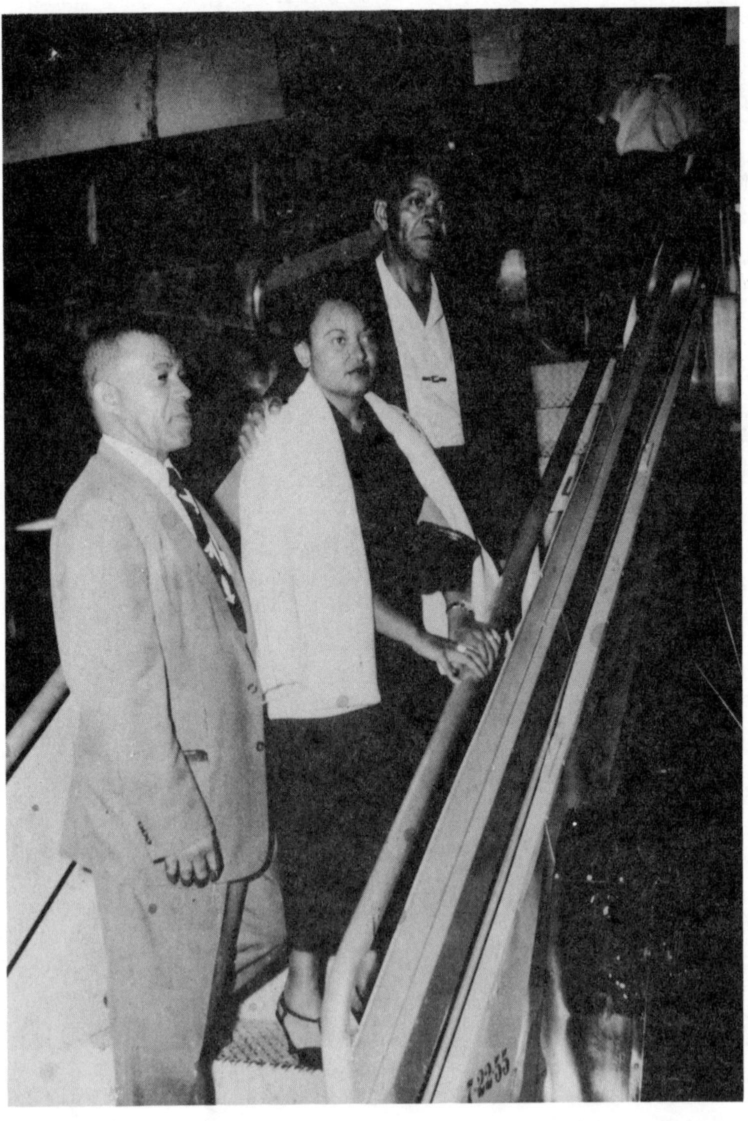

Photograph 12. **Boarding plane for departure to trial (September 19, 1955).** [Rayfield Mooty]

and released him.

The five defense attorneys for the half-brothers, "all the legal brains in the town,"[2] were Harvey Henderson, J. W. Kellum, John W. Whitten, Jr., J. J. Breland, and C. Sidney Carlton. The three prosecuting attorneys for the state were Gerald Chatham (of Hernando, Mississippi), Robert B. Smith III (special attorney general), and Hamilton Cardwell from Tallahatchie County.

> *Chatham and Smith, a former FBI agent and Marine officer, shocked the crowd on the second day of the trial when they abruptly sought and received a recess from Swango [the circuit court judge] after the final juror was selected. The prosecutors said they needed additional time to locate and interview new witnesses which Smith said were of major importance.*[3]

The state produced three surprise witnesses—all members of black sharecropping families in the area—whose testimonies contradicted Bryant and Milam's story. A. J. Reed had seen Till on the back of Milam's truck headed in the direction of the farm belonging to Leslie Milam's (J. W.'s brother). Before daybreak, Amanda Bradley (no relation to Till's mother, Mamie Bradley) had heard Till wailing for his mother and pleading for mercy inside Milam's barn. And Willie Reed, A. J.'s nephew, had been fetching water when he saw Milam, Bryant, and others loading a bloody tarpaulin—with what appeared to be a body underneath—back on the truck shortly after the commotion in the barn.

The deciding factor in the case was the claim by defense lawyers that the body could not be proven to be

---

[2] *Jet*, October 6, 1955, p. 7

[3] Tom Brennan, *The Clarion-Ledger*, August 25, 1985.

Till's. Dr. L. B. Otkins, a white doctor, testified that the body seemed to have been in the water longer than three days and that he could not tell whether it was the body of a white or a black man. The defense prevailed in spite of Mamie Bradley's positive identification of her son upon close examination of the corpse in Chicago. The jury ignored the factual evidence of a ring with the initials *L. T.* found on the victim, a ring that had been passed on to Emmett from his deceased father, Louis Till.

> *"I knew it (was Emmett) without a shadow of a doubt," she said on the stand.*
>
> *Mobley also identified a ring removed from the body as belonging to her ex-husband, Emmett's father Louis Till, which she later gave to her son. The silver band carried a simple inscription of May 25, 1943 and the initials "L. T."*
>
> *Whitten said that the ring caused a furor among defense attorneys. "We didn't know about it and she made such a good impression that the ring was their (the state's) key," he said.*[4]

The atmosphere at the trial, according to Ruby Hurley, director of the first NAACP office in the Deep South who investigated the Till case for the NAACP magazine *Crisis,* was "just like a circus. The defendants were sitting there eating ice-cream cones and playing with their children in court just like they were out at a picnic."[5] The accused came to court in the morning, "accompanied by Sheriff H. C. Strider of Tallahatchie County who liked to demonstrate his friendliness with Negro reporters covering the trial by greeting them each day with: 'Good

[4] Tom Brennan, *The Clarion-Ledger*, September 25, 1985.

[5] Howell Raines, *My Soul Is Rested*, p. 132.

morning, niggers.'"[6] At the Jim Crow Negro press table sat, among others, *Jet* magazine's Simeon Booker, Congressman Charles C. Diggs, Jr., of Detroit, Mrs. Mamie Bradley, her father, and Rayfield Mooty.

Although Circuit Court Judge Curtis M. Swango remained fair and impartial throughout the murder and kidnapping trial, he was helpless to stop an all-white male jury that carried out the prescriptive course of action for southern racism and returned verdicts of not guilty on both charges. The reporter for *The New York Times*, Paul Burton, stated that:

> *The jury acquitted the defendants largely on the basis of defense testimony that the body found in the Tallahatchie River was not that of Till.*
>
> *The body, which Mrs. Mamie Bradley said was that of her son was found three days after Till was abducted.*
>
> *Defense testimony said the body had been in the river much longer than that.*[7]

Law was already Till's adversary because he was black. According to Judge Leon Higginbotham, Jr., in his book *In the Matter of Color*:

> *Ultimately, the legal process has always acted as an expression of social control ... The mechanisms of control through judicial decisions and statutes span the sanctioning of slavery and the special limitations imposed on free blacks, to the prohibitions against interracial marriage and sexual activity, to the eliminat-*

---

[6] *Jet*, October 6, 1955, p. 8

[7] Paul Burton, "Mose Wright Prepares to Leave Home," *The New York Times*, 1 Oct. 1955, p. 2.

ing of the legal significance of blacks' "conversions to Christianity," to generally restricting any activities or aspirations of blacks that might threaten the groups in control. The law is usually perceived as a normative system, founded on a society's custom and convention.[8]

Records Lost and Found

Of all of the legal activity surrounding the five-day trial to evaluate the murder charges and later the hearing on the kidnapping charges there are only seventeen brief legal documents still extant. The others, including the trial transcripts, were destroyed. The existing documents provide both factual and attitudinal information.

The first document is a true bill, presenting the opening statement of an indictment by the district attorney, Gerald Chatham, and it reads: "The State of Mississippi, Tallahatchie County, Second District Court District. In the Circuit Court in and for said District of said County, at the September Term thereof, in the year of our Lord, 1955, the Grand Jurors of the State of Mississippi ... present that Roy Bryant and J. W. Milam ... did wilfully, unlawfully, feloniously, and of their malice aforethought kill and murder Emmett Till, a human being."

The second document is a true bill that lists the witnesses; the third document is the first criminal subpoena: "The state of Mississippi, Second Judicial District, Tallahatchie County. To the Sheriff of Leflore County, Greeting: You are hereby commanded to summon George Smith, J.

[8] A. Leon Higginbotham, Jr., *In the Matter of Color: Race and the American Legal Process* (New York: Oxford Univ. Press, 1978), pp. 13-14.

E. Cathran, Mose Wright, Sonny Wright, Simeon Wright, Maurice Wright, Mose Wright's wife, Dr. L. B. Otkin, Chick Nelson, Garland Milton, H. C. Strider, if to be found in your county, to be and personally appear before the Circuit Court of the Second District of the County of Tallahatchie, in said State, at the Court House in the Town of Sumner, Mississippi on the 9th day of September 1955 at 9 o'clock A.M. and there testify on behalf of Defendants (at whose instance this writ is issued) in a certain case pending in said Court, wherein the State of Mississippi is Plaintiff and J. W. Milam and Roy Bryant are Defendants." The second criminal subpoena adds: "You are hereby commanded to summon Charles Fred Mims, W. E. Hodges, Robert Hodges, if to be found in your County, to be and personally appear" at the same place and time "and there testify on behalf of State." The third subpoena adds Mamie Bradley, to be and personally appear and testify on behalf of the State. The fourth subpoena adds Johnnie Jennings, Mamie Bradley, Mrs. J. W. Milam, Mrs. Roy Bryant, Mrs. Erika Bryant, Chester A. Miller, Charles Fred Mims, W. E. Hodges, and Robert Hodges, to be and personally appear at the court to testify on behalf of Defendants.

Next follow seven instructional procedures for the jury regarding the defendants, Roy Bryant and J. W. Milam. Instructions No. 1 through 3 for Defendants read: "The court instructs the jury to find the defendants, Roy Bryant and J. W. Milam, not guilty." Underneath is written by hand "Refused and filed Sept 23 1955 Charles Cox Clerk."

Instruction No. 4 for Defendants reads: "The Court instructs the Jury for the Defendants that although you may believe from the evidence, beyond every reasonable doubt, that the Defendants did kill and murder Emmett Till, the person described in the indictment in this cause, and the person whose body was taken from Tallahatchie River, as shown in this cause; but unless you further believe from the evidence, beyond every reasonable doubt, that the said Emmett Till was killed and murdered by the Defendants in the Second Judicial District of Tallahatchie County, Mississippi, then, in such event, you would not be authorized under the law to return a verdict of guilty in this cause." It seems the court was instructing the jury that they could not find the defendants guilty because the crime was not committed in Tallahatchie County. Underneath is written by hand "Refused and filed Sept 23 1955 Charles Cox Clerk."

Instruction No. 5 for Defendants reads: "The court instructs the jury for the defendants that the defendants at the outset of the trial are presumed to be entirely innocent of the whole charge against them and every part thereof, and that this presumption attends them through out the trial of the case, and the court further charges you that they are not required to prove themselves innocent, but that the burden is upon the State to prove them guilty beyond every reasonable doubt, and the court instructs you that if from the evidence or want of evidence it should appear that the defendants are even probably innocent, it is your duty to acquit them." Underneath is written, by hand "Refused and filed Sept 23 1955 Charles Cox Clerk."

The sixth instruction reads: "The Court instructs the Jury for the Defendants that the body taken from Tallahatchie River as testified to in this cause, as a matter of law, is not shown to be that of Emmett Till, the person described in the indictment in this cause." Underneath is written "Refused and filed Sept 23 1955 Charles Cox Clerk." The seventh instruction reads: "The Court instructs the Jury that any statement against interest made by either of the Defendants, out of the presence and hearing of his Co-Defendant, is not admissible against such Defendant who was not present when such statement, if any, was made." This was also refused and filed September 23, 1955.

Then comes a statement *Nolle Prosequi,* which reads: This day this cause came on to be heard, came the District Attorney for the State and moved that this cause be *Nolle Prosequi.* And the Court considering the same finds that this motion should be and the Court hereby sustains the said motion. It is therefore ordered by the Court that this cause be and it is hereby *Nolle Prosequi.* And it is further ordered by the Court that the Sheriff of Tallahatchie County, Mississippi, deliver to the Sheriff of Leflore County, Mississippi, the said defendants, J. W. Milam and Roy Bryant. So ordered and adjudged this the 23rd day of September, 1955. In other words, if we cannot quickly acquit these defendants without a fuss (because the clerk keeps refusing our instructions), then let us not have to deal with the case at all, since the crime was not committed in our county.

The final two documents are a handwritten note, which reads: "We the Jury find the Defendants 'Not Guilty,'" and a Statement of Trial and Verdict of Jury, which reads: "This day the trial of this cause continued to be heard with all concerned present as of the day before and with the defense continuing its presentation of evidence to the Jury by its Witnesses until the counsel for defendants announced that they REST, after which the District Attorney announced that the State RESTS. And this cause continuing to be heard this day with the jury hearing the arguments of counsel for both the State of Mississippi and the defendants and receiving the instructions of the Court, the said jury retired to consider of their verdict and having duly considered the same returned into open Court in the presence of the Defendants and their counsel and the District Attorney and Special Prosecuting Attorney for the State this their Verdict to-wit: 'We the jury find the Defendants "Not Guilty". It is therefore considered by the Court and so ordered and adjudged that the Defendants, Roy Bryant and J. W. Milam, be and they are hereby discharged from this cause and that they go hence without d[el]ay. So ordered and adjudged this the 23rd day of September, 1955."

All these documents, and the missing documents including the trial transcripts, reveal the attitudes of the official participants in the trial. It was not the tradition of the South to place whites on trial for anything they did to blacks, and the whites, in general, were no doubt appalled that such a trial could even be held.

The information in two documents is particularly significant. The first one is the statement of discovery by District Attorney Gerald Chatham in which he, using the language of the constitution of the United States, states that Till, "a human being," had rights as such. These liberties are a part of the Fourteenth Amendment to the Federal Constitution, which guarantees "due process" including, but is not limited to, a fair and impartial jury, a fair *voir dire* (to speak the truth) examination of the prospective jury, and a judge who is unbiased.

The district attorney also states that Till was "willfully, unlawfully, feloniously, and of their malice aforethought" killed and murdered. In an issue denying someone his constitutional rights, these charges were critical, which suggests that the southern officials were apathetic and hostile to blacks and the trial. Till and blacks in general had already lost the case. He serves, then, as a catalyst for exploring a brutal form of legal racism.

Repercussions

The news of the Till case internationally shocked, horrified, and sobered reasonable minds and alerted people to the fact that something had to be done about racial injustice in America. Till's lynching rapidly became a subject of daily conversation in every household of the African-American community, and the image of his mutilated face became permanently etched into the conscious and unconscious memories of Americans. Ironically, complete and accurate documentation of the case has been lacking. Despite its importance to African-American consciousness, the Emmett Till murder case has never been fully examined by historians. In a sense, when Till was laid to rest in his Chicago grave, the knowledge of his legacy was also laid to rest.

The National Response

After the trial, Mamie Bradley and Rayfield Mooty were flown directly to New York. Congressman Diggs returned to Detroit, and Willie Reed went to Chicago. In each city, they spoke of what they had seen at the trial in Sumner. "More than 10,000 persons jammed a NAACP mass meeting at Chicago's Metropolitan Community Church where lanky Willie Reed, 18-year-old cotton picker who became the trial's star witness, urged 'northern Negroes to quit shouting and begin working to help their people in the South.'"[9]

A boycott was called by New York representative, Adam Clayton Powell, Jr., Democrat of Manhattan:

---

[9] *Jet*, October 6, 1955, p. 4.

Demands for a national boycott of all products from the State of Mississippi were cheered yesterday at a rally protesting the recent murder there of 14-year-old Emmett Till, Chicago Negro boy.

The rally [20,000 people] was held in Thirty-sixth Street between Seventh and Eighth Avenues under the auspices of District 65. Retail, Wholesale and Department Store Union, C.I.O., The National Association for the Advancement of Colored People and the Jewish Labor Committee cooperated.[10]

The New York Times provides an omnibus report of activities in major cities in "100,000 Across Nation Protest Till Lynching":

Detroit

Interest in the injustices of Mississippi reached its zenith here on Sunday when between 50,000 and 65,000 people jammed the streets here in an attempt to hear reports from those being made by Rep. Charles Diggs and Medgar Evers, NAACP field secretary of Mississippi.

Baltimore

More than 2,500 persons jammed Sharp Street Methodist church Sunday as the local NAACP staged a mammoth rally in protest of the current wave of terror and injustice going on in Mississippi. The civil rights fighting organization collected $3,001.50 from the attendants and gained hundreds of new memberships.

New York

---

[10] "Case of Emmett Till," *The Nation*, 25 Sept. 1955.

> *A throng of 12,000 gathered inside and all around Williams Institutional CME church Sunday as they rallied to a call made by A. Philip Randolph of the Brotherhood of Sleeping Car Porters, to protest the brutal killing of little Emmett Till in Mississippi ... One hour and a half before the dramatic program began, hundreds of indignant, irate Negroes began filling the church and by the time the program was ready to begin, all standing room was taken and others continued to pour into the avenue. As the crowd swelled, a detail of 30 policemen arrived to keep order ... Key figure and speaker along with Randolph, Roy Wilkins of the NAACP, City Councilman Earl Brown, Rev. David N. Licorish and others, was Mrs. Mamie Bradley, attractive mother of the slain lad who came to town straight from the trial in Sumner, Miss. ... Randolph termed the trial and killing a national disgrace ... He called for full support of the NAACP and thousands milled around the booths and took out membership.*[11]

Bringing the focus of the activities to the home of the victim, Robert Birchman notes that

> *Three thousand Chicagoans packed Metropolitan Community church, 41st and S. Parkway, Sunday and 7,000 more spilled out into the street in a mass meeting to protest the lynching of Emmett Louis Till [this was the meeting Willie Reed spoke at].*
>
> *Sunday's gathering was described as the largest and most enthusiastic civil rights mass meeting ever*

[11] *The New York Times*, "100,000 Across Nation Protest Till Lynching," October 1, 1955, p. 40.

> *sponsored by the NAACP in Chicago. The rally was attended by people of all races, colors and creeds.*[12]

It is clear that national organizations were joining forces in spearheading the demands of the people for justice.

The Hush-up: Till's Father

The defiant spirit of Mamie Bradley was to be quashed by discrediting the source. The momentum against racial injustices continued to escalate, until there came a move to extinguish the flame. In the headline story of October 22, 1955, the *Chicago Defender* pictured Till's mother pointing toward the Capitol, saying, "Maybe I can get justice here."[13] After the alleged murderers were acquitted, the sensational story of Till's father (Private Louis Till) was revealed with a photo of the twenty-three-year-old soldier. John Popham, reporter for *The New York Times,* asserted that, "Perhaps the most explosive of the developments was the disclosure two weeks ago by *The Jackson Daily News* that Till's father, serving in the Army in Italy in World War II, was hanged for the murder of one woman and the rape of two others."[14] This information was made public for the first time by Senator James Eastland of Mississippi, who probed into Louis Till's records, revealing that General Eisenhower, the commanding officer at that

[12] Robert L. Birchman, "10,000 Jam Till Mass Meet Here," *Chicago Defender,* 1 October 1955, p. 1.

[13] "Looking For Justice," *Chicago Defender* (Chicago, IL, 22 Oct. 1955), p. 1.

[14] John N. Popham, "Kidnapping Case Revived in South," *The New York Times,* 30 Oct. 1955.

time, had signed authorization papers permitting this execution.

An article in *Jet* (November 3, 1955) covers the response to this negative publicity from Private Till's World War II unit buddies in Chicago. Former non-commissioned officers and men of the Jim Crow 397th Port Battalion, composed mostly of Chicago draftees, contended that he was "railroaded" to his death in a "strange hush-hush atmosphere" in Italy. They said:

> *Till and three other Negro GIs were whisked from the unit and carried to a stockade in another area. Later, all of Till's records were taken from the company and none of the outfit's Negro leaders was allowed to see any material on the case ... [One] Negro non-com said: "Till never confessed the crime and we felt he was innocent. It is inconceivable that the big, playful fellow could be a criminal. If the facts stood up, the Army should not have been so hush-hush about killing him."*
>
> *Said another former corporal: "A group of 127 of our Negro non-coms were 'busted' following North African riots when white MPs sought to enforce non-fraternization bans. We were known as 'the most militant unit' in Italy but we also established new tonnage records in unloading ships under fire."*[15]

Whether he was guilty of the conviction will never be known. Mrs. Bradley recalls,

> *I've heard all of the nightmarish things that went on. The fellows would have to come out of the bed; they would have to fall out. The women [white] would go*

[15] *Jet Magazine,* "GI Buddies Say Till's Dad Was `Railroaded' in Italy," 3 November 1955, pp. 4-5.

> *through the line pointing "this one." And some of them would say "I know that one. He sleeps right next to me. He hasn't moved all night long." They'd never see that one again.*[16]

Whites were resentful of black soldiers overseas because blacks were known to date white women, and that was enough to threaten the white men. It was rumored that many black soldiers were accused and killed for such activities, as a scare tactic for discouraging interracial dating.

The first time Till's mother, wife of the accused who should have been advised of the nature of her husband's death some ten years before, was informed of his execution was reading about it in these newspapers. The only information she had been given prior to this was that he was killed.[17] In spite of her many attempts to secure more information, she had been left in the dark until Emmett Till's lynching.

In an effort to countervail southern white efforts to mar the credibility of Till's mother and even Till himself (suggesting that he was a potential rapist) by disclosing the execution of Till's father, a black *Chicago Defender* newspaper reporter, Ethel Payne, wrote the following:

> *The execution ten years ago of slain Emmett Till's father was headlined in the southern press this week in what a Chicago attorney described as an effort to influence the grand jury that is to weigh kidnapping charges against J. W. Milam and Roy Bryant ... William Henry Huff of Chicago declared Sunday that the disclosure that the slain boy's father did not die a*

---

[16] Tape-recorded interview with Bradley-Mobley, Chicago, IL, 6 January 1988.

[17] Bradley-Mobley.

> *hero's death "does not justify the youth's lynching nor discredit either the dead boy nor his mother," Mrs. Mamie Bradley.*[18]

For Payne and Huff, the need to clear the air on the matter of Louis Till was critical. The tactics of the southern journalists were nonetheless effective, for after this public exposure, many began to judge Emmett Till and his mother on moral grounds, asking "What can she say now?"[19] in view of the alleged history of her husband.

The two accused half-brothers were subsequently acquitted on the kidnapping charges. Further, to counter the information from the southern white presses and the decision of the jury, a story from a University of Illinois publication, entitled "University Students Rap Till Verdict" appeared in the October 22, 1955, *Chicago Defender*. The story held to the following position exemplifying the wide range of support against Till's lynching and the court decision: "The verdict rendered by the jury will be remembered as one of the most notorious miscarriages of justice ever handed."[20]

The intensity (especially the ingenuity) of the publicity of the Till case posed a threat to existing institutionalized racism, which had to be minimized. The quieting of the Till case was not an unusual or isolated occurrence in American history—Malcolm X was also effectively whiteballed by the media in the early sixties.

---

[18] Payne, p. 1.

[19] Unidentified voice, Mamie Bradley's last speaking engagement under the auspices of the NAACP, Indianapolis, October 1955.

[20] Payne.

3
The Modern Civil Rights Movement

Historians will talk about the good and the bad, but they don't want to deal with the ugly...The ugliness of racism is not a white man's telling a black woman to give him her bus seat—bad as that is—but the —confident home-invasion, kidnapping and murder of a fourteen-year-old black youth and the exoneration by jury of the youth's apparent killers.

—Rayfield Mooty[1]

The subject here is the history of the Civil Rights Movement with regard to the Till murder case and how this case has been treated or ignored by traditional historians. Since the involuntary migration of black people from Africa (the motherland for all blacks), throughout the bloody transatlantic slave-trade, to the seasoning islands of the Caribbean, to the incomprehensible atrocities of American slavery, blacks have been struggling for human rights. During the earliest stages of American slavery (near the beginning of the seventeenth century) to its final legal

---

1 Video-tape-recorded interview with Rayfield Mooty, Chicago, Illinois, April 1986.

period in the mid-nineteenth century (marked by the Civil War and the signing of the Emancipation Proclamation in September 1862, which went into effect January 1, 1863), emphasis on physical freedom from human bondage characterizes the black American struggle. Subsequent white retaliation and bitterness, resulting from the whites' displaced ownership of black people and their stubborn sense of white superiority, ultimately evolved into the establishment of the Jim Crow laws in the early 1880s. These laws, which according to Woodward were "the public symbols and constant reminders of his [black's] inferior position," legalized what W. E. B. DuBois metaphorically designates in *Souls of Black Folk* as the "veil," the wall or curtain of segregation.[2] Just as blacks rose up against forms of oppression then, they continue to do so today. Extreme white opposition to the black resistance to oppression, in the form of heinous, brutal crimes such as rape and lynchings, clearly validates the need for black people to continue and even to intensify their struggle as a proud and historically determined people. This act of self-determination in turn would protect blacks against a designed vulnerability to which they are assigned in this dehumanization and blatant denial of their "inalienable rights" as fellow human beings.

The fifties mark the beginning of the era of the widely publicized struggle for the civil rights of African-Americans. No longer a question of emancipation, the key issue for the early part of that decade was the notion of being "separate but equal" as a way of life. This aspiration proved to be both hypocritical and unrealistic within the American system. The Supreme Court's landmark decision in the 1954 controversial *Brown versus Topeka Board of Edu-*

---

[2] C. Vann Woodward, *The Strange Career of Jim Crow* (New York: Oxford Univ. Press, 1957), p. 7.

cation, established the unconstitutionality of the "separate but equal" public school systems. Thus, desegregation in the public schools was officially ordered. Blacks, like any other people, desired to share in all the benefits American society had to offer—educational, political, economic, as well as social rights. However, the resolution to demand boldly their civil rights did not come without a high price. As in the past, blacks were severely dehumanized; but they were to be now alarmed into consciousness of the urgent need to remedy the powerlessness and insignificance of their lives as perceived by the dominant white culture. Such was the case in the infamous murder and mock trials of the Emmett Till.

From 1877 to 1965

The Till murder case has been vastly underappreciated as a main stimulus for the modern Civil Rights Movement, despite the fact that it was one of the most important events that occurred in African-American, and even American, culture in the fifties. It embodies the ugliness of American racism, effecting the most vicious form of violence to be bestowed upon a human being. Lynching is an atrocity that finds its victims both powerless and, more important, too often guiltless. After reflecting upon the nuances of the scores of atrocities heaped upon African-Americans between the years 1877 to 1965, marking the beginning to the end of the Till scenario, it appears that symbolically the stage for the Till slaying was set by Rutherford Birchard Hayes's infamous 1877 Compromise. The nineteenth president of the United States, Hayes won by only one electoral vote. As a strategy to win the presidential election, he agreed to a "laissez faire" policy on the matter of the laws and practices of the southern conservative states. One of the ramifications of the Hayes Compromise was that the North ignored the plight of the African-American in the South, and the Till case, seventy-eight years later, forced America to take another look.

The ramifications of the Hayes Compromise would not be legally concluded until Lyndon Baines Johnson, the thirty-sixth president of the United States, signed the 1965 Voting Rights Bill, that removed the legal shackles from African-Americans. Mooty has this to say:

> *I have to go back to the presidential election of 1877 ... when all of the rights that we had (President Abraham Lincoln did give us a little relief of freedom) were taken from us by the stroke of one pen and only by one vote! One electoral vote! ... In 1877 Rutherford B. Hayes made a compromise with the South that "if you give me your vote and make me president, I will pull the troops out of there." And the troops were what they called a toothache to the southerners, and he said, "I will pull that tooth out, and then you can do whatever you want to."*

Just prior to the Hayes election, whites were retaliating against the legal progress of the African-Americans, directly related to Lincoln's signing of the Emancipation Proclamation. They particularly resisted the newly acquired freedom of African-Americans in Reconstruction to exercise voting rights, so they used terrorist tactics at the polls.

During the mid-twentieth century, Till became part of that historical continuum, although voting was not the issue with him. The climate was much the same just before his lynching, when voting registration drives in Mississippi were posing a threat to the white power system. As in the 1870s, whites used lynching as a means of intimidation and of discouraging African-American participation in the voting processes. The Thirteenth, Fourteenth, and Fifteenth Amendments provided constitutional rights and protections for African-Americans; however, the established institution of black servitude and white supremacy was a way of life, and one that whites were not willing to surrender peacefully.

The Jim Crow Laws

Another critical event in the history of the modern Civil Rights Movement was the emergence of the Jim Crow laws of the 1880s. These were various laws that sprang up in different states, culminated by the *Plessy versus Ferguson* case in 1896, which was decided by the Supreme Court and which gave federal and constitutional sanction to "separate but equal facilities," thus making racial segregation both legal and constitutional. This legally established second-class citizenship for African-Americans during the nadir of the post-Reconstruction period. These limitations on African-Americans culminated in countless lynchings as terrorist political tools for social and economic control. And the lynchings continued, legally uncontested in the courts, until the Till lynching in 1955: the first of its kind to hold a trial of whites for the lynching of an African-American.

The Till lynching was a culminating experience in African-Americans' feelings of powerlessness. Demonstrations erupted and continued. Ten years later, in 1965, President Lyndon B. Johnson, with the stroke of a pen, granted African-Americans the voting rights that were needed to change this abject victimization. He cautioned that every African-American must register and vote, for one is not truly free until then, until one can ensure oneself proper protection through proper political representation. Johnson knew that the dominant culture would stop at nothing to secure the votes of African-Americans, once the latter had that privilege. And since over half of the African-American population lived in northern and western states where they had voting rights already, southern whites knew that once southern blacks had that right too, the whites would have trouble. Realizing that much of the power of the dominant culture as American citizens in a democratic society lies in the voting power, Johnson moved all the more on the potential of the ballot for African-Americans. This represents the true meaning of the signing of the Voting Rights Bill, reflecting its significance to the plight of all African-Americans, and reversing Hayes's earlier regressive act.

As for Till, his death carried that race and sex inference. His murderers had the security that the law would not be implemented against them. The point of the trial following Till's lynching is that African-Americans did not and could not become jurors in Mississippi, and whites would not convict any other white for murdering any African-American. According to John Popham of *The New York Times*, race was a key issue with John C. Whitten, one of the defense attorneys, who established his confidence in the all-white jury: "Every last Anglo-Saxon one of you has the courage to free these men in the point that several people who handled the dead body testifies they thought it had been too decomposed to be identified."[3] That was just what happened: the jury unanimously found the defendants not guilty.

---

[3] John N. Popham, "Mississippi Jury Frees 2 in Killing," *The New York Times*, 24 Sept. 1955, p. 38.

The Fear Beneath

There is something beneath the surface in the meaning of Till's murder. It has always been said that opposites attract—men are attracted to women, women are attracted to men, and in some cases white men are attracted to black women, and black men are attracted to white women. According to Calvin Hernton, "Out of his [white man's] guilt [because of his relationships with black women] grew fear—if he found it difficult to stay away from the 'animal' attraction of black women, was it not possible that his wife felt that same attraction to the black 'bucks'? Something had to be done."[4] Given the time period, the location, and the state of race relations during the pre-Civil Rights era in the South, the attraction between the different races (particularly of African-American men to white women) was not only illegal and unacceptable, but abhorred and dangerous. This was true because the fear that Hernton analyzes on the part of white men is that, given the freedom of choice, their women may demonstrate a mutual attraction to the African-American men. Wells explored this concept earlier with the following conclusions:

> *I also found that what the white man of the South practiced as all right for himself, he assumed to be unthinkable in white women. They could and did fall in love with the pretty mulatto and quadroon girls as well as black ones, but they professed an inability to imagine white women doing the same thing with Negro and mulatto men. Whenever they did so and were found out, the cry of rape was raised, and the lowest element of the white South was turned loose to wreak*

[4] Calvin C. Hernton, *Sex and Racism in America* (New York: Doubleday & Company, Inc., 1965), p. 16.

> *its fiendish cruelty on those too weak to help themselves.*[5]

Winthrop Jordan takes the fear to another level in *White Over Black,* in which he examines the white man's attitudes toward the African-American man. He contends that the white man fears the African-American man's sexual aggression:

> *The concept of the Negro's aggressive sexuality was reinforced by what was thought to be an anatomical peculiarity of the Negro male. He was said to possess an especially large penis ... If a perceptible anatomical difference did in fact exist, it fortuitously coincided with the already firmly established idea of the Negro's special sexuality; it could only have served as striking confirmation of that idea, as salt in the wounds of the white man's envy.*[6]

The white, therefore, finds the need to prove to himself that he is the master.

According to William Bradford Huie, a white investigator of racial atrocities who wrote the celebrated story of Till's murderers for *Look* magazine after the trial, "They didn't take him out to kill him. They killed him because he had a white girl's picture in his pocket, and he told 'em that she was his girl. It was at the time that they thought that this sorta thing had to be stopped in order to defend the 'Southern way of life.'"[7] The thought that such an at-

---

[5] Duster, p. 70.

[6] Winthrop D. Jordan, *White Over Black* (Baltimore, MD: Penguin Books Inc., 1968), pp. 158-159.

[7] Quoted in Howell Raines, *My Soul Is Rested* (New York: Viking Penguin Books, 1983), p. 393.

traction might get out of hand and cause widespread miscegenation was regarded by the dominant culture as a critical problem, and hence was treated with utmost urgency and drastic measures. The scenario surrounding the Till incident was indeed explosive.

Arnold Rose asserts in his condensed version of Gunnar Myrdal's *The American Dilemma* that "a lynching is not merely a punishment against an individual but a disciplinary device against the Negro group."[8] Although the reaction and response of Till's murderers to such an issue was both extreme and unwarranted, it was, nonetheless, the trend. It was easy to repeat such an act, since it had happened over and over again. The difference with Till was that he was a teenager who could not have had the same ultimate intentions as a grown man. His lynching was called to the public's attention, and the ugliness of American racism became known to the world.

These insights into the socioeconomic and psychological ramifications of lynchings confirm that the motivations behind them are multifaceted, complicated, and intricate. The lynching of Till symbolizes the ultimate deterioration of race relations. His death reflects a threefold victimization: of a human being denied his life, of an African-American man deprived of dignity, and of a child robbed of his future.

The Till Case and the Modern Civil Rights Movement

It appears that, for a number of reasons, there has been a conscious effort to neglect the fact that this incident

---

[8] Rose, p. 185.

is a key historical event in the record of the movement. To begin with, the victim of this incident was not a member of the upper-middle-class bourgeoisie, and his experience was more prone to happen among the lower and working classes than among the upper class. On the whole, established historians, as is the case of academicians in general, were members of the upper-middle class, the bourgeoisie, and generally tended not to focus on the particular plight of the lower or working-class African-Americans, except as their plight affected the whole race. In other words, the neglect of the Till case stems from a class issue.

Then the nature of Till's "crime"—wolf-whistling at a white woman—was ambiguous. At that time, it was considered taboo behavior, particularly in the Deep South. Finally, because Till was an outsider (a northern African-American youth visiting in the South who did not conduct himself according to white people's expectations, according to southern etiquette), the whole Till case posed an embarrassment to the movement, both for African-American leaders and whites. The respected black leaders and historians possibly feared that the incident would alienate them from white culture. For example, there has always been that segment of the African-American population who seeks approval of and direction from the dominant culture. During slavery they were generally among the "house niggers" and later they were identified among the "black bourgeoisie." Having been accepted by the dominant culture, this group directs its energies toward protecting that relationship to maintain the alliance, which necessitates protecting whites through avoidance of the embarrassment of having their shortcomings exposed. Therefore, in avoiding the Till incident as a significant part of the fabric of American culture, they protect both their established relationships with whites and the reputations of the whites as well.

Another possible explanation for the lack of attention to the Till case is that those historians, leaders, and reporters of the Civil Rights Movement had more to gain from a "peaceful" movement. This is true because they could that way appease both blacks and whites: the former by articulating and spearheading their demands to end segregation in the social and educational spheres, and the latter by addressing the eradication of their acceptable chosen issues of concern. The historians in particular acted to downplay Till's lynching, to downplay the embodiment of racial violence and the ugliness of racial victimization. They chose, instead, to celebrate the refusal of Rosa Parks to relinquish her bus seat to a white man, a morally acceptable act of proclaiming one's common humanity through integration, a major issue with the NAACP. Unlike Till, Parks was not the object of brutal racism. Her symbolic act was a peaceful one and a more appealing media image than the slaughtered Till. Had the Till case continued to receive maximum attention, under the leadership of organized labor (with its legacy of marshalling the demands for economic parity as well as civil rights for blacks since the early forties), the direction of the then-evolving Civil Rights Movement would have probably taken on another dimension or even direction.

Ranking Till with Established Leaders

Although Till, technically, cannot be included among the martyrs who gave their lives in the pursuit of African-American freedom (for instance, two black Mississippians murdered shortly before Emmett, Rev. George W. Lee, who had just delivered a sermon giving a review of the history of black Americans' struggle for freedom on the

Sunday before he was murdered by members of the white Citizens' Council for registering to vote, and Lamar Smith, also involved in voter registration efforts), Till's untimely death, and the public's reaction to it, helped set the stage for the Civil Rights Movement. Richard Aubrey McLemore in the second volume of *A History of Mississippi* concludes that "the effect of the crime and its aftermath was to intensify an already emotional atmosphere, and the state's preoccupation with a politics of race increased."[9]

Indeed, even Rosa Parks herself acknowledges the uniqueness and importance of this case. She asserts that "it [the Till murder case] was a very tragic incident ... Many such incidents had gone unnoticed in the past."[10] Dr. King, too, referred to the Till case twice in *Stride Toward Freedom*. Discussing the impermanence of publicity and popularity, he asserted, "Today it is Emmett Till, tomorrow, it is Martin Luther King. Then in another tomorrow it will be somebody else."[11] Later he alluded to the fact that Till's murder is ever present in the minds of the oppressed who fear that there is no recourse for their victimization: "With the Emmett Till case in Mississippi still fresh in our memories, the Negroes held little hope of conviction."[12] Undoubtedly, this case bore heavy on their minds, as it did on the minds of many others.

Although Juan Williams does not postulate that the Till incident was the catalyst for the movement, in his work *Eyes on the Prize*, he does acknowledge that "the

---

[9] Richard Aubrey McLemore, *A History of Mississippi, Volume II* (Hattiesburg: Univ. & College Press of Mississippi, 1973), p. 153.

[10] Rosa Parks, "Slain."

[11] Martin Luther King, Jr. *Stride Toward Freedom* (New York: Ballantine Books, 1958), p. 127.

[12] King, p. 145.

Montgomery Advertiser in Montgomery, Alabama, picked up the Till story and gave it prominent display. Three months later, the black population of Montgomery began an historic boycott of their municipal bus system."[13] He investigates the motivations behind the prime movers of the boycott, such as Rosa Parks's continuous refusal to relinquish her bus seat at times dating back as early as 1944; Jo Ann Robinson's traumatic and dehumanizing experience of being forced to relinquish her bus seat during the Christmas rush in 1949; and Edgar Daniel Nixon's leadership in waiting for the "right person" and soliciting the black ministers (one of whom was Martin Luther King, Jr., then a new minister in the town).

It should be noted here that, for a number of reasons, Till was not the "right person." The leaders of the Civil Rights Movement have always made choices. For example, according to Taylor Branch in *Parting the Waters*, approximately seven months before Rosa Parks's demonstration, there was the case of

> *a feisty high school student named Claudette Colvin, who defended her right to the seat in language that brought words of disapproval from passengers of both races ... Colvin was crying and madder than ever by the time the policemen told her she was under arrest. She struggled when they dragged her off the bus and screamed when they put on the handcuffs ... Prosecutors had thrown the book at Colvin, charging her with violating the segregation law, assault, and disorderly conduct.*

Unlike Parks, Claudette did not surrender peacefully. On May 6, Judge Eugene Carter

---

[13] Williams, p. 57.

> *sentenced Colvin to pay a small fine—a sentence so much lighter than anticipated that it ruined her martyr status. Many Negroes who supported her case nevertheless came to believe she was lucky.*[14]

The black leadership did investigate the situation. However, after the discovery that the teenager was also pregnant and unmarried, they decided that she would not be the proper model to rally behind. In other words, because her character and sense of morality were questionable, she was not selected as the perfect model for a movement against institutionalized racism.

Parks, on the other hand, was another story. Nixon, a black leader in Montgomery, went to Clifford Durr, an attorney and one of the few white liberals in the town, for consultation.

> *He asked for Durr's legal opinion: was this the case they had been waiting for? Could they use it to win a victory over segregation on appeal? ... The only flaw with the case as he saw it was that the charges would first be heard in state court rather than federal court. But there were ways to move cases. Otherwise, the circumstances were highly favorable. There were no extraneous charges to cloud the segregation issue, and Rosa Parks would make a good impression on white judges. This was enough for Nixon, who already knew instinctively that Rosa Parks was without peer as a potential symbol for Montgomery's Negroes—humble enough to be claimed by the common folk, and yet dig-*

---

[14] Taylor Branch, *Parting the Waters: America in the King Years 1954-63* (New York: Simon and Schuster, 1988), 120, 123.

> *nified enough in manner, speech, and dress to command the respect of the leading classes.*[15]

A respectable, light-skinned gentlewoman, Parks was a perfect model, both impressive and appealing.

As for Till, particularly with his bloated brutalized face, and the whole white woman/black man sex scenario, he was not the proper model to choose. There were still those who said that Till should have known better, and who were angry with him for being mannish, and for stepping out of line. Williams' investigation in *Eyes on the Prize* (which is the most detailed account of Till in the traditional historical canon) is a demonstration of individual or personal history, reflections on the lives of the heroes or "great" people (or, as in the case of Parks and Robinson, established, respected citizens), rather than the history of the masses. His study would have been strengthened had he attempted to include an assessment of the mood of the black masses who in fact carried out the Montgomery Bus Boycott.

It seems that since blacks had been subjected to the segregated bus system there for sixty-five years, something more dramatic or traumatic than their "tired feet" was needed to carry them through this unyielding yearlong bus boycott. And it seems plausible and natural to suggest that a people would react in the manner they did only after a supreme insult to their race—the racially motivated murder of a black youth, for example. Indeed, after Till's death, blacks in large numbers bravely demonstrated and publicly confronted the racial immoralities in the American system. Even though all were moved by the Till murder case, the movement itself physically needed a Rosa Parks, the symbolic impetus for the movement.

---

[15] Branch, *Parting the Waters*, 130.

Till and Traditional History

Prior to the Till case and the Montgomery Bus Boycott, the *Brown versus Topeka Board of Education* case had in a sense established a mood of optimism. The Till case exploded approximately a year after this legal landmark and jarred people back too the realization that black freedom would be achieved only through independent black efforts, since the Till case made it once again obvious that the courts would not take up the fight for equal justice. Moreover, the Till case occurred about a year before the Montgomery Bus Boycott, which points to the fact that there was the need for another vehicle—mass demonstrations—by which to achieve justice and exposure for black victims.

Until *Eyes on the Prize,* black and white historians alike have failed to recognize the significance of the Till case and even this work does not do it justice. Even though Williams's work introduced Till, still there has been no official full-length scholarly discussion of the implications of the Till case on the future development on the Modern Civil Rights Movement, particularly from an endemic perspective. Williams implicitly corroborates the thesis of this work: that Till's contribution to the growing militancy of the black community was significant, and worthy of a full-length scholarly examination.

Consider the historical account of the black American struggle in the fifties and the sixties as documented by the foremost black historian, John Hope Franklin. In his most recently revised edition, the 1994 seventh edition of *From Slavery to Freedom,* there is only one reference to the Till case, and it is not even indexed. Franklin wrote, in a brief catalogue of black victims during that period: "Near Greenwood a fourteen-year-old Negro boy from Chicago was murdered for allegedly whistling at a white storekeeper's wife."[16] He failed to even identify the victim. So much for the Till murder case in this standard textbook.

Consider Kenneth G. Goode's *From Africa to the United States and Then: A Concise Afro-American History*. Nowhere is Till mentioned in the text, not even in the chronological table of events, which appears in the back of the book.

Consider Peter M. Bergman's *The Chronological History of the Negro in America*. Here Till receives minimum coverage, as he appears in the list of three victims of lynchings occurring in Mississippi in 1955: "Lynching returned to the South. Mississippi accounted for three: Rev. George W. Lee at Belzoni, Lamar Smith at Brookhaven, and Emmett Till near Money."[17] While there is some elaboration on the other two, Rev. George Lee and Lamar Smith relative to their involvement with the Mississippi voter registration drive, no additional comment on the Till case is made.

Consider co-authors Albert P. Blaustein and Robert L. Zangrando who wrote *Civil Rights and the American Negro: A Documentary History*. In the entire 671-page book on the African-Americans' civil rights from 1619 until 1968, only one reference is made to Emmett Till: "Moreover, segregationist and states' rights opposition had encouraged the formation of such organized groups as the White Citizens' Councils and the initiation of such unorganized violence as the kidnap-lynching of fourteen-year-old Emmett Till at Money, Mississippi, in the summer of 1955."[18] Even then,

---

[16] John Hope Franklin, *From Slavery to Freedom: A History of Negro Americans* (New York: Alfred A. Knopf, 1980), p. 459.

[17] Peter M. Bergman, *The Chronological History of the Negro in America* (New York: The New American Library, 1969), p. 542.

[18] Albert P. Blaustein and Robert L. Zangrando, *Civil Rights and the American Negro: A documentary History* (New York: Washington Square Press, Inc., 1968), p. 471.

the reference does not reflect the impact Till's murder and trial had on the American people, particularly African-Americans. On the contrary, it merely emphasizes intimidation of the black community by the dominant culture.

Consider one of the greatest black historians of the twentieth century, Benjamin Quarles and *The Negro in the Making of America*. Nowhere in his entire book is the Till murder case mentioned. In recapitulating the activities of the fifties, he asserts that "This movement [Civil Rights Movement] started on December 1, 1955, when seamstress Rosa Parks boarded a bus in downtown Montgomery, took a seat in the section reserved for whites, and refused to surrender it to a white man who subsequently entered the bus."[19]

Consider the recently published co-authored historical account of the black American by two highly credible black historians, Mary Frances Berry and John Blassingame, *Long Memory: The Black Experience in America*. Again the reference to the Till murder case is limited to one sentence, and like other historians they fail to put this case in the historical perspective of the Civil Rights Movement. Hence, "Emmett Till, a fourteen-year-old boy, was kidnapped and killed in Money, Mississippi, in 1955 because he allegedly whistled at a white woman."[20] Their reference to the Till case only exemplifies the taboo of the black man and the white woman in the long debated issue of sex and racism.

According to Gunnar Myrdal, who devised what he called "The Rank Order of Discrimination" in *An American*

---

[19] Benjamin Quarles, *The Negro in the Making of America* (London: Collier-MacMillan Ltd., 1969), p. 250.

[20] Mary Frances Berry and John W. Blassingame, *Long Memory: The Black Experience in America* (New York: Oxford University Press, 1982), p. 124.

Dilemma, he found that whites contended that blacks wanted sexual relations and intermarriage with white women more than other forms of equality. When he questioned blacks, he found that they contended that they valued the sexual attraction least.[21] Calvin Hernton discusses this issue in *Sex and Racism in America,* in which he concluded "that the race problem is inextricably connected with sex ... The sexualization of the race problem is a reality, and we are going to have to deal with it even though most of us are, if not unwilling, definitely unprepared."[22]

Finally, consider the interpretive historian Vincent Harding in *The Other American Revolution.* Till is not mentioned at all.

Others, too, have been guilty of side-tracking or bypassing the Till case, as reflected in the records of both *The World Almanac* and the *Reader's Digest.* In recording the significant events of the month and year, the World Almanacs cite the Rosa Parks incident, but fail to mention Till. The *Reader's Digest,* too, mentions Parks, but not Till. Clearly, the Till murder case is a lost chapter in the history books on the Civil Rights Movement.

There is a discrepancy between the underplayed account of the Till case in history and the detailed media coverage it received. Only through reviewing the Till case as interpreted by journalists, as well as everyday people, photographers, creative writers, singers, and autobiographers, can the oversights of historians be corrected. One important publication (important because of its accuracy on the Till murder case), which documented testimonies

---

[21] Gunnar Myrdal, *An American Dilemma* (New York: Harper & Brothers, 1944).

[22] Calvin C. Hernton, *Sex and Racism in America* (New York: Doubleday & Company, Inc., 1965), pp. 4-5.

by persons with insights on it, was one of several small pamphlets covering this atrocity. Published in 1956, *Time Bomb* was written by Olive Arnold Adams, editor of *Global News Syndicate*, with a foreword by Dr. T. R. M. Howard, the civil rights activist in whose home Till's mother, grandfather, and cousin Mooty resided during the murder trial. This book relates detailed information surrounding the murder. Mooty attests to the insights in this book, as he was an intricate part of the case from its inception. In all these testimonies, one crucial thing comes out: that at the outset of the Civil Rights Movement, a fourteen-year-old northern black youth fell prey to the treachery of American racism, both in his death and in the subsequent mock trials. The unrelenting restlessness, fervor, and anger of the African-American established on that day that obsequiousness, helplessness, and complacency had passed, at least for the moment.

In spite of it all, Till has yet to receive his deserved place in the historical chronicles of the African-American struggle. As Simeon Booker observes, "Today, only one statue of Emmett Till exists in the entire nation. That being, in a city park in Denver. The black mother who changed the course of history is almost forgotten—except for a three-part series on the lynching, broadcast by Chicago's WMAQ-TV station's Rich Samuels."[23] Although Till has not been properly remembered or immortalized by Americans, Congressman Gus Savage of Chicago wrote in a moving letter addressed to the fallen victim that, "A monument to serve as a shrine has been suggested in your memory; but we know the only monument not decayed by

---

[23] Booker, p. 14.

time is freedom. So we shall fight for freedom in your memory."[24]

Sacrificial Lamb

Emmett Till has been called the sacrificial lamb of the Civil Rights Movement. As Jordan asserts: "There was no way for progress to be made without someone dying ... There had to be sacrificial lambs and that is what Emmett Till was." The editor of *Freedom*, Louis E. Burnham, said shortly after Till's death: "The fight to avenge the murder of Emmett Louis Till has become a symbol of the Negro people's bitter struggle for first-class citizenship."[25]

Although many regard the Parks incident as the beginning of the Civil Rights Movement, it is a mistake to ignore the earlier impact of the Till murder, which occurred just three months and three days before the Parks incident. Inundating the world press, the Till murder case was thoroughly covered by the news media, but it has not been adequately chronicled in history books. In a 1956 *Ebony* article, Clotye Murdock wrote:

> *The state [Mississippi] has been referred to in the foreign press as the "land of the Till Murder." Racial clashes between Negroes and whites there have made headlines in a Babel of languages. In lands far distant from America, where Mississippi is only a word, a name, for a state or a city or a province—many know*

---

[24] Gus Savage, "30 Years Ago: How Emmett Till's Lynching Launched Civil Rights Drive" in *Jet* by Simeon Booker (17 June 1985), p. 18.

[25] Louis Burnham, *Behind the Lynching of Emmett Louis Till* (New York: Freedom Associates, Inc., Dec. 1955), p. 5.

> *not which—people frown in bewilderment as they hear it, and say: "Is that not the place where the Negro boy was killed?"*[26]

Labor Unions Take Up the Case

Since Till was neither the first nor the last black to be lynched, one may question why this case became a big issue. First of all, the Till incident happened at the right time, just as the age of modernity with mass media technology reached an all-time high in the area of communication. Radio, newspapers, and television ushered the news of the Till lynching into the homes of countless American citizens, making a traditionally isolated incident public information. With this new technology, events that would not have reached the national public were now known to all.

Another reason is that a major national labor-union organization, the AFL-CIO, had just merged in August, bridging the gap between the two most prominent black labor leaders—A. Philip Randolph, president of the Brotherhood of Sleeping Car Porters, and William S. Townsend, president of the Former Red Caps, president of the Transportation Services Employees—who embraced this case from the outset and obtruded it upon the American society for public censure. The following memorandum, dated September 27, 1955, from labor-union official Boyd L. Wilson to David J. McDonald, the president of the United Steel Workers Union, and I. W. Abel regarding the labor meeting on the Till case states that:

---

[26] Clotye Murdock, "Land of the Till Murder," *Ebony* (April 1956), p. 91.

> *Monsignor Cornelius J. Drew, pastor, St. Charles Roman Catholic Church, before an impressive crowd of ten thousand people in New York City last Sunday, made an impassioned plea that the decent, right-thinking people of the United States rise up and make a repetition of the Till case impossible in America.*
>
> *He was joined by A. Philip Randolph, president, Brotherhood of Sleeping Car Porters; Roy Wilkins, executive director, NAACP, and City Councilman Earl Brown, before a rally sponsored by trade unions and instigated by the Brotherhood of Sleeping Car Porters, AFL ...*
>
> *Resolutions were adopted calling upon Governor Hugh White of Mississippi, and the United States Department of Justice to investigate and establish the whereabouts of two missing witnesses. Likewise, to establish, beyond the shadow of a doubt, as to the identity of the body discovered in the river, if indeed it was not that of Till.*
>
> *The Till case has been a rallying point for liberal movements and peoples within the United States in recent weeks, and it has been my considered judgement that it is to the best interests of the Steel Workers' Union to carry its share of the responsibility and to do what it can to further the case of justice of all people.*

Mooty had much to say about the labor-union involvement: "The whole labor union was involved in it [the Till case] before it [public exposure] happened."[27] A relative of Till through his uncle Henry Spearman, Rayfield Mooty, a member of the Community Services Committee and the president of a steel labor-union local in Chicago, had spent years in the labor movement and was in the position to

[27] Mooty.

make the necessary contact with the right people who had the influence to expose this case nationally. As Mamie Bradley-Mobley recalls, "Mr. Mooty was the one who was sort of like steering me which way to go because he was quite active in the labor movement and he knew the politicians. I didn't know a politician."[28]

He first contacted one of the most influential blacks in the United Automobile Workers, vice-president of the Cook County Industrial Union, vice-president of the newly merged AFL-CIO, and vice-president of the NAACP (Chicago branch), Bill Townsend. Townsend, in turn, was able to bring the entire United Automobile Workers and the Cook County Industrial Council into the case. Some other influential persons who were drawn into the case included Boyd Wilson (personal representative of the United Steel Workers of America), Bill Abner (vice-president of the Cook County Industrial Union Council and vice-president of the NAACP Chicago branch), David McDonald (president of the United Steel Workers Union), Doug Anderson (former chairman of the Community Services Committee and manager of Senator Paul Douglas's office in Chicago), Senator Paul Douglass, Congressman William Dawson (of the First Congressional District of Illinois), and three executive board members of the union, Lucius Love (staff member of the United Steel Workers and executive board member of the Cook County Industrial Union Council), Charlie Hayes (Cook County Industrial Union Council), and Hugh Lewis (public school teacher with the school union). And finally the president of the International Brotherhood of Sleeping Car Porters himself, A. Philip Randolph, was brought into the case. These people had worked together for years and thus, as

---

[28] Tape-recorded interview with Mamie Bradley-Mobley, Chicago, IL, 6 January 1988.

Mooty asserts, "It was easy to swing them into place."[29] Clearly they could together influence the entire labor movement to act.

Demonstrating the commitment of the Steel Workers' Union, it was revealed in *Steel Labor: The Voice of the United Steelworkers of America—C.I.O.* that "the brutal slaying of a 14-year-old Chicago Negro boy ... was vigorously condemned in a resolution on Civil Rights adopted by delegates at the annual conference of District 31, United Steelworkers."[30]

The following telegram to Rayfield Mooty from Theodore Brown, director of research and publicity for the Brotherhood of Sleeping Car Porters in New York, dated September 23, 1955, documents the national involvement of the labor union:

> *Would appreciate deeply your acceptance of invitation of New York division of the Brotherhood of Sleeping Car Porters to attend and speak at mass meeting occasion to protest and organize New York public opinion against the brutal lynching of your nephew in Mississippi. This meeting first organized effort in New York on this unfortunate incident to take place this Sunday, September 25, at Williams Institutional C.M.E. Church located 2225 Seventh Avenue, New York City. Time is 2:30 pm. The organization's international president, Mr. A. Philip Randolph, will be chairman and speakers will include some of New York's distinguished citizens, white and colored. We would also deeply be very happy to have Mrs. Mamie Bradley. I*

---

[29] Mooty.

[30] "Steelworkers Condemn Racial Slaying of Boy," *Steel Labor: The Voice of the United Steelworkers of America--C.I.O.* (Indianapolis, Ind., Oct. 1955). p. 11.

> *have talked to our mutual friend Boyd Wilson, of your union. The Brotherhood of Sleeping Car Porters will be happy to pay all expenses for you and Mrs. Bradley if it is possible for you to accept this invitation. Kindly wire or telephone me collect at Monument 2-5079.*
>
> Theodore Brown, Director of Research and Publicity, Brotherhood of Sleeping Car Porters
> 217 West 125th Street, Suite 301
> New York 27, New York.

The involvement of the National Labor Union and particularly the Brotherhood of Sleeping Car Porters offered an interesting diffusion of sentiments and information. In the case of the porters, they talked to the passengers on the trains, which was assumed to be a part of their job. People had heard about the Till case and naturally wanted to talk about it, and so, oftentimes for hours at a time, the porters, who had become themselves involved in the national movement against this murder, would share their information with the passengers.[31] This sort of activity, passing the information by word of mouth, served as an information channel from the North to the South, from the East to the West.

Communist organizations, too, expressed demands for action against the Till lynching; however, efforts to conceal their interest were undertaken, as revealed in the following memorandum from Boyd Wilson dated September 28, 1955, to Mr. Mooty:

> *Reliable information from New York supports the suspicion that the meeting now being arranged for that city, October 2nd, involves some questionable possibilities.*

---

[31] Mooty.

> *You probably noticed a number of telegrams received at last Sunday's meetings. You will recall none of them were read. The reason was some of these wires were from known communists. We could not properly read some of these telegrams and not read others without having demands made for reading all of them, hence rather than read communists demands for action, none of the wires were made public.*
>
> *I am reliably informed that next Sunday's meetings will provide an opportunity for these communists telegrams to be read, thereby furnishing an opportunity for communists to be identified with our movement. I fear this will tend to kill the support and give hundreds of liberal people an excuse to refuse to support our demand for redress in the brutal murder of an innocent boy in the State of Mississippi.*

To be sure, the labor-union officials knew that involvement from the communists could alienate other legitimate organizations, which considered communists as illegitimate and un-American, from continuing their involvement in the case.

The NAACP and the Till case

It should be noted that (in keeping with the tradition of intervening in racial incidents) the NAACP did embrace the Till case, although not until late October.

Photograph 13 (p. 102) documents the key participants in the first demonstration meeting, September 1955, after the trial for the Chicago Chapter of the NAACP. Seated at the table is Vivian Moore, the Chicago secretary of the Chicago Chapter, with Mamie Bradley and Rayfield

Photograph 13. **First meeting of the Chicago Chapter of the NAACP after the trial.** [Rayfield Mooty]

Photograph 14. Mamie Bradley, Rayfield Mooty, Elizabeth Wright, and Bishop Isaiah Roberts at the Capitol in D.C. [*Chicago Defender*]

Mooty seated to the left behind. In all of their faces, the message of the story of Till is the same—that this senseless act should not have taken place. They (the family and the officials of the NAACP) came together to devise a strategy for ending such racial atrocities. It was noted that the membership drive for the NAACP escalated following their involvement with the Till murder case, thereby empowering them more in their war against racism.

In a letter dated September 23, 1955, the president of the West Side Unit of the Chicago Branch of the NAACP wrote to Rayfield Mooty: "We would be honored to have you as a guest on the platform at our Mass Rally on Sunday, Oct 2, 1955, 3:00 P.M. at Stone Temple Baptist Church, 3622 W. Douglas Blvd., to protest the lynching to Emmett Till." This was after Roy Wilkins, the executive director of the NAACP at that time, was persuaded to undertake the case by Henry Maloon, director of public relations for the NAACP, and Theodore Brown, public relations director for the Brotherhood of Sleeping Car Porters, who set up the meeting with Wilkins, Mamie Bradley, and Rayfield Mooty in New York. Bradley recalls in a recent personal interview that Wilkins's primary reluctance about taking the case on stemmed from the fact that too often the organization had taken on people and their cases who later demanded too much money. As it turned out, a financial dispute between Mamie Bradley and Roy Wilkins did ensue. She agreed to a $3,500 honorarium, an amount with which one of the NAACP leaders, Mr. Odum of the West Coast, had also agreed. However, when she discussed the financial matter further with Roy Wilkins, "He became very distraught ... Roy Wilkins just put his foot down, and he said he would not do it, and he accused me of capitalizing on my son's death, and he broke the relationship, and that was the end."[32] Wilkins withdrew his support and subsequently canceled all her scheduled engagements under the auspices of the organization. This act discredited her with the organization, and thus the NAACP's supporters likewise pulled away.

Alphonse Lewis, Jr., president of the Grand Rapids branch of the NAACP, said the following in a letter dated October 31, 1955, to Mr. Mooty:

> *Please acknowledge our thanks for the fine down-to-earth message that you brought to our mass meeting on Friday, October 21, 1955. I truly hope that Mrs. Bradley's bravery through her long suffering will not be forgotten by this or any other community in this nation. I trust the message that Mrs. Bradley and you bring will be long remembered.*

Everywhere, the Till murder case was discussed; according to the *Chicago Defender*, it had become an international "cause célèbre."[33] Not only were there written denunciations of the Till lynching, but there were financial commitments as well, most of which were channeled through the NAACP, early on before it pulled away from the case, to combat injustices against blacks in the South and elsewhere. For example, the display of Till's body, according to Juan Williams in the book *Eyes on the Prize*, "without question, it moved black America in a way the Supreme Court ruling on school desegregation could not match. Contributions to the NAACP's "fight fund," the war chest to help victims of racial attacks, reached record level. Only

---

[32] Tape-recorded interview with Mamie Bradley, Chicago, IL, 24 March 1988.

[33] Ethel L. Payne, "Army Gave Till Facts to Eastland," *Chicago Defender* (Chicago, IL, 22 Oct. 1955), p. 1.

weeks before, the NAACP had been begging for support to pay its debts in the aftermath of its Supreme Court triumph."[34] After the mock trials, there were numerous speaking engagements under the auspices of the NAACP.

Simeon Booker, the Washington bureau chief for *Jet* magazine, asserted thirty years later, that "a black Chicago mother, Mrs. Mamie Till Mobley [Mrs. Mamie Bradley] unknowingly, but decisively jolted 'the sleeping giant of black people.'"[35] The young thirty-three-year-old grief-stricken mother, Mamie Bradley Mobley, emerged heroic, publicly vowing to honor her son's memory with a lifetime commitment to the black struggle. The Rev. Smallgood Williams of Washington, D. C., arranged the speaking engagement in which she "spoke before a crowd of 6,000 who filled the Uline Arena in Washington. Four thousand more who waited outside were given a chance to hear her at a second special service that evening ... The Uline rally launched a spiritual nation-wide mobilization drive against intolerance and racial bigotry in Mississippi and elsewhere."[36] Clearly the strength of this mother to define her loss as public and political was unusual. The numbers were there to witness this; the crowd was evidence that the Till murder case had a profound impact upon the black masses. While in D.C. Mamie visited the Capitol, and Photograph 14 (p. 104) of Mamie Bradley, Rayfield Mooty, Elizabeth Wright (wife of Mose Wright), and the Bishop Isaiah Roberts in October 1955 at the Capitol Building in Washington, D. C., makes a powerful statement. The Capitol Building is at the center for obvious rea-

---

[34] Juan Williams, *Eyes on the Prize: America's Civil Rights Years, 1954-1965* (New York: Viking Penguin Inc., 1987), p. 44.

[35] Simeon Booker, "30 Years Ago: How Emmett Till's Lynching Launched Civil Rights Drive," *Jet* (17 June 1985), pp. 12-13.

[36] Payne, p. 2.

sons. Moreover, Mamie Bradley collaborates with the photographer, in this posed photograph, by pointing to the Capitol as the others, at an angle, face both her and the Capitol with the American flag of justice and freedom waving in the background. Given the fact that she had just experienced one of the greatest injustices to befall a mother, whose child's brutal death was ruled non-consequential, it is ironic, as well she knows, that she should be standing on the steps of this building which supposedly houses the executors of American justice, smiling as she muses to the others that "Maybe I can get justice there." Justice was never rendered in the murder case of Till and, thus, it remains an unresolved issue in the minds of many Americans.

Emmett Louis Till lived and died. His murder and trial were a mockery of the value of African-American life. This incident exemplified racial atrocities in modern history. As the people were keenly cognizant of this case then, through mass media, so should they be today through recorded history. Indeed, it so pressed upon the minds of Americans then that it ultimately exploded into the Civil Rights Movement. It is crucial for the civil rights struggles of today, yesterday, and tomorrow that the importance of Emmett Till to the Modern Civil Rights Movement be written, understood for its merit, and become a focal point for positive, consciousness-raising thought and action for all American citizens who love the ideas of trust, truth, integrity, and justice.

4
Artistic Responses

Even though historians, on the whole, have underplayed the significance of the Till case in relation to the modern Civil Rights Movement, the legacy of this historical figure has been graphically captured through literature. The image of Emmett Till serves as frontispiece for several examples of African-American literature produced during and after the modern Civil Rights Movement.

Partly because the case of the murder of the black youngster from Chicago was so widely publicized through the media, it is easy to imagine that the name Emmett Till had a high recognition quotient in households throughout America. In the homes of African-Americans, it was more than the repetition of news of the demise of Till that etched the name of the victim into the black consciousness. It was those elements in the story that had about them the familiar ring of history, learned by rote and repeated as a ritual memory exercise: black male allegedly makes passes at white woman; he's later found in the river, mutilated. For many of the black writers of the period, the image of Till is an image as old as American Negro slavery for, since that time, the black male has been, in the white mind, a danger, a threat to white racial purity, and hence to be derided in white folklore for his physical (black) ugliness and feared for his capacity to destroy the sexual innocence of white womanhood. What attracted African-American writers to the Till case was the youth and innocence of the victim, his northern, urban street savvy, and his utter ignorance of the folkways and mores of the white South. On the other hand, these writers recognized that the murder of the northern black child in the South pointed up, once again, the extent to which whites continued to exert their values into twentieth-century American life to the detriment of black people.

Three dominant features characterize the spirit of this era—persistence, resistance, and endurance. At the core of African-American life, these forces propelled the Civil Rights Movement into what literature characterizes as the Black Revolution. These forces are, in fact, keys to exploring the nature of the opposition to racism during the Civil Rights era. The image of Emmett Till has in its quality something that suggests the art of that resistance, an art that seems to be a carrier of the germ of resistance, a pride in resistance. Although it speaks to the resistance of oppression itself, the art of resistance also has full artistic play. The murder of Till is the focus, and the literature that utilizes the facts of this demise illuminates a haughtiness, a pride, a dialectic of hope and despair, rendering a synthesis as powerful as DuBois's double consciousness. The literature of the Civil Rights Movement that utilizes Till offers easy and open access to existence beyond the barriers of segregation, subjugation, and despair. If Till surfaces in all this as a force, it is as a force that focuses both on his death and on that easy gesture of confidence in the face of adversity. Thus, in a sense, the image of Till emerges as a blend of images: of fourteen-year-old kid leaning into that gesture of confidence and of battered man-child in an open casket.

Like other black folk heroes, Till, though just a child, emerges larger than life. The fear in the minds of whites of what he might have become, but for the tragedy, is exceeded only by the horror evoked in what he was. African-American folklore best explains Till whose folk traits are part of a long celebrated tradition. The attributes in him, as he was fixed in our minds, serve as a source of determination of the Civil Rights Movement for blacks to rise above oppression.

While literary selections illuminating Till and the movement are numerous, this study will be restricted to representatives from four genres—short story, poetry, autobiography, and drama. It includes Arthenia J. Bates, "Lost Note"; Gwendolyn Brooks, "The Last Quatrain of the Ballad of Emmett Till"; Anne Moody, *Coming of Age in Mississippi*; and James Baldwin, *Blues for Mr. Charlie*—all of which artistically illustrate and dramatize racism as a brutal and insidious force in American culture, with Till as the focal image. This study provides a close contextual analysis, with a perusal of the compelling history outside the texts.

A significant factor of American culture during the fifties is that the American system was monolithically violent and oppressive. Unless there were periodic sacrificial victims, such as Till himself, realized through vigilante violence, the system could not continue to work. Every so often, whites had to make an example out of a black, to show blacks what would happen to them if they stepped out of line. According to Arnold Rose, "The causation is such that, when the time is ripe, almost any incident may touch it off. The incident is usually some crime, real or suspected, by a Negro against a white, or merely a 'racial insult,' such as a Negro's buying an automobile or stepping beyond the etiquette of race relations in any way. Rumors will often start or quicken a lynching."[1]

This was a practice that came out of the tradition of American slavery, one which kept the slave system intact. It was the threat of force and its application that maintained slavery. There were trumped-up charges and illegalities that could be alleged, and which could have no meaning outside the context of southern, racist politics. The very social foundation of the politics demonstrated in the Till case represents the way violence against blacks is created as social conditions that sustain racial problems. It was not Till himself, but rather the dynamics of an oppressive system, that dictated his life.

Arthenia Bates, Short Story

To begin with, I would like to quote in full Arthenia Bates's own words concerning her reaction to the Emmett Till murder case:

> *I was teaching at Mississippi Valley State University (then called Mississippi Vocational College) in Itta Bena at the time of the incident. There was an old mill at the edge of the campus, and they took the wheel from the campus to weigh him down. Reporters were here from everywhere, London, everywhere, trying to get the story. I remember some saying that this isn't anything new; it happens all the time. But it was so tragic. At that time, things were very tedious: They had a hit list. Medgar Evers was doing a lot of things there. I wanted to do something, but I was so full of terror. It*

---

[1] Arnold Rose, *The Negro in America* (Boston: The Beacon Press, 1948), p. 186.

> *was only after I was away from Mississippi that I was able to put this case in perspective, that I could realize the sadness and the tragedy of it all. One of my students' grandmother had said to him, "Boy, you bett not whistle no mo." That was so sad to me; a boy could not even whistle for fear that it may get to the wrong ears. I kept thinking how sad that was. It made me think of my brother who always loved to whistle. That was an expression of joy. Then I reflected back on Till and wrote the short story "Lost Note."*

Arthenia Bates's short story "Lost Note" from her collection *Seeds Beneath the Snow* is one example of the black literature of the period that offers a dramatization of the senselessness of racist lawlessness in America, which blacks have been forced to respect, particularly in the South, if they hoped to survive. Whites were content with things as they were and became retaliatory when blacks insisted upon attaining equal rights. They inflicted pressure on blacks in order to "keep them in their place."

Bates's narrative treats the process of acculturation that both the grandmother and the young male protagonist, Son, must undergo. Her theme is similar to Richard Wright's concept of mandatory subservience, which is the prescribed method for black survival in a white society. Wright's essay, "The Ethics of Living Jim Crow," explains the painful physical and emotional process that all southern blacks had to suffer for survival.

In "Lost Note," Bates presents a profound commentary on the haphazardness of the southern environment in which Till's crime—wolf whistling at a white woman—occurred. One must note that the primary reason his whistling was a crime was that, as Bates describes it, it fell on the "wrong ears." Thus, Till's gesture got "lost" in the elements, for had it not gotten to the white woman, it would have been safe.

This meaning echoes the theory of a social anthropologist, Mary Douglass, who contends that dirt (like Till's gesture) is merely misplaced matter: "If we can abstract pathogenicity and hygiene from our notion of dirt, we are left with the old definition of dirt as matter out of place."[2] For example, dirt in a flower pot becomes fertilizer while dirt on a clean table cloth becomes pollution. Similarly, Till's gesture was "matter out of place"; for had the circumstances been different, so would have been the meaning. Had Till been an affluent white man whistling at the same woman, his action would have possibly been construed as a compliment. As it turned out, however, he was a black boy, young and unsophisticated, and his gesture became dirt, misplaced matter, as it were.

The traditional reaction to a racially subjugated people, there had to be sacrificial lambs, whose function was to serve as examples for southern blacks, to keep them in their assigned place. Till obviously had no control over the situation. In fact, as revealed in the testimony of the "offended" subject, Carolyn Bryant, Till's crime was not so much that he whistled at her (as was the allegation) but rather that he squeezed her hand and asked for a date. He could have done any number of things—whistled at her, squeezed her hand, asked for a date, or even looked at her the wrong way; it would not have mattered. All these gestures were equally "misplaced matter" in the sense of a black male's demonstrating unacceptable familiarity toward a white woman. This was a serious American taboo. The conflicting testimony of Carolyn Bryant, who contended that Till put his arms around her waist, squeezed

---

[2] Mary Douglass, *Purity and Danger* (London: Routledge & Kegan Paul, 1966), p. 35.

her hand, and asked for a date, and the alleged crime of wolf whistling reveal just that. Someone and something had to serve the needs of the system of racial oppression by posing as an example in order to perpetuate abject subjugation.

The pivotal issue in "Lost Note" is the dangers of the black man's whistling when it may reach the wrong person. This becomes the lesson that one of the main characters, Clara Atkins, must teach her grandson, Son, so that he will not risk sharing the tragic fate of Till. As the story line goes, two elder black women are discussing the lynching of a youth, an international issue now, and their fear that their loved ones, young Juny Boy and Son, may become the next victims. They must find a way to keep this from ever occurring. Nursery need only to warn her child of the danger, while Grandma Atkins must find a more convincing strategy. As Clara Atkins reveals, Son's mannerisms pose a possible threat to his life, particularly in a southern, hostile environment. She admits that "as hard as I try to teach him manners, he goes telling the wrong folks 'yes' and 'no.' Besides, he whistles when he gets good and ready to, in season and outa reason. And so far, I can't stop that."[3]

It is clear to her that a fate similar to Till's would be inevitable, unless she is able to redirect this habit. And a habit it was, indeed, for "She realized, then, that he whistled for everything; to ignore people, to soothe anger, to hide fear. He whistled his way in and out of everything."[4]

After tricking him into a dark closet, she locks him in and leaves him there in order to reflect on his ways. This experience becomes a symbolic death for Son, a death of

---

[3] Arthenia J Bates, "Lost Note," *Seeds Beneath the Snow* (Washington, D.C.: Howard University Press, 1969), pp. 115-16.

[4] Bates, p. 117.

innocence, a kind of buried-alive experience, symbolically burying his inability to understand and adapt to the limitations inflicted on black males. When she finally releases him, realizing how traumatic and confining the experience was to him, she reveals the lesson to be learned:

> *"You haven't started feeling, yourself, yet, but you will. When that happens, I don't want you to see nothing but black when it comes to womenfolks ... Whether you're thinking about them or not, I mean for you to check on that whistling. Every time you whistle, you just think back and make pretense like you were locked up to not ever get out."*
>
> *"I swear, Grandma Atkins, if I have to think about your joke every time I whistle, I don't care if I ever whistle again."*
>
> *"You can whistle. That's the way your heart talks. All I want you to do is to make sure your tune don't catch up with the wrong ears."*[5]

Bates's story, like Wright's sketches in "The Ethics of Living Jim Crow," illustrates black victimization—the danger, the pain, the degradation, and the constant threat of death—which American racism absurdly forces upon the black race. Although Till himself is absent from the story, he is permanently etched in the mind of the adults. Son must learn the lessons that Till failed to learn, lest his innocence, too, becomes "lost," and his life aborted.

[5] Bates, p. 121.

Gwendolyn Brooks, Poetry

According to Darwin Turner, for decades Gwendolyn Brooks, a 1950 Pulitzer prize winner for her *Annie Allen* poetry collection, "has earned praise both for technical artistry and for her sympathetic revelations of the Afro-American experience."[6] Writing from a woman's perspective, she artistically demonstrates acute sensitivity to the victimization of African-Americans, both as a black and as a poor people. In "The Last Quatrain of the Ballad of Emmett Till," Brooks, in the absence of Till himself in the poem, has created a portrait of his mother. In keeping with the tradition of the ballad, Till's presence is strongly implied in the missing stanzas, reflecting on the single episode of his tragic death. By stressing the mother's strength and pride, this poem attributes to her son the same potential. The poem sketches one dominant characteristic of the mother. She is engaged in cerebral activity, in which she reflects upon her reactions to her son's victimization by American racial oppression.

While the poem ostensibly suggests the calmness and helplessness of a grief-stricken mother, close scrutiny reveals that underneath there is tension, that, in fact, passivity is not the demeanor of this mother:

after the murder,
after the burial
Emmett's mother is a pretty-faced thing;
the tint of pulled taffy.
She sits in a red room
drinking black coffee.
She kisses her killed boy.
And she is sorry.

[6] Darwin Turner, *Black American Literature* (Columbus, OH: Charles E. Merrill Publishing Company, 1970), p. 257.

Chaos in windy grays
through a red prairie.[7]

Poignant in its simplicity, the poem abounds in ambiguity.

The first two lines set up an obvious mood that has been determined by the preceding activities, murder and burial. While the words connote violence, destruction, and fragmentation, Till's mother here, amid the unpleasantness of death rituals, remains strong. She is not destroyed, certainly not in a physical sense, for she "is a pretty-faced thing;/ the tint of pulled taffy," but the reader is encouraged to make the awful associative contrast with the dead son's puffed, mutilated, and colorless face, which the mother kisses. The word "taffy," gains further resonance in describing this mother, for it suggests strength and resilience, both dominant qualities of the candy whose very shape is created only through much pulling and stretching. Like the candy, the ultimate posture of the mother is realized through the tugging that she must undergo. The empowering ordeal enables her to "become," to evolve into the undaunted person she ultimately does. It is, in fact, the very pulling that molds them (she and the candy), which in turn creates the form that both must assume in their ultimate stage. Hence, form is essential to survival.

Color is significant and suggestive in this short poem. Note the "red" that the author assigns the room in which the mother sits, "drinking black coffee." The term itself connotes fervor, heat, even anger, all emotions that the mother must have in view of all that has happened. Moreover, as Gladys Williams surmises in "Ballads of Gwendolyn Brooks," "The 'redness' of the room conveys much

[7] Gwendolyn Brooks, "The Last Quatrain of the Ballad of Emmett Till," *Selected Poems* (New York: Harper & Row, Publishers, 1963), p. 81.

emotion and many facts: Emmett's blood and pain," for example.[8] Thus, the presence of Till reigns high. The idea that Till's mother is able to sit quietly after such a horrible ordeal suggests perseverance, a quiet determination to carry on, to survive the evils of a violent system that offers no recourse for victimized black people. The determination to overcome destruction, to live on ("red" also suggesting life here), serves her well. This is the same determination that served as the major impulse throughout the black struggle in America.

There is striking imagery in the statement, "she sits ... drinking black coffee." She, like "black coffee," is strong, and she is dealing with something that, like the black coffee, is bitter. Pensiveness and an element of perplexity are also evoked here as one senses that the mother is struggling with and even contemplating just why such an act took place and, more important now, what course of action she must take. The statement "she is sorry" then becomes ambiguous, for not only is she sorry for what has happened to her only child, but also she is sorry for the subsequent violence that must inevitably erupt from her ultimate resolution to expose the mutilated body to the public for its response. Indeed, "she is sorry" for both these reasons—the former, which should not have happened, and the latter, which surely must happen.

The poem culminates in a sense of pandemonium resulting from this bloody deed, thus, a strong anticipation of endless, bloody upheaval—"chaos in windy grays/ through a red prairie." According to Gladys Williams, "Mrs. Till is desolate ('gray'). The desolation boils, writhes,

---

[8] Gladys Williams, "The Ballads of Gwendolyn Brooks," *A Life Distilled: Gwendolyn Brooks, Her Poetry and Fiction*, edited by Maria K. Mootry and Gary Smith (Urbana and Chicago: University of Illinois Press, 1987), pp. 220-221.

rises. All other mental conditions are overcome by the rising and boiling ... The desolation of aborted human community, the barren black and white lives are expressed in the final lines."[9]

The "Red prairie" also evokes the myth and symbol of the wild, open, vast frontier (the prairie) as nurturer. Although this concept is mythologized in Henry Nash Smith, *Virgin Land: The American West as Symbol and Myth,* ironically the prairie, historically controlled by the "red" man (Indian), becomes anything but a nurturer for the Native American, who has sacrificed much blood in his futile struggle to maintain dominion over his land. However, in the case of Till, who becomes the "sacrificial lamb" for the black race, the victim does not suffer a totally futile death. Once the public views the battered body of this young victim, slain for his wolf whistle at a white woman, demands are made that such insidious murders be stopped. (In a recent personal interview, Rayfield Mooty revealed that, after Mrs. Bradley viewed her child's body, her crying subsided, and soon afterwards she began to speak out publicly in an effort to affect change for blacks in America.)

Anne Moody, Autobiography

One of the most impressive ways of recording or recounting history is through the literary form of autobiography. One of the most insightful autobiographies tracing the significant Civil Rights Movement is Anne Moody's *Coming of Age in Mississippi,* in which the author narrates her politicalization and involvement in the movement. This literary piece proves to be extremely effective in

[9] Williams, p. 221.

communicating the evolution of the ideas and consciousness of the writer, and it also offers some valuable insights into the ideals and hopes of the American society in general. Tracing the racial tension in the Deep South, Mississippi, during the pre-Civil Rights and the Civil Rights eras, Moody's autobiographical piece lends invaluable insights into race relations and even human relations in America. She discloses the multilayers of oppression for black Americans whose resistance ultimately awarded them their right to a decent life.

Moody devotes two chapters to Till's murder. Although Till is not actually present, she discusses in detail the reaction of both black and white citizens to the tragedy: the former exuding fear and intimidation and the latter expressing disgust and outrage that such a thing had to take place. While still in high school (and fourteen herself), Moody is interrogated by her white boss, Mrs. Burke, as to why she thinks Till was murdered. Pretending not to know, Moody then receives a long lecture by Mrs. Burke on what happens to blacks who get out of their place with whites. She voices her attitude toward Till's death, which is pretty much that of whites in general:

> *"He was killed because he got out of his place with a white woman. A boy from Mississippi would have known better than that. This boy was from Chicago. Negroes up North have no respect for people. They think they can get away with anything. He just came to Mississippi and put a whole lot of notions in the boys' heads here and stirred up a lot of trouble ... It's a shame he had to die so soon."*

> *She was so red in the face, she looked as if she was on fire.*[10]

The most compelling section depicts the spirit of the black youths, the new breed, the leaders of tomorrow and their logical response to the murder:

> *"Man, what in the hell do you mean?"*
>
> *"What I mean is these goddamned white folk is gonna start some shit here you just watch!"*
>
> *"That boy wasn't but fourteen years old and they killed him. Now what kin a fourteen-year-old boy do with a white woman? What if he did whistle at her, he might have thought the whore was pretty."*
>
> *"Look at all these white men here that's fucking over our women. Everybody knows it too and what's done about that? Look how many white babies we got walking around in our neighborhoods. Their mama's ain't white either. That boy was from Chicago, shit, everybody fuck everybody up there. He probably didn't even think of the bitch as white."*[11]

In this passage, Moody addresses the problem of race, sex, and politics between blacks and whites. The characters express disenchantment over contradictions and inconsistencies regarding these issues as they relate to the black community. Moody uses Till as the controlling image of black victimization.

---

[10] Anne Moody, *The Coming of Age in Mississippi* (New York: Dell Publishing Co., Inc., 1968), p. 125.

[11] pp. 121-22.

Endesha Ida Mae Holland and James Baldwin, Drama

Drama is highly effective in expressing sociopsychological ideas. Even a minimum reference can carry layers of meanings of profound significance. For example, although Endesha Ida Mae Holland in her play ***From the Mississippi Delta*** makes only one direct reference to Till, in the opening of the play she gives it a power that is overwhelming. It frames the entire story in that it sets up the atmosphere, thereby foreshadowing the nature of racial oppression to which all three of her characters, found in the midst of the Civil Rights Movement, are subjected:

> *The region of the country where I was born and raised, the Mississippi Delta, is a testament to African American inferiority. My town is famous for the infamous "wolf-whistle." In the mid-1950s, a young boy, Emmett Till, was standing on the corner with a couple of his friends. A white woman passed and claimed that young Till had whistled at her. Later that night, a mob of white men took the black Chicago youth to the river. They put a millstone around his neck, they cut his penis off and stuck it in his mouth; and then they lowered him into his watery grave. That's the town I'm from.*[12]

Although Holland's facts are not accurate to Till's specific lynching (the description of one includes facts from many), the fact she mentions the Till murder at the very outset of her play suggests its importance.

---

[12] Endesha Ida Mae Holland, *From the Mississippi Delta* (Unpublished, 1987), p. 1.

James Baldwin, on the other hand, makes more obvious use of the Till story. In his "Notes for *Blues*" (*for Mr. Charlie*), he announces that the play was based on the Till murder case. He also establishes his intention in writing the play, which is to "draw a valid portrait of the murderer."[13] Although he feared he would not be able to realize his goal, he does. In exploring the psyche of the murderers, Baldwin hoped to understand him (them). Like Bigger Thomas, Wright's protagonist in *Native Son*, the murderers of Till, as Baldwin sees them, are products of the American racist society.

The fact that the dominant culture would frequently, without reservation, inflict the cruelest forms of violence on an oppressed people, as in the case of the Till lynching, clearly establishes the fact that blacks are the most despised group and are more victimized by such heinous crimes, as tools of social control. Although other groups experience lynching, some whites included, the percentage among whites was disproportionately smaller than that among blacks. The intent of the dominant culture is to control the African-American and hold him or her in a subordinate position. In the final analysis, as American people share in the responsibility of the crime, they "have the duty to try to understand this wretched man [the murderer]; and while we probably cannot hope to liberate him, begin working toward the liberation of his children."[14]

As both a writer and a fellow human being, Baldwin empathized with the victim and his family. He communicates the impact of this slaying on him in a docufilm by Rich Samuels: "It was myself in that coffin. It was my brother in that coffin. I can't describe it precisely because it

[13] James Baldwin, *Blues for Mr. Charlie* (New York: Dell Publishing Co., Inc., 1964), p. 6.

[14] Baldwin, p. 6.

had been so mutilated, so violated. It was him but it was all of us."[15]

Baldwin's play was published nine years after Till's death. It is not known exactly how long after the incident he began to write it, but the profound impact on him certainly suggests, at least, that the mental writing process started almost immediately.

There are several startling observations in this play about the nature of racism that need be explicated. To begin with, the opening quotation demonstrates the terror tactics of the dominant culture: "And may every nigger like this nigger end like this nigger—face down in the weeds!"[16] This cynical message is given by the white store owner in Baldwin's play, Lyle Britten. Like the white store owner Roy Bryant, Lyle Britten is charged with defending the honor of his wife against the advances of a black man. His mission, which is to protect the white woman, is expressed by three other white men as they explain their position to the white women:

> *Ellis: Mrs. Britten, if you was to be raped by an orang-outang out of the jungle or a stallion, couldn't do you no worse than a nigger. You wouldn't be no more good for nobody. I've seen it.*
> *George: That's right.*
> *Ralph: That's why we men have got to be so vigilant.*[17]

Moreover, he and white men in general are charged with the responsibility of using this incident as a lesson for all

---

[15] James Baldwin, *The Murder and the Movement* by Rich Samuels (Chicago: WMAQ TV, 1985).

[16] James Baldwin, *Blues for Mr. Charlie* (New York: Dell Publishing Co., Inc., 1964), p. 13.

[17] Baldwin, p. 71.

black men who dare to think of getting familiar with a white woman. The lesson is that the honor of the white woman must be protected at any cost, including life. The fear of encouraging possible miscegenation is manifested in the white man's fear and his reaction to Till's encounter with the white woman. The notion of sex and race is a critical preoccupation for the white man and as Lyle asserts, "I'll be damned if I'll mix with them. That's all. I don't believe in it, and that's *all*. I don't want no big buck nigger lying up next to Josephine and that's where all this will lead to and you know it as well as I do! I'm against it and I'll do anything I have to do to stop it, yes, I will!"[18]

Although *Blues for Mr. Charlie* is a dramatization of the Till incident, Baldwin stays true to the facts of the real story. With the exception of certain superficial things, such as identifications and location, there are many similarities. First there is the similarity between Mother Henry, the grandmother of the victim in the story, and Till's mother regarding their attitudes toward the murderers. Both come to pity rather than hate the murderers. Mrs. Bradley-Mobley in a recent interview said, "Toward these people, I had no feeling whatsoever. I went completely into neutral. I do not hate them; I have on occasions felt sorry for them because I know that if they could have undone it, that was one tar baby they touched they wished they had never touched."[19] Mother Henry, too, has no hatred for the murderers: "I used to hate them, too, son. But I don't hate them no more. They too pitiful."[20]

There is also the similarity between the scenario surrounding the unacceptable lifestyle of Till at home in Chi-

---

[18] Baldwin, p. 27.

[19] Tape-recorded interview with Mamie Bradley-Mobley, Chicago, IL, 6 January 1988.

[20] Baldwin, p. 29.

cago before he went to Mississippi and that of Richard Henry. Like Till, who reputedly bragged about the picture of the white girl he carried in his pocket as being that of his girlfriend, Richard claims a relationship with white women: "You remember that chick I was telling you about earlier, lives in Greenwich Village in New York? ... She's *white,* man. I got a whole gang of white chicks in New York ... Wait—I got some pictures. That's the one lives in the Village. Ain't she fine?"[21] Of course, the situation here is exaggerated, mainly because the victim in the play is older and Baldwin gives him more experience with white women.

Another crucial issue concerning color is dramatized here, which reflects the attitude of some whites toward light-skinned blacks. This is reflected in the conversation between two of the white characters:

> *Ellis: They got one interest. And it's just below the belly button.*
> *George (Laughs): You know them yellow niggers? Boy, ain't they the worst kind? Their own folks don't want them, don't nobody want them, and you can't do nothing with them—you might be able to scare a black nigger, but you can't do nothing with a yellow nigger.*
> *Rev. Phelps: That's because he's a mongrel. And a mongrel is the lowest creation in the animal kingdom.*[22]

This issue, coupled with the fact of the victim as a Northerner, are important for understanding the added source of hostility in the whites. Frustrated because the townspeople do not understand the ramifications of these threatening qualities, Lyle interjects, "I don't know what's

[21] Baldwin, p. 41.
[22] Baldwin, pp. 70-71.

come over the folks in this town! ... Raising so much fuss about a nigger—and a northern nigger at that."[23]

Richard, like Till, was undesirable and a threat to the southern way of life, both because of his color and because he was an outsider. The greatest fear in the whites in both the true story and in the play was that they could not control the northern mulatto, whom they surmised had become accustomed to some semblance of equality.

Still another important aspect is that the fictional character, like Till, exhibits no fear toward the whites:

> *Maridian: What was the last thing he said? Did he beg you for his life?*
> *Lyle: That nigger! He was too smart for that! He was too full of himself for that! He must have thought he was white. And I gave him every chance—every chance—to live!*[24]

As verified by Till's cousins, Wheeler Parker and Simeon Wright, Till showed no fear. In fact, he even used the wrong language ("yes" and "naw" instead of "yassar" and "nossar") when answering the white abductors, which enraged them even further.

In conclusion, therefore, as we reflect on these literary creations, we realize that although literature, by its very nature, cannot render a totally factual historical account of life, it does immortalize a given experience. Unlike history, it is not pure documentation; it does not deliver empirical evidence. Instead, literary history is a creative perspective, which treats facts and issues from another realm. Subjective and emotional, it is sometimes difficult to document;

---

[23] Baldwin, p. 26.
[24] Baldwin, p. 154.

however, it draws upon the imagination and, thus, becomes a successful combination of fact and fiction. Hence, art transposes information in the factual world and brings facts to bear for a proper assessment of things in society.

Although literary history reveals difficulty in verifying and recalling facts, it is interesting. Like life itself, it suggests more—idealism and hope—that is needed as much in our hopes and aspirations for a reality. Thus, the creative framework, offering a different kind of evidence, renders the artist as an accomplished articulator of ideals of the society, which is particularly true as we strive toward understanding and appreciating the African-American's realities as they are interwoven in the American culture.

The interesting thing about all these artistic creations is that they are true to the real scenario of an innocent black male youth who falls prey to American racism. Like one of Wright's characters in the short story "Big Boy Leaves Home," published in 1938, the fate of Emmett (alias Bobo) parallels that of the fictional character, also called Bobo. It is as if the fictional character comes to life in the Till murder, almost as if Wright had predicted it. This tragedy reflects a compelling fear and preoccupation within the white male psyche, which has created one of America's greatest taboos—the possible attraction between the black man and white woman.

5
Testimonies from the People

No one tells the story of Till's murder more vividly than Rayfield Mooty, with such minute details as if it happened just yesterday.

> *No one who was old enough to be aware could forget that quiet Sunday morning, August 28, 1955, when the flame in the Civil Rights Movement that was burning low suddenly blazed following the reports of every newscaster on TV and radio and of telephone calls from friend to friend that Emmett Louis Till, fourteen, had been dragged from Moses Wright's (his uncle's) house in Money, Mississippi, by two white men in the middle of the night at gunpoint. One kidnapper's wife had accused Till of "wolf-whistling" at her in a grocery store. Four days passed, as blacks hoped that what seemed all too familiar and true, would prove to have been a nightmare. But on that fourth day, grim reality surfaced—Southern style. In an area where it suddenly runs 30 feet deep, the Tallahatchie River had become sick of something it was forced to swallow and heave up—the mutilated body of Emmett Till. A seventeen-year-old white fisherman, Robert Hodges, saw the feet sticking up. He got a motor boat, rode to the corpse and pulled it out. Till had*

been lynched, shot through the head and tossed, naked, into the river with a seventy pound cotton gin fan tied around his neck with barbed wire.[1]

The recalling and recounting of the past by an actual participant is one way history can be evoked for reinterpretation. In fact, because much of the past that people remember is not recorded, according to Barbara Allen, it "can be salvaged only by tapping the memories of those who lived through it or remember hearing older members of the family or community talk about it."[2] In reconstructing the past through words, one is able to verify facts and figure out what really happened. Indeed, "When newspaper files, court records, and other written sources normally utilized by historians have been destroyed by fire, flood, thievery, political chicanery, and simple neglect, the only remaining source materials may be the oral recollections and personal reminiscences."[3]

While most scholars tend to rely upon written records, such as letters, diaries, and journals as well as legal documents, many broaden their informational base to include the often unrecorded accounts of the past. Journalism, too, relies upon words of common people, which is demonstrated by the use of personal interviews by newspaper reporters, in which the interviewee shares certain insights about a given incident. According to Ellen Catarow, "There is a democratic idea at the learning of oral history:

---

1 Tape-recorded interview with Rayfield Mooty, and a passage he had earlier written, Chicago, IL, April 1986.

2 Barbara Allen and William Lynwood Montell, *From Memory to History: Using Oral Sources in Local Historical Research* (Nashville, Tenn.: The American Association for State and Local History, 1981), p. viii.

3 Allen, p. 67.

because the people who have lived through particular events are the ones best qualified to talk about them."[4] Oral history offers an effective means of recapturing the feelings of the moment, which is necessary in order that an untouched generation may better appreciate historical events.

While there are several drawbacks regarding the dependability of oral history as a reliable source of information—some consider it unreliable because it depends upon the memory of the informant, who may intentionally or unintentionally exaggerate facts—it can bring to bear its unique strengths, many of which are compatible with and serve to enhance written sources. For example, in *From Memory to History,* Allen and Montell's opening statement holds that "Orally communicated history is a valid and valuable source of historical information, as oral tradition and formal history complement one another. Each body of knowledge possesses qualities that, taken together, form a fuller historical record. Alone, each one is incomplete."[5]

The Voices of the People

In order to recall the spirit and emotions of the past during the tense moment of Till's lynching, a range of people—black and white, poor and affluent, men and women, young and old have been interviewed. Recalling and sharing a past event can offer a healing effect, in that it can offer the informant a discharge of pent-up feelings of fear and anger, a catharsis of those emotions. Blacks and whites alike need this opportunity to say what they feel.

---

[4] Ellen Catarow, *Moving the Mountain* (Old Westbury, New York: Feminist Press, 1980), p. iv.

[5] Allen and Montell, p. 3.

Invariably, they seem to seize the opportunity to share their feelings when asked about the case. In fact, some volunteer this information even if they are not asked. In sharing their emotions, their testimonies somehow encourage others, too, to experience and express their own private purgations.

In a general sense, these collective expressions, both positive and negative, represent the spirit and the privilege of American culture in its freedom of expression. As all people must assume the glory of their people, they must likewise assume their degradation. Hence, the American society and its race relations must acknowledge this crime as one of the most hideous in its culture. These private testimonies serve as revelations for a better understanding of the Till incident and, more important, a better understanding of how American race relations continue to affect individual realities and those of American culture in general. In turn, these revelations will render clues for improving race relations today and in the future. In order to correct social ills, one must necessarily understand them and admit that they do, indeed, exist.

Presented here is a collage of impressions from people of various walks of life, all of whom were born by 1950, so they were at least five years of age at the time of the Till incident. When asked what the Till murder case meant to them (given their ethnicity, profession, age, and geographical locality at the time of the incident), they spoke, some more freely than others, of their personal reactions. Their accounts often carry great authenticity. In alphabetical order in Appendix 3, "Voices from Outside the Story," presented are the accounts, virtually verbatim. This study and interpretation of culture using oral history methodology is employed here because it allows certain truths about the Till murder case to be realized for the first time.

As the informants remember the case, their testimonies strike certain thematic congruencies of significance.

All assess the lynching of Till as having insufficient cause. They speak of knowing what the code was (a black male whistling at a white woman was a "no-no"), but they still see the act of murder as senseless, perpetrated by white males following out a prescriptive response. They view the society that made and justified the code as demonstrating the hypocrisy of Christianity. However, regarding Till's gesture as a potential threat to white womanhood, those whites like Susan Brownmiller who regard Till's whistle as "more than a kid's brash prank ... no small tweet of hubba-hubba or melodious approval for a well-turned ankle ... It was a deliberate insult just short of physical assault."[6]

More realistic about it, most blacks and some whites regard the gesture as typical of teenage males and, therefore, morally harmless. They concur that Till's gesture was ultimately excusable, thereby viewing his punishment as morally wrong, in spite of the fact that whistling at the white woman was a taboo.

Till's naivete, his tragic downfall, allowed for his error and, hence, when it was made clear, he was afraid. But the fact that Till was a child runs throughout these accounts as a crucial concern, since his intentions could not have been the same as those of a grown man. His gesture was exemplary of the puberty *rites de passage* of most males.[7] In the southern environment, however, his gesture was a threat to the sanctity of white womanhood, and, in the final analysis, what happens to Till makes a striking contrast to

---

[6] Susan Brownmiller, *Against Our Will: Men, Women and Rape* (New York: Simon and Schuster, 1975), p. 194.

[7] For further explication of the *rites de passage* see Arnold van Gennep's *Rites de Passage.*

what would happen to a fourteen-year-old white kid without such restraints. Given the locale and Till's ethnicity, for obvious reasons, he could not afford the "mock ritual."

The Black Man at Risk

The most critical theme in these accounts is the vulnerability of the black male to white aggression. The warnings are for black men to keep their distance, and especially from white women. As H. E. Newsum puts it, "the most memorable thing about it was the feeling as a young boy that I was unsafe and that white women were taboo." Theo James Carver says:

> *During the time when I was coming up, there were many lynchings of young black men who had been accused of saying sexual words to white women, like "Baby you look fine and sweet." This was back there in the fifties in Brunswick, Georgia. Mama always said that you never mess with a white woman anyway, 'cause you get yourself in trouble or killed for nothing and a white woman ain't worth it.*

Alvin Chambliss remembers his grandmother warning "Don't say anything to white folks, and especially white women."

Black men were at risk even because of their eyes: they must not even look at a white woman. "Y'all hide, y'all hide. Now you see why I been telling y'all don't be looking up in no white women's faces 'cause you see what happened to the boy from Chicago."[8] James Scott King remembers:

> *their mentioning it in school; we were told that there was a lesson to be learned and that we should avoid encounters with white girls. The term reckless eyeballing came up as a sort of joke among black boys. This incident served as a kind of general warning that we were still in the South and that we still had to be careful in all of our actions and that the same thing could happen in Marion, South Carolina that happened in Mississippi.*

Lucy Grigsby remembers:

> *Some of the newspapers called it eyeball rape. I thought it was one of the more outlandish situations involving blacks and whites. Here is this kid whom nobody accused of actual, physical rape. He looked at a white woman and lost his life ... Those white folks had no sense of the humanity of black folks, which is a comment on human relations. The teaching was that many black persons were taught as a child not to look directly at white people. And especially black men were taught not to look at white women. Here was a kid from the North who was not taught that.*

Richard Hill recounts how closely Emmett Till affected his own life: "At that particular time, I think I was traumatized; he was close to my own age. I had a friend who was a white girl who picked cotton along with me. And after

---

[8] Telephone interview with Endesha I. M. Holland, November 1987.

the incident, my people became frightened for me because she was a white girl and she liked me and indicated that."

Several voices mention a change in attitude toward whistling. Kathy Gibson recalls, "I couldn't believe that anybody could get killed for whistling, or whistling at any body at all. I remember being more shocked than angry. Whistling—that's regular, that's minor." Charlotte Kuh recalls, "To an eleven-year-old, a fourteen-year-old wasn't that different and we knew kids that whistled. It was a terrible shocking thing." Carolyn Banks Thompson remembers:

> *It really hit my mother because my own father had been lynched and burned alive in Arkansas because they [whites] wanted his land and that was their way of taking it; he refused to sell. The rationale they used to justify my father's death was that he whistled at a white woman. As a result of the similarities, my mother was more horrified and appalled. It was like pouring salt on an open wound. My father had been killed only two years before [1953] and my mother hastily remarried (about a year later) so that we could move to Chicago.*

Molefe Asante remembers:

> *The Emmett Till case was the most awesome event that occurred in my childhood because it revealed to me in the most profound manner how fragile I was as a black boy in America. The impact made me aware for the first time of all that my grandfather Moses and my father, Authur, had told me about black manhood being at risk in America. It came together with the most deafening sound of despair.*

Racism

In many instances, the Emmett Till case reawakened awareness in northern blacks who had become complacent that racism was still a dreadful reality.

Some see it as just a facet of the South: as Richard Barksdale says, "The Till case is a reminder of the southern way of life—racial violence." James Croft underlines the way this violence is hushed up in the South: "It was hush, hush ... You actually didn't learn too much about it until you began to grow up and read about it .... I lived in Webbs, just nine, ten, or twelve miles actually from where it happened ... The person that was sheriff at the time, his son is about to be sheriff again. So you can see how much progress we've made, not very much."

Sandy Kravitz was struck by the anonymity of racism: "My immediate reaction was that they were just looking for an excuse to kill a black. Anything would have triggered the reaction to kill. I don't think that it had anything to do with what they said. It was no different from the Germans, the Nazis, no reason except inbred hatred—a pretty damn feeble excuse for killing unless you just want to kill." Elza H. Minor remembers how his awareness of racial problems was given a new dimension by Till:

> *I was born and raised in New Jersey. My mother was a teacher and she told me that race was just one more obstacle to overcome. I had had no serious confrontations with racism. When the headlines hit about Emmett Till and I read the events that led up to his murder, I realized that I was reading about someone the same age as I was, who evidently represented a threat to white maleness to the extent that they felt that they needed to murder him. That shocked me into the real-*

> *ity that my blackness was more than just a barrier to overcome. This made me reexamine all of my relationships with white people.*

The Feelings

Horror is one of the strongest emotions experienced. Cheryl Leggon says, "I just remember that it was just horrifying ... I don't even think that they considered him human. It was a gut reaction, what the whole lynch-mob psychology was about—the unbridled, the base emotions without any social or moral element. The reason I got into sociology was to get answers to these sorts of issues, which were social rather than psychological." Annette Dunzo expresses the everyday aspect of this horror: "I was very shocked and frightened as a pre-teenager. I knew him as about the same age I was; it was similar to having it happen to a friend of mine ... Whenever I go through Mississippi, I have a lingering memory of that kind of terror that befalls blacks in a black/white situation." George Barlow discusses the way this horror is hushed up by society:

> *The Emmett Till lynching ... hasn't lost its horror ... It makes me ask what I don't hear anybody else asking and that is where are all those people, those citizens who participated in those "festival" events. The common American myth is that this is a handful of drunken rednecks, but the real horror is that these people were "normal citizens." I think it is the deepest, darkest taboo in our country's past and present.*

Another immediate and overpowering sensation is that of fear, the terror of knowing oneself in danger, danger that comes from all sides and that seems to have no reason.

Evelyn Reaves expresses horror that this befell a child: "I was terrified when I first heard it. I was a child myself and was appalled that someone could do that to a child." Juanita Hudson remembers, "It was frightening and it was also sad to know that people could be that cruel and get away with it. I felt that it was totally unnecessary and it was an injustice. It made me feel that white people were just sick."

This fear had natural consequences; it was too strong to remain a passive sensation. Erma O'Hara considers the courage that comes from terror:

> *Living in Mississippi, I had experienced some harsh treatments from whites myself and thinking of my personal experiences and what had happened to him terrified me. Then I noticed that in the black community there were feelings of courage and strength and togetherness that really encouraged me at that young age. And somehow I was able to cope with that fear because I felt so secure in that community, with my black relatives and friends and teachers and church folks. I shall never forget.*

Joyce A. Ladner expresses clearly the evolution from this fear to commitment to the modern Civil Rights Movement:

> *I remember crying over it, and the tremendous fear. I think that it was one of the greatest influences that ultimately led me to becoming a scholar, a sociologist. It was impossible for me to become a dispassionate observer ... A very important thing is that it followed the Supreme Court decision in 1954. It's like the*

> *whites said that they don't care what rights we were given ... It served as a grave incident that showed people how intractable a problem could be and how difficult a solution would be. So when the spark came in Mississippi to sit in the public library, for example, people who participated had been incensed by the Till incident and were just waiting for the spark to come. The Till incident was the catalyst.*

Of all the natural consequences, most often this fear turned to rage. A common thread throughout these testimonies is the anger. Richard Hatcher: "It was very frightening, very intimidating to think that white people were capable of doing that to a young black boy. It made me very angry and bitter towards white people." Mary Harris: "I thought it was terrible. Just because he whistled at the lady, they killed him. I was just real angry."

Evelyn Conners remembers, "They said Till was an 'uppity nigger' from up North. That's what we read in the *Cedar Rapids News Gazette* or the *Iowa City Press Citizen*, one or the other. It got quite a bit of coverage in Iowa. I can remember talking to a friend and she said, 'Why did he go down there?' I got so angry with her. Why can't he go down there; he had relatives there, didn't he?"

And this rage was sometimes not to be controlled by peaceful means. Doug Davidson says "I was one of those who, after that, wanted to get a gun. I'd always thought that was the only way we'd get respect from them; if they killed one of us, we'd have to take one of them. 'An eye for an eye.' Like my grandmama said; that's what the Bible said."

Some people describe these feelings as setting the fire of conviction. Tommie Hudson: "It puts fire in you. I was angry about Caucasians doing that, angry about anything they did to blacks like that. You know when something like that happens something ain't right." Ola Kennedy: "That [incident] lit a fire that probably made others not able to take what they were able to take in the past."

The anger affected work relations; blacks in many walks of life found themselves unable to work as before. Katie Thompson Lacky: "We were just angry to the point where as it was so tense at the hospital. We just couldn't work well and this was all that we could think about is what happened to the child ... We didn't even feel like communicating with the white people we were working for. It was to that point." Silas Thomas: "They tell me the people, especially blacks, down there wouldn't work. They couldn't get no cotton picked, no work done there ... they paid for it; they lost their crops 'cause black people wouldn't work for 'em ... They couldn't hire them [the blacks] for no amount of money. One of the black workers said that before this thing is over with, blacks and whites will all be as one." And King Henry: "When I went back to work, I detected some negative reactions from the black workers. I noticed productivity among black workers went down. It also affected race relations among blacks and whites. It promoted sloppy workmanship among blacks who normally took pride in their jobs. It promoted job absenteeism."

Politicization

Rage is the most powerful force mentioned in these testimonies as the inspiration and source of commitment to the modern Civil Rights Movement. The experiences are expressed from many different angles. Walter Williams expresses the personal view with vigor.

> *The Till incident struck me as something offensive. It galvanized black people to focus their outrage against those kinds of injustices. One thing it did to me; it did lead me to punch one of those rebels in the face when I was stationed in Fort Jackson, Florida, in 1959; I was twenty-three. One guy in my union, a real redneck, said to me, "I'm from Parkersville; that's where we lynched Emmett Till." It led to a fight, but then it wasn't really a fight. I punched him hard in the face. I had been sent to the South from Philadelphia without being educated about the nature of the Southern life style.*

Minnie Walker Logan describes her personal commitment, "My first response when I heard it was anger because of what had happened ... I also felt when I finally could calm down that I had to do whatever I could to keep those things from happening again. Whether small or large, I felt that I had to do something for my race. Those feelings have still not left today." Alvin Chambliss also describes his personal commitment:

> *Till, Charles Mack Parker (lynched in Pearl River County in Popularville, Mississippi), Verner Damer (lynched in Hattiesburg, Mississippi), Noah (a black man who was light-skinned and apparently had been wronged in some manner and decided to fight back; he took a rifle and killed several whites and got away. When he was caught, he was placed in an asylum. We all saw him as a hero, like John Brown) all of these lynchings motivated me to being a civil rights attorney, committing me to a life-time struggle for black people.*

Talmadge Anderson asserts:

> *The Emmett Till lynching brought me to a realization of what America was really like. Before then, I had known that black people were under foot in the American society. After Till, it brought to me the focus of what the inhumanity of racism was/is. For all blacks at that particular age and time, it brought to us a realization of how brutal and atrocious racism is. I think it shook blacks in America. Without Emmett Till, King would not have been successful ... It was the nucleus, the impetus of the Movement, not the Rosa Parks incident.*

Billie Campbell sees the Till incident as raising the national consciousness of whites as well as blacks:

> *some whites saw the injustices which made them come out of the wood works to fight for civil rights. I think a lot of those bizarre cases where people could see the injustices, could see the cruelty, where they didn't have to dig out and think it through, raised the consciousness ... It struck me as a cruel thing but it raised the national consciousness as to the injustices to the black race.*

Arkela Revels describes one of the rallies that took place after the Till case hit the media:

> *I heard about the rally at New Bethel Baptist Church, headed by the Rev. C. L. Franklin (Aretha Franklin's father). He had been announcing the rally, the purpose, and was providing leadership at a very crucial time. At the rally they had speakers; the mother of Emmett Till was there and people had the opportunity to meet her, which gave people a more realistic identification with this case. People wanted to contribute ei-*

> *ther time or money to draw attention and awareness, creating enough friction that the whole city of Detroit was very much riled up to the point that masses of people that had never formally been really active (they had been passive protesters) protested. Although I was only fifteen, the horror of the incident was such that the arousal of people in Detroit included young people like myself. I rose up for the occasion and was in attendance at New Bethel Baptist Church for the rally to hear and see for myself and share the pain of his mother.*

King Henry describes another:

> *When this news first hit in this particular area, a crisis orientated community [St. Louis, Missouri], they [blacks] came out of the shell and cooperated. It takes a tragedy to arouse them. Most of the people got very upset about it. They had planned a meeting at the Masonic Hall, one of the largest places owned by blacks. I had never seen a crowd so large. The place was just packed. Some of the relatives from Chicago were the main speakers. Afterwards they starting to collecting money for legal expenses to try to bring about justice. The people gave very generously and they collected bushels of money. A lot of churches collected money also.*

Emmett Till and the Modern Civil Rights Movement

Irene Thompson describes the transformation most clearly of all, speaking from a personal angle:

> *It was singularly the most grotesque event in my life. It came to full fruition in the death of Emmett Till. I was just coming out of college, full of dreams of freedom and awareness of life and still in the "I pledge allegiance to the flag ... with liberty and justice for all" stage. All wrapped up and then flung right down in my guts. It was an age of awakening, the catalyst for the thirst for freedom, the catalyst that precipitated the yearning for real freedom, the right to stand up and say, "I am and I am going to be." This was the thing that led me into the sixties. The death of Emmett Till catapulted us into the Civil Rights Movement.*

Several others express opinions about the effect of the Till case on the modern Civil Rights Movement. James Stewart considers:

> *Although the Civil Rights Movement was not in full bloom until later on, we knew then that something had to be done. And you wanted to do something but did not know what to do. The revolution hadn't caught fire yet. I think it was leading towards it. Till did more to galvanize blacks since the day of Marcus Garvey. Frankly, I think this did more to rekindle it. The Movement is up and down and always has been. I think this was one of the incidents that sparked it more so than the bus boycott.*

Ola Kennedy continues:

> *I think that that turned people on to the fact they had to really start thinking and doing something about civil rights. The hurt and the shock of it went so deep that I think that it moved me more to wanting to be committed to the struggle to change the unjust situation more so than the Rosa Parks's refusal to move because that had really happened before ... I think really the climax, if there was any doubt in your mind, was when the body was brought back to Chicago ... It kind of really shook you up so that you really wanted to do something. That lit a fire that probably made others not able to take what they were able to take in the past. The Emmett Till death really started the fire that really made us know that we had to make changes.*

These personal reflections of Emmett Till are a form of oral folk tradition, which clearly reveal a dimension not to be found in traditional documents. They represent one way of getting at more details and facts about the lessons to be learned from the Till murder through the voices of the people, attesting to its horror and its devastating effect on people, how vigilante violence holds an oppressed people in place. Reflections from the people are an effective method in the crucial challenge to modern society for self-criticism as a means of self-improvement.

Indeed, with powerful heart-relieving testimonies like these, one cannot question the tremendous impact of the Till murder case on countless American lives, both black and white. Invariably, these voices reveal that most Americans share the feeling that this tragic act was inhumane and should never have occurred. Moreover, they suggest that the sense of direction for many Americans because of the lynching was indelibly altered and that American society on the whole, too, was affected. To be sure, America was forced to adhere to the outcries and demands for the eradication of such atrocities and the amelioration of life-threatening, deplorable conditions of the oppressed. Ultimately, the undaunted struggle for civil rights reached its peak and became intense and hence, the critical era for the modern Civil Rights Movement ensued, making its permanent mark on American culture.

Part 2

Voices from Inside the Story

6
The Spiritual Force of Till's Lynching

Communal experiences are an intrinsic part of the cultural heritage of the African-American, and it comes as no surprise, then, that the tragedy of Emmett's death became a tragedy for all African-Americans. Emmett's mother herself, Mamie Till Bradley-Mobley, proclaimed that Emmett did not belong to her alone, but rather that he was "a universal child." During a personal interview with Mamie in her home in Chicago on January 6, 1988, she recalled the funeral of her son and remembered that almost every other person would scream out in anguish or faint when paying his or her last respects.

Even before the display of the body, the African-American community had rallied around her, supporting her both physically and emotionally when she went to the train station to receive the body of her only child. A powerful bonding took place within the black community at the Roosevelt Railroad Station in Chicago that Friday before Labor Day. The community came to the station to share the tragic loss of Emmett's grief-stricken mother. Among the supporters were the two ministers, Bishop Isaiah Roberts and Rev. Louis Henry Ford, who played major roles in the funeral arrangements. Their presence dramatized the centrality of the Africana church in this communal outrage. At the funeral, too, there was striking testimony of the spiritual autonomy of African-Americans, a kind of strength that dates back to American slavery.

Although Mamie had the support of the African-American community, she had to spiritually reconcile herself to her son's tragic death. In an eight-part biographical interview conducted by Ethel Payne of *The Chicago Defender* entitled "Mamie Bradley's Untold Story," she reveals her life up to the lynching and its aftermath. Demonstrating a special dimension, Mamie's story, which reflects why Christians must experience suffering, is a testimony of how her own religious faith helped her to cope with the devastation of her son's death. Part of a religious tradition in which one testifies one's trials and tribulations, this testimony of her endurance and faith is characteristic of the Africana religious experience. Similar to the spiritual rewards in many denominational churches, the benefits derived from Mamie's story afforded both her and the listener a kind of catharsis, a purgation.

First, Mamie relates a number of divinely inspired premonitions of Emmett's death, the first of which was the reaction of Till's grandmother Alma Spearman to a letter of praise from his great-aunt Elizabeth Wright, from whose home Emmett was abducted. Ironically, the letter was received on the same Saturday that Emmett was abducted. Mrs. Spearman commented, "It was so beautiful that I'm going to put this up carefully. This could be his obituary."[1] That same night, as Till's mother bragged about her son to some of her friends, incongruously she interjected, "If Bo Till could get his feet on Chicago soil, he would be one happy kid." The irony is that Till at that

1 Ethel Payne, "Mamie Bradley's Untold Story," *Chicago Daily Defender* (Thursday, 8 March 1956, p. 8).

moment was in the hands of the kidnappers. According to Rayfield Mooty in a recent interview, Till was heard early that morning by Walter Reed crying, "Mama! Mama! Lord have mercy! Mama!" and pleading for his life.[2]

Another demonstration of the spiritual folk tradition is Mamie's version of Christ and redemption and her son's death. This is revealed in the section called "Strange Experience" in which Mamie, distraught, relates how she was able to finally reconcile herself to Emmett's death. Alone in her bed, unable to sleep and questioning God, she relates that

> *The presence said to me, "Mamie, it was ordained from the beginning of time that Emmett Louis Till would die a violent death. You should be grateful to be the mother of a boy who died blameless like Christ ... Have courage and faith that in the end there will be redemption for the suffering of your people and you are the instrument of this purpose. Work unceasingly to tell the story so that the truth will arouse men's conscience and right can at last prevail."*[3]

In a Biblical mode, she presents the story of the rise of humanity by connecting her unfortunate experience with the universal truth of unconditional love and the promise of redemption. God is forgiving and merciful. Mamie, like Mary the chosen mother for Christ, is forgiving. She demonstrates this forgiving nature, interweaving her ultimate mission in life, which she relates in a later interview. When asked if she harbored any hatred toward her son's murderers, she responded,

---

[2] Mooty, Interview, 1986.

[3] Payne, p. 8.

> *To tell you the truth, it was almost as if I had a heart transplant at the time. One of the experiences I had was that if I were to go around harboring hate, that that hate would eventually destroy me. And it was just as if the whole thing was just lifted. Toward these people, I had no feeling whatsoever. I went completely into neutral. I do not hate them; I have on occasions felt sorry for them, because I know that if they could have undone it, that was one tar baby they touched they wished they had never touched ... Ever so often I get revelations, or dreams, or whatever you want to call them. But it is as if the Lord is reassuring me that I have nothing to harbor, to feel guilty about. I have no guilt; they have the guilt. For me to just put them aside. Leave them to Him. He will handle them. There's nothing I can do about them anyway. My job is to do exactly what I'm doing. And in doing what I'm doing, I'm molding character ... Most everyone who came through Sister Mobley is doing something worthwhile in the church [the Evangelistic Crusaders Church of God in Christ] and in life. And how it happened so fast, I can't understand it ... That's the most unique feeling.*[4]

Mamie's testimony has all the elements of struggle that are common to every Christian believer in God. It is a story that strikes the depths of human despair, but it ends with a triumphant shout of victory. From beginning to end, it is the testimony of a mother's faith in God, like Job's relentless and unswerving in its strength. She speaks of her deep love for the Lord and gives thanks that He has heard her prayer for deliverance from her suffering. Her

---

[4] Tape-recorded interview with Mamie Bradley-Mobley, Chicago, IL, 6 January 1988.

faith never waning, she prayed, stumbled, blinded by her tears, knocked down to her knees, and she sought the face of God to comfort her in her hour of loss. She tells of a good, gracious, and merciful Lord who rescued and delivered her soul at that moment. She felt His presence in an absolute peace. She came to understand that her son did not die in vain. God spoke to her heart, with the universal truth that God is Love and that He causes all things to work together for the good of those who are called according to His purpose.

The multifaceted faces of human suffering are as sweeping in scope and as certain as is day and night. Human suffering is unavoidable. Just as we cannot postpone the rising of the sun or delay its setting, neither can we choose the time, place, degree, or method of our suffering. We can, however, choose our response. Mamie contends that it is only as we look to Jesus Christ that we have the right attitude toward our suffering.

She has spent her life since the death of her son helping kids to grow up spiritually. These kids grow to have a sense of purpose through the activities of a group she founded and named after her son, the Emmett Till Players. Their presentations, which are the recitations of Rev. Dr. King's speeches, are designed to raise the level of consciousness of the power of the love of God and its opponent, the monstrous horror of racism.

It is appropriate now to go to speeches given by Mamie Bradley and Rayfield Mooty, in October 1955 in South Bend, Indiana.

MAMIE BRADLEY-MOBLEY:

I would like to extend my appreciation to all of you for coming out tonight, to hear what has happened and to find out what you can do about what has happened. I would like to thank the youth group. How impressed I am by the beautiful job that they are doing here. You young musicians and you young children everywhere. Surely the things that we do here tonight is going to make the way for a better tomorrow. And only the foundation that we lie here that they can build upon. So it's up to us, to us grown-ups, to get together and build a foundation for them to build a future upon.

At this particular time, I would like to introduce to you a gentleman who has stood by during this entire ordeal. We called him the very first day that we found out that Emmett had been kidnapped. He, like so many others, [has] stood by and given of himself and his time very unselfishly. Mr. Mooty and my father went with me to Mississippi to face the trial, or at least a mock trial of Emmett Louis Till's murder. I would like to introduce you to Mr. Rayfield Mooty. He will speak to you for a few minutes, allowing my mother a chance to come.

RAYFIELD MOOTY:

Mr. Chairman, honored guests, I'd like to extend you my appreciation for the warm invitation you have extended to Mrs. Bradley in bringing her up to your city. I know that you have been waiting patiently to hear what's happened in the case in Mississippi. And she just mentioned to you that we have been going so fast since this incident occurred, so we haven't had time to hardly catch our breaths.

I'm not going to tell you the mother's reaction, she will explain that to you herself. I am only going to brief you on some of these things that occurred in this case, and before I leave here I hope to be able to tell you what you can do to see that this doesn't happen again in America. Especially this same kind of event. Because I know that you are interested in hearing her story, but also you should be just as much concerned knowing where in this program do you fit. And when you learn what part you have to play in this program, the rest of it will be up to you. There isn't anything that we can do for Emmett Till. Emmett Till is dead and buried. But direct something we can do to see that the rest of the Emmett Tills don't meet with the same fate.

As Mrs. Bradley pointed out to you, I came into this case, the first day this thing happened. We went all the way through, all the way through, even down into the depths of Mississippi to where the trial was. I want to stop for a minute here to talk about what happened when Emmett's body arrived in Chicago.

This was one of the most trying times that I have ever witnessed. When we looked and found out this casket had come into Chicago, we met it, and we had no idea, no idea of imagination, what that casket held until we followed it to the undertaker's shop. When he got there, the undertaker was looking at the body, he pleaded with Emmett's mother to not look at what was in that box. She had made up her mind definitely before, when she first heard that her child had been murdered, it made no difference what it looked like, she would have to see it. When she gave that determined stand, and I took it upon myself to lead her to that casket to see what was in there. Some of you saw the pictures, but you didn't see the real thing. I saw it. And when I looked into that casket, and she looked into that casket, we stood side by side along with her father. Something happened to her. If you would have been there it would have happened to you too. Something happened to me so severe until I can't explain what it was, but there's one thing that keeps ringing in my mind, that this has got to be the last time this kind of a thing happens in America. I don't know what I'm going to do to see to it, I don't think I can handle this whole job by myself. I think it's going to take everybody in America to see that this doesn't happen again.

A lot of things started rolling in my mind. How could I rile up the people of America to know what has happened? Oftentimes (this is not the only murder that has happened in the South, it's not the only link), it just appeared to me that if a hundred thousand people, if a million people could see that body, that it would be enough to keep you up late at night. It would be enough to start you to thinking. When you start to thinking, then you are going to start acting.

MAMIE BRADLEY-MOBLEY:

You probably have heard snatches of the speeches that we have been making through the country. I don't know how you reacted to them, perhaps you're wondering how I'm standing up here doing it. Well, I'm wondering the same thing, but I haven't really had time to sit down and analyze what was going on. It just seemed that I was caught up in a whirlwind and there was only one thing to do and that was to go and do the best that I could. In doing so, the NAACP had me to come to their New York office, they have sat down and talked to me, they have started to arrange these tours for me, which has really and truly taken a great burden off of my mind. In all of the turmoil, upset, and the daze of what had happened, it was just almost impossible to make a telephone call.

Back on August 28 when the call first came to the house that Emmett Till had been taken from my uncle's house, I had had no way of knowing or preparing myself for what was fixing to happen. I really didn't know what to do. The first thing that I did was to call my mother, because that is where I had been taking all of my burdens all of my life. When I called her, she said, "Sister, you come right over." And I think that I broke just about every speed record in the city of Chicago getting over to her house. I certainly ignored stop signs and red lights, I just had to depend on the horn to clear the way. For some reason, there wasn't a policeman on the street that morning. I only saw one car and no one was in it. I had decided if anybody did stop me I was going to tell them that I didn't have time to argue—just clear the way to 1626 West Fourteenth Place and I'll talk to you when I get there. But as God would have it, there was nobody to interfere with me that morning and the street was just about deserted.

Then I walked in mother's house, and I just knew that I was going to go in there and throw this burden all on her shoulders and sit down there and see what she was going to do. But as God would have it, when I walked in her door, I found out that she was in worse shape than I was. And for the first time in my life, I was going to have to stand up and take care of my own problems, because there wasn't a soul there who could do it for me.

We had made numerous telephone calls. The first thing we did was to call Crosby down in the state of Mississippi who had lived down there for nine years. We had been wondering for nine years why Crosby went to Mississippi. He had a home in Argo, he had the use of my mother's car, and he ate all of his biscuits and cakes over at our house, so we really didn't see why he wanted to go to Mississippi. But God sent him down there nine years ago and prepared him—helped him to go among the people to be uncle, to be strong, to be a man, to be man enough to get Emmett Till's body out of the state of Mississippi. Out of our family there must be hundreds and perhaps even up to a thousand, but that was the only man in this entire family that could have done the work necessary to get Emmett Till back to Chicago. At last, we know why Crosby went South.

When we started making calls to Mississippi, we got through to Crosby, we got through to one or two other people, but the first thing we noticed was that nobody wanted to talk to us. We called the gentleman on whose place my Uncle Mose lived, and we asked him to take a message to Uncle Mose. He said he couldn't hear good over the telephone, he didn't have a pencil, he didn't have any paper in the house and besides he was old and couldn't see and he couldn't even hear. There was nobody else there to take the message. Well, I don't think much of people who go off and leave an old man in that condition.

We tried calling other people that we had known through the years, name families down in Mississippi. They too had other business. They couldn't get a message to anybody. Their cars were out of fix. Pretty soon it got so that when we put a call through down there we would hear the person on the other end say that I have nothing to say, I don't want to talk to them. The cotton curtain in Mississippi is tougher than the Iron Curtain in Russia. It's that cotton *curtain that we're going to have to penetrate.*

We went on like that for several days, from Sunday until Wednesday. During that time I just really can't tell you what all didn't happen. I went out to take care of something, but most of the time I spent there at the telephone taking messages trying to put through calls and just trying my best to find my baby. But Tuesday I had to leave. I got back and the family was all in smiles. They had had three telephone calls. My mother had taken one of the calls, my cousin had taken one, and my stepfather had taken a call. And they met me at the door and said, "Emmett Till's on his way home." For some reason, my heart didn't skip a beat, I said, "How's he coming?" Nobody knew. I said, "Well, is somebody bringing him?"

Well, it was a pretty hard time around there for awhile. Everybody just seemingly gave up all sorts of hope. But I said to my mother, "We can't give up now, if we stop hoping, we'll stop living. We've got to keep going." I sat down again and started taking care of the telephone. I said, "If you will just let me, I'll answer the phone myself, and I'll write everything down" (because I didn't trust my memory, but I would be able to get the message perhaps as good as anybody else). And I had to be doing something; I couldn't just sit still.

When I would go and lie down it felt like I had no right to be in a bed when I didn't know where my baby was. I sent him away from me happy, cheerful, a normal boy, a boy that was excited about a vacation in Mississippi. I got a letter from my aunt and from my son, one week from the day he left home. And she was just amazed at the job that I had done of bringing Emmett up. And, frankly I was a bit amazed myself, because he had turned out to be a very nice boy. At the age of thirteen, he took over the laundry for me. I guess I've been down to the laundry room six times since last Christmas. And when I went then, it was under protest, because when Emmett started doing the laun-

dry, I found out I wasn't able to do it anymore. About two years ago, Emmett took over my housecleaning. I don't think there are many eleven-year-old boys that take over the mopping and the dusting and the waxing for their parents. But I found out after Emmett went on his vacation, that I couldn't even mop a floor anymore. I was going to leave the house really nice for him. I was supposed to leave the Tuesday after he left. I was going to leave it for him as nice as he had left it for me when he took his vacation. We depended on one another. He said, "Mother, if you go to work, and cook, I'll clean up and wash." And that was the way it was. And not only did he do those things, but if I had painting to be done, or a wall to be washed, that was Emmett's job. He didn't think I could wash the wall good anyway, and I was very happy for him to do it.

As we lived together, we grew up together and I'm sure that I learned just as much from Emmett as Emmett learned from me. One of the things that Emmett taught me, or that I know that he knew, was that he didn't realize that he was a black boy and had to look up to a white boy. I was taught in school that I was as good as I wanted to be. If I excelled in something in spite of the fact that I was dark, that still made me hold the top spot. It didn't matter that a colored person or a white person were vying for the same position. Whoever earned it was the one that got it. Consequently, it wasn't until I looked down, that I realized that I was dark. Out of a class of a 130 white children, there were only three colored that graduated. I happened to have been at the head of that class. And nobody wanted to hold me back because I was dark. I earned my spot and I got it. I have never been race-conscious. I had white friends that I loved just as much as I did the colored—perhaps even a little bit more.

And I still have white friends that I love. And I wouldn't take anything in the world for them. Because they have stood by me, and I know that you can't judge a race by one or two people. Because I know some people in my race that I wouldn't want to be judged by.

I think that the only way that we're going to be able to be a nation, is to get ourselves together because divided we cannot stand. Anybody knows that when there's friction in a house, there's no peace there. Any outsider can walk in and tear everything up. That's just the position we have our country in today. It's the white man against the black man, the red man against the green man, and everybody is against everybody. It's even the black man against the black man. All some of these other countries have to do is just walk in and take over because we are so stupid. We are arguing among ourselves until we can't see what we are doing to ourselves. As long as we keep those people down in Mississippi ignorant, we're going to have white men killing colored boys. And we're going to have other people killing white boys. And we can't have that, because the other nations are looking at us.

I said that I sent Emmett Till down South. I sent him down there a happy boy. He usually went to Argo on the weekends to spend the weekend with my grandmother. And he came home one night, a little bit later than usual and I was waiting for him, I was pretty mad. When he came in he knew about the only way to get around me was to out-talk me. He said, "Mamma, I think the people pick on me when I ride the bus." I said, "What do you mean?" Because I was ready and as soon as he got through, I was going to let him know just what I thought of him coming in late. He said, "Well, I think all the women stand over me because they'll know that I'll give them a seat." I said, "Uh huh, who would you give your seat to if a white lady and a colored lady stood up by you?" He said, "I'd give the seat to the one who had the most packages or the one who was holding a baby." I thought that was a pretty good answer. I mean, I was mostly testing, I didn't know really how Emmett thought about the race problem. Except that I know he's brought many a little white boy to our house, and he has always treated them nice. He has pushed them around as much as he pushed the little colored boys around, and he's treated them as good as he did the little colored boys. I just knew that he was a normal well-adjusted child, and that's why I thought that I could let him go to Mississippi. But I did warn him that he had a place down there that was a little bit different than Chicago. I told him that if anything happened, even though you think you're perfectly within your right, for goodness sake take low. If necessary, get on your knees and beg apologies. Don't cross anybody down there because Mississippi is not like Chicago. What you can get away with here, you might not be able to do it there. I said no matter how much it seems that you have the right, just forget your rights while you're in Mississippi.

In time, I called the uncle that was going to take him down there, and I asked him, "When you let the boys go to town, please go with them. Take the car keys. If you get six teenagers together, anything can happen." I didn't really think all of these things, it just seemed that I had to say them. If I exaggerated a little bit, maybe I would make Emmett conscious that he was going to a different place and to be reasonably careful.

But I, like everybody else, felt the conditions were changing in Mississippi. I certainly thought that everything was getting better. I couldn't really tell though because I was confining myself to my house and my job. I didn't go out and see what the city's problem was. I felt that I had done pretty good when the government gave me two hours off and I used a half hour of that time to vote. I really thought I was making a noble sacrifice. I didn't go to the different civic meetings and listen to what was happening all over the world. I depended on what I might happen to read as I was rushing through the morning paper just before leaving for work. Now I know that that was very wrong. If I had sat down, if I had made the problems of the nation my problems, maybe I would have had something to say, or maybe I could have done something about the situation before now. Maybe I could have done it without having to lose a son to find out that I had a part to play.

Even though I've lost my son, crying won't get him back. Nothing I can do will get him back. But now I realize that other people's sons are going to go that way. There's a great job that's going to have to be done. People are going to have to be awakened. I certainly was no more than an average citizen—perhaps even a little below average because, just a boy and his mother (and a government worker at that), he didn't have too much. There are many of you sitting here tonight that are in far better condition than my son and I were in. Everything we got we struggled for. So that's proof positive right there that race haters don't care, they don't have a particular group to pick on. If I had been rich, then it could be assumed that they wanted ransom or that they wanted any number of things. But I could have given them anything under the sun hardly if they had asked me for it in return for his life. I was just as average as any of you. And inasmuch as they walked up to my door, you might say, and took my son, and I know beyond a shadow of a doubt that he was not guilty as accused, then they can do the same thing to your sons and your daughters.

But it's not for us to get up and hate one another. Rather we're going to have to stand together and love one another, share the problems, and try to work them out together. Because in the United States of America there can be nothing but Americans. We can't have Negroes, and white people, and Jews, and Indians, and Greeks, and whatnot. We have to be one. Because only as one unit can we stand.

Finally, I got the news that Emmett Till was dead. The Chicago Tribune *called, but they didn't feel like they wanted to give me the message. They just didn't have the heart to do it. They called a girlfriend of mine and asked her to break it to the family as gently as possible. When she called I was on the phone. She didn't want to talk to me either. But it seemed like I just knew what had happened. So I told her, "For God's sake, whatever it is, let me have it, because I can probably take it better than anybody around here anyway." And that's when she told me that Emmett was found dead in the Tallahatchie River. That his skull was beaten in on the left-hand side, and that he had a gin fan around his neck tied with barbed wire. I wrote the message down on the paper, and I turned around to my mother and my aunt (those were the only two I can remember being in the house). I read off what I had written. My aunt started to break down. I said, "Take her out, and don't let her start. For some reason, we don't have time to cry, there's something we've got to do. Maybe tomorrow, maybe the next day—" (and someone said, "Well, maybe you'll never get to cry.") "But right now it's just necessary to think." Well, I really didn't know what to think about because after the child was found dead, I had no doubts that I would get the body. Surely they would let me have that.*

By holding ourselves together, my aunt remembered to call the undertaker, my mother left the house to call Crosby again. She informed Crosby that Bo's body had been found. The potentates down in Mississippi said the minute they got any news of that boy they would notify my uncle. Instead, when Bo's body was found, it was in such horrible shape when the sheriff called an undertaker and ordered him to bury that body immediately. He didn't even have time to let that undertaker go and wash the mud off the body and prepare it for burial. The main thing to do was to get that body in the ground so nobody could see it.

As God would have it, we didn't stop and cry, we didn't cut ourselves off. Only by not wasting any time were we able to get that body on the way out of Mississippi. We got hold of Crosby and Crosby went and got a sheriff and went down to where they were burying the body. There were twenty men that had dug a two-foot grave. They were getting that body away as fast as they could. Believe me, if night had fallen, with that body in the ground, nobody would have ever seen it again. Because it wasn't going to stay there very long. Crosby went down and asked the undertaker if he would take the body and prepare it for shipment. The colored undertaker said, "Well, Mr. Smith, I'll tell you the truth, I'm afraid to let Nate catch that body in my undertaker's shop. But I will take it back there and you will get somebody to get it out of there before night. My orders are to bury it and bury it immediately."

They went on back to town, and my uncle called a white undertaker in Charleston, Mississippi. That undertaker came over to look at that body, and he said, "Yeah, I could embalm it. And I will do so. But you'll have to promise that this top will never come off of this box, otherwise I'll have nothing to do with it." Well, Crosby wasn't in a position to argue about anything. But he promised, and he intended to keep that promise. When Crosby called me, he said, "I'm coming. I'm bringing Bo with me. I'll be at the station at such-and-such a day." I said, "Okay, we'll meet you." But I didn't know how I was going to react when I saw that big box come off of that train. It just seemed terrible that I would send my boy down there happy and alive, and he would come back to me in a pine box. And that's one of the times that I broke down. But that still was nothing, really.

They took that body to the undertaker shop. We went in there to see if we could see the body. The undertaker met us, and he said, "For God's sake, Mrs. Bradley, don't look. I'm a friend of the family, and as a friend, I'm telling you don't look." I said, "Mr. Rayner, I have to see it if I have to break it open myself. I'm not asking you to, I'm telling you to." He shook his head, and he turned around, and he went back. I think Mr. Mooty went and looked first. When they came back to me, he said, "Well, if you insist, you come on." I turned to my father, and I turned to Mr. Mooty, and I said, "Will one of you get on each side?" because I just didn't know if I was going to be able to make it or not. I wanted to, but I didn't know how long my strength was going to last. They got on each side, and we started walking. That was about the longest walk and the hardest walk I've ever had to make. When I stood up over that casket and looked down in that box, the thing that I saw down there changed my mind completely. I started crying then. And, as Mr. Mooty said, I got real mad. And I've been mad ever since.

What I saw in that box was not like anything I've ever seen before in my life. I had been reading funny books because Bo read them. I read them too. Not so much to see what he was reading, but because I liked to read them. We read the spooky kind until they were taken off the market. In these spooky books I have seen everything that I can imagine—things beyond the imagination. But what I saw in that casket hadn't been touched in a funny book. I looked down, and I saw that there was a hole in my son's head that was big enough to stick your hands through. It looked like it had been made with an ax. I said, "Oh, my God!" And then I looked a little bit further, and I saw that there was a hole in his jaw. You could see that every tooth in the back of his head had been knocked out. And he had twenty-eight real nice ones; I was very proud of them. I looked at his mouth, and it was choked open, and his tongue was bulged out of his mouth. His lips were pushed back, and only a few teeth remained right in front there. I shook my head again. They even had the nerve to put a bullet hole right up over his ear. I do remember asking, "Was that bullet necessary, because surely he was dead before they did all of that." You just wondered what kind of a person, or what kind of people, or would they be human beings who would do a job like that. The more I looked, the more confused I became. Finally, I said, "Well I've got to look down here and really look good and see if I can find Emmett, because that's not the Emmett that I knew." After looking, and after searching, I found my boy. I tried not to, I didn't want to. But it had to be, and it was. I asked Mr. Rayner if he would be good enough to take the body out of the casket and lay it on a board, because I wanted to look at it real good. I couldn't see it down in those satin covers. He looked at me again, as if to wonder what on earth in the world—is she crazy or what? But he just shook his head and went ahead and did as I asked him to do. When the body got here, it didn't have any clothes on it. It was just covered up in a whole lot of white powder, because nobody was supposed to see it anyway. But I couldn't look through all of that steel and tell whether that was Emmett. I couldn't say that I was burying Emmett until I looked to see for myself. I worked around that body, and that's when I ran into another shock, when I looked at the left side of Emmett's face. And I looked at that left side, it looked like somebody had taken a knife through, it was made in a crisscross shape. They had just sat down and had chop, chop on the side of his face. And the right eye had been picked out. It seemed like it had been picked out with a nut picker. And the right eye was almost out, it was just hanging. I had to examine that eye, examine those teeth. I started to examine the ear, and that's when I found out that the entire back of the head had been knocked off.

I said, "Roy, anybody that wants to look at this, can see it. I'm tired of stuff being covered up. If some of these lids had been pulled off of Mississippi a long time ago, then something like this wouldn't be happening today. So far as my personal feelings are concerned, they don't count. Because the thing that has happened to me now is more than I will ever have to face again. I can take it just a little bit longer. I have lost the only thing that I held really precious and dear beside my mother and father." And if my son had sacrificed his life like that, I didn't see why I should have to bear the burden of it alone. There was a lesson there for everybody. Because if it happened to him, it can happen again. And I've never been one to sit by and accept defeat anyway. Not if I could see a way out of it. And if I couldn't do anything else but raise a lot of sand, I would do that. So that temper, or whatever you want to call it, came in a little bit handy this time.

I know my mother has been trying to get me to shut up for about twenty-nine years. Every time I go to shut up it looks like that's about the best opportunity to go to talk, and so I start all over again. Well, I'll tell you. As long as somebody wants to hear what's going on in our United States that's the land of the free and the home of the brave, as long as you're willing to try to get up and do something about it (and I don't think you would be here tonight unless you did want to do something about it), as long as that condition exists, then I will be before you. I will try to tell you, because I think that we all have children, and I think that we want to leave them a heritage a little bit greater than ours. We want to leave them a land that they can be proud of. Some of the letters that I have gotten have told me that we should go back where we came from. I don't know where I came from. My mother told me that I was born on the Tallahatchie River. Well, I don't want to go back there, that's for sure.

And if they're talking about Africa, well I don't know anything at all about Africa. The climate might not agree with me. This is where I was born and this is where I was raised. This is where I intend to stay. But I'm not going to stay here backed up against the wall afraid to open my mouth. Because if I have to live in fear then I think that I'm a lot better off dead. That little baby sitting on that floor—she shouldn't ever have to know that she's black and that she's inferior. If she grows up and she's smart enough to work a crossword puzzle, she should be given credit for working that puzzle. If she's able to sew a fine seam, then surely she shouldn't be denied a job because her face is black. I feel that we should stand up and be counted. I don't know how the men feel, but I know that when women die to bring a child into the world, we don't want anybody to bother that kid. We're going to discipline him or her the best that we can. But we don't want anybody kicking them around. You'll fight more for your children than you will for yourself. Because I know a lot of things I have taken on the chin. I've fought a little bit, I said that I wasn't going to take it, but I learned how to live with it. But when they picked on Emmett, they just did the wrong thing.

And so help me God, until my dying day, I'm going to be fighting that thing. I'm not going to be fighting color, I'm not going to be fighting creed, I'm not going to be fighting anybody's belief, so long as it's a safe and sound one. So long as it doesn't reach out and destroy me or destroy somebody else. But I feel like we should stand up, we should make a stand once and for all, we should say that we're going to live as men and women, as long as we're paying these first-class taxes, we're going to demand this first-class citizenship that goes with it. I don't feel like going down to the Bureau of Internal Revenue on taxpaying day and they tell me, "Come on and pay your tax." And then I ask for just a little bit of freedom and I'm told, "You can't have it." If they were telling me, "You're black, Mrs. Bradley, you'll only have to pay second-class taxes," then I would expect that second-class citizenship. But they're not making any allowances for me on income tax day. They're not making any conces-

sions for me on any other things either. They're asking me to pay, they're asking me for the best that's in me, and I want the best in return. Oh, my God, if our children have to come along, if we have to be afraid of the man next door or the woman over there, then we don't have very much to live.

We buried Emmett. The state of Mississippi said that that was not Emmett. They said that it was impossible for a body to deteriorate that much in that length of time. But what they didn't say, they didn't bring out that the body was badly beaten, that the river water had busted the skin and it had pealed off the body. The water was hot, the beating was brutal. Then to beat him, they didn't hear his cries. They didn't touch them whatsoever. This one little colored boy that did hear them said that he heard screams coming from that barn about an hour and a half. He cried for God, he cried for his mother, he pleaded with them. But they were having such a good time, so they didn't consider that he was a human being. I don't see myself how he stood the beating. But when they got good and through, when they got good and tired, then they took Emmett and put a canvas over the truck and dumped him in the Tallahatchie River with a [ginmill's] band around his neck. Oh, Emmett wasn't supposed to show up anymore. If they had thought he was going to show up, they never would admit they had gone to my uncle's house and taken him away.

But as God would have it, three days after he was dumped into that river, his feet came up, and a little white boy saw his feet sticking there. He called the people that he knew—his friend, his father, or somebody. They got a man with a boat, they went out there, and they got Emmett, they took this band from around his neck and put it in another boat and got him to the shore. They called the sheriff. The sheriff already knew that a little colored boy from Chicago was missing. But he didn't bother to report to anybody that he had found a body or that my Uncle Moses Wright had identified Emmett by the ring on his finger that said, "L. T." Louis Till was his father, who died overseas.

As God would have it, they didn't get the body in the ground. But this sheriff stood up in the courtroom and said that when he saw this body he didn't know if it was a white man or a colored man. They called a doctor to the scene. He signed the death certificate, that this was a Negro. His name was Emmett Louis Till, age fourteen, resident of Chicago, Illinois. He did all of that. But when he stood up on the witness stand, he too, didn't know if it was a white man or a colored man. Still, the state of Mississippi sent me three death certificates, and it was on the basis of these three death certificates that I collected his Metropolitan Life Insurance (and they don't pay off unless they know they're paying on the right individual). They made so many mistakes, but God wouldn't let it be a perfect crime. In a way I feel that it had to be. Because if that hadn't happened, I wouldn't be standing up here tonight, I wouldn't be worried as to whether the NAACP had fifteen million Negroes and as many whites as possible joining their forces to fight for democracy. I would be home perhaps arguing with Emmett about wearing out shoes so fast because that's the way I spent most of my time. I had never done any public speaking before.

People have asked me how I do it. And as I told you before, I don't know how I do it. But it's something I believe in, I feel that it's through the NAACP, and through we people who will get behind the NAACP, that's going to make the difference in our to-

day and in our tomorrow. And I'm with them one hundred percent. It's not a job that they can do by themselves. I, too, have sat aside and criticized the way things were run, but it never had occurred to me to get in there and try to help run. Well I'm in here now and I'm willing to perform any services they ask of me. I feel like when my job is done, when there's a better place carved out of this democracy for us, when justice and freedom and democracy last until they get to you and me, then I will feel it is time for me to go home and try to make a new life for myself. I feel like I have fifteen million sisters and brothers that I'm partially responsible for and every child in this United States, part of him belongs to me. So with your help and with my help and with the help of the NAACP and mankind as a whole, we can make this United States the place that it was originally intended to be. We can make it what our forefathers and what the other people who came over here from the other countries, to carve out was a life where everybody could be free and equal.

Well, we'll have to help them do it. There's a job for us to do too. And there's one thing that we'll have to remember. Nobody is going to walk out and hand you anything on a silver platter. Just because you're good, nobody walks up and hands you a Cadillac. You go out and work for it. You're going to have to work for your freedom, and you're going to have to buy it. To me it's just as important to buy five hours' worth of freedom as it is to buy a fifth of Scotch, because you can do more with the freedom than you can with the Scotch.

I want to thank you all for listening so attentively.

7
Mooty's Story

This information is taken from a personal interview with Rayfield Mooty, the second cousin of Emmett Till, in Chicago, Illinois, in July 1986. In the first meeting with Rayfield, we discussed the Emmett Till case, and in the second meeting we discussed Mooty's activities with the labor union, as a labor-union leader.

CH: *In this third meeting that we are having here today (this is of course July 19, 1986), we are going to discuss the Civil Rights Movement and see if we can put the Emmett Till case into proper perspective. Let us focus on the Emmett Till case and see if we can actually shape the whole case, and place it into historical perspective in reference to the modern Civil Rights Movement of the fifties and the sixties, which has been historically marked with the Rosa Parks's bus incident.*

So, could we have you explicate briefly how you feel about the modern Civil Rights Movement and, of course, how Emmett Till fits into that whole era or movement?

RM: *Whenever I start discussing the Civil Rights Movement with people, I always get lost, and I have to go back, think about and talk about and learn what happened prior to even the 1900s. When I talk about that, I have to review a lot of things that happened in The American Negro Slave Revolt by Herbert Aptheker. This will give you some of the background of what people have gone through—like Nat Turner, Denmark Vesey, and Gabriel Prosser, and others—and all of the struggles that have been going on over the years.*

Most of us get lost as to why these things are. I have to go back to the presidential elections of 1877. In 1865, President Abraham Lincoln did give us a little relief of freedom. But that was all taken from us. All during the fifties and sixties, we were just feeling in the dark, not knowing why; most of us didn't know why we were in the shape we were. But all of the people that were killed and murdered and lynched and everything is recorded in this book by Aptheker, but he also reflects on the election of 1877, when all of the rights that we had were taken from us by the stroke of one pen and only by one vote! One vote! One electoral vote!

Those Southerners held up their vote, and they didn't give their vote until they got assurance. Because when Abraham Lincoln gave us some type of freedom, it was a portion of freedom that we enjoyed, and we voted, and we went and made a lot of gains—but he also at the polling places had troops in the South to protect us, and we used our vote. And we sent people to Congress; we had more people in the Senate then than we've got now. We still don't have a senator in the Senate yet. But that was all done with the stroke of one pen, just with one vote in 1877 when Rutherford B. Hayes made a compromise with the South that "if you give me your vote and make me president, I will pull the troops out of there." And the troops were what they called a toothache to the Southerners, and he said, "I will pull that tooth out, and then you can do whatever you want to."

And at that time, every state set up their own laws. Ten days after he was elected, he started pulling the troops out of the South. And within twenty days, he had all of the troops out of the South, so we couldn't go to the poll and vote. And out of all of the struggle that we had, the only thing that we had going for us was that one thing: the right to vote. And we didn't get that right until after all of the killing, all during the years trying to go to the polls and vote, including Lamar Smith and all of that kind of stuff.

President Johnson made that clear after Martin Luther King and the Kennedy brothers, and Johnson came heir to the White House. Just before he left he said, "I am going to give you what you have been needing, and this is what you need." And when he signed that Voting Rights Bill in 1965 "giving you the right to vote," he said, "I am going to say it to every Negro. You must register, and you must vote. And then you must learn, because if you don't have the right to vote all other rights you have are null and void." If you don't have the right to vote. Your future depends on it, and your children's future depends on that.

Now once we learned that—and it took us a long time to even consider that—from 1965 to way down here now in the last election when we began to really vote, we began to feel our muscles. But it took us a long time, because 350 years is a long time to be beat down, and every time you raise your head up, somebody would knock you right back down.

So that brought me up to this Till case. A lot of people got involved in the Till case, because they thought that was scandalous. But that wasn't the worst thing that happened to black people. There was a lot of murders that were worse than that, but there wasn't nothing done about it because every state set up their own laws.

In the Till case, it didn't make any difference what Carolyn Bryant said that Till did; it wouldn't have made any difference. Milan was what you called a "Nigger breaker," just like the man that broke [Frederick] Douglass. When a plantation owner had a lot of blacks out there that he couldn't control, he hired him as a breaker. You have to read all of these conceptions of what the Till case was all about, and what happened in Mississippi. You have to read most of them in order to learn that that was the law of the land, and it was not against the law to kill that boy and tie that chain around his neck with barbed wire and throw him in the river. It wasn't against the law, so it wouldn't have made no difference what anybody said.

So I have to think about what went on before, not just Emmett Till. When I talk about Emmett Till ... I took his mother to the courthouse; those are the pictures there. I forgot to tell you who Crosby was. That was her uncle, and that was why he was so deeply involved.

CH: *When you say that you took her to the courthouse, you mean in Mississippi?*

RM: *In Sumner, Mississippi.*

CH: *How did her family view the whole thing? People have always been, especially northerners, apprehensive about the Deep South, particularly Mississippi, and particularly with her son's being slain there. How did the family react to her decision to go to the trial?*

RM: *Well, they were a religious family, very religious. And there was mixed emotions in the family about her going to Mississippi. And she really didn't agree to go to Mississippi until her father came in. That's the only three people who went to Mississippi in that photo—she and her father and myself. He got there about nine o'clock. I guess she wouldn't have left to go to Mississippi had he not got there to go with her.*

CH: *So he was definitely pro going?*

RM: *Yeah, he was definitely pro going.*

CH: *So the two of you were the ones who were pretty much instrumental in getting her to go?*

RM: *Yes, we had to persuade her to go and to persuade her mother to agree to let her go, because her mother didn't want her to go because there was a lot of disturbance in the air. But to talk about things and to go is two different things. And we couldn't bear no arms. She tried to get the armed guard to go with her, and they wouldn't allow that. No armed guard, couldn't even have a pocket knife. You had to go on pure, cold nerve. So we agreed to go.*

And it's a good thing that we did go to hear the case. I think it was the first time that a black man had pointed his finger, accusing a white man, and Ole Man Moses stood up in the courtroom, and he identified the man, but that wouldn't have made no difference.

CH: *Moses, Ole Man Moses, is the great-uncle that Emmett Till was visiting at the time he was abducted?*

RM: *Right. But to talk about fighting, the civil rights struggle, unless we know what went on previously, then you're fighting in the dark. When you know that you didn't have a right, then the first thing that you've got to do is like Johnson said—and we got that right. Now we're beginning to feel that instead of jumping out here and getting killed and getting beat up and getting bit by dogs and wet by a firehose, you don't have to do that but one thing. Vote. Vote 'em in or vote 'em out.*

CH: *Well, of course, there's a white population that sees a problem with that. That's why there's so much happening around the time of Emmett Till case, for example, with the murders of those two men. Both of them, Lamar Smith and George Lee, were active in the voter registration. In fact, I think it was Strider—what's his name?*

RM: *Sheriff Strider.*

CH: *Sheriff Strider was the one who commented that they had never had any problems with what they called their Niggers until they went up North and then came back down South. It was the South that was holding on to keeping the blacks out, keeping the power from them, the voting power. The stage was set for Emmett Till. They were already antagonistic because of the series of demonstrations revolving around their voter registration that year. It was the spring of the year, and then, just a couple of weeks before Emmett Till, were the two slayings of Smith and Lee. Both of those persons were active in voter registration.*

RM: *But you see, they were trying to vote without the right to vote. The people that sat in, if you look back in there, in American history, you will find pictures of people standing at the polls with shotguns. And people daring you, if you talk about voting, drag you out of the house at night, burn your house down at night, while you were trying to vote without the right to vote.*

The people in the South were already mad. I have to go back to the Civil War; a lot of things happened in the Civil War. When Sherman marched down through Georgia, he really did the South up, and the South was mad about it. Abraham Lincoln let a lot of Negroes go into the northern army. The South could have won the war if they would have given a Nigger a gun, but they weren't going to give no Nigger no gun. For every ten Niggers they had, they had one white person over them. And they wouldn't give them no gun. So when the North got them and gave them guns, and they came back down through there with Sherman and the raiders that Sherman had, he told them we're going to set everything afire, sixty miles wide. From the Chicmonga Rock Quarry in Tennessee clear to the Everglades of Florida. He said, "We're going to burn up everything between here and there. If y'all want anything ahead of that thing, go ahead and get it."

And I was just reading an article the other day where an old lady said that when they come down there, they come down there just like wolves, they took all of her chickens, all of her cows, all of her hogs. Said they run them hogs down just like they were soldiers themselves. Said she was trying to tell them not to take all her stuff—she had eighteen turkeys, so they took all eighteen of them turkeys and put them in a wagon and hitched up her old gray mare that was too old to breed, but they still had her there for breeding purposes. But they hitched her up to a wagon, put everything they had in a wagon, took all of her fruit jars, everything that she had in the cellar, put it in that wagon and drove off with it. So you know they was made, and when they took that land away from them, they put the Negroes back in them homes, you know. So they were mad. So they showed their resistance.

So if you don't know that, you don't know why you was being killed! So it didn't make them any difference about how many Negroes they killed. They hung a man in my home, in Franklin, Georgia. Went into the house and got him, took him down there to the Chatahootchie River, cut a limb off there, hung him up on a tree and shot him, so they tell me. And I was just a little boy at that time, and they told me he just had enough flesh on his bones to hold his body together. Every little boy that could shoot a shotgun shot him.
So all the records that's being shown here, they don't show all the people that's been killed.

CH: *There was no way they could.*

RM: *Wasn't nothing done about it because every state set up their own laws. Wasn't no law that said you got a right to vote. You got a right to vote now; there's a lot of people today that won't vote.*

CH: *Well, see, this is the whole thing with the Till case. They were able to take that one to trial. That was something that was significant, not that they were going to win anything, because, as you say, they had not broken any laws. The jurors and many people said (long before the end of the trial) that there was absolutely no way they would ever convict a white man for killing a black in the state of Mississippi, so it was nothing alarming or shocking about the decision. In fact, if it had turned out otherwise, I think, they probably would have been shocked, because they'd already stated they were within their rights.*

RM: *If you read back all through the slave revolts, there has always been somewhere, as I wrote in one of my articles, that the one thing they forgot, they forgot the human element. And you cannot forget the human element. What was so disturbing about the Till case? These people had been doing that so long until it just looked right to them. They didn't see where they could make a mistake. Same way with the Watergate case. They had been doing that so long—they made one mistake. One!*

CH: *I think the fact they were able to get that body to comment, they opened it and showed the world the ugliness of racism.*

RM: *That's what I'm fixing to tell you now. And I think I took the stages one by one. Number one, they had to kill that boy. They had to beat him up, so they had to kill him—they had no choice. Because inside that house, that woman and those kids heard that kid in there crying, "Mama, Mama, Mama!" So they began to ask their mother (talking about Lester Milan's wife), "Mama, who are they beating? Somebody's calling Mama!"*

So she knew who it was. So she had to go out and get him, according to the Willie Reed statement, and I showed you Willie Reed. Because they were standing in old lady Milan's house looking out the window. When she came out, she pulled both of them guys right out in that yard, and she said she put her finger in their face, and she gave them the scolding of their life. So it's a Sunday morning, and it's around ten o'clock, exposing her kids to all that, so what you gonna do?

So they had to go in there and kill him; they couldn't bring him out and show the kids that that kid was being beat up. So they had to kill him and cover him up with that tarpaulin.

Now that's what you mean about the human element. Now that would have settled the case if they had just taken him over there, tied that gin wheel around his neck and thrown him in the river. That would have settled it. But that didn't settle it. The news got out that this boy got killed. And I wouldn't be surprised, not one bit, if the truth was really told, if that was the woman that called that old Sheriff Strider to go down there, because they went right straight to Roy's house that same Sunday and got him out of the bed and took him down there and interviewed him. And he found out then (Sheriff Strider) he told him, "I got to arrest you, Roy." And he wouldn't tell who was in there with him, but he went on down there and got Milam, and interviewed him and put him in jail. "I got to hold you, I got to hold you for murder."

But that would have been all right, now we got to fix up the tale. What we gonna say? We turned him loose? Yeah, they turned him loose, but when they turned him loose, he hit the water! That's when they turned him loose. And when that wheel hit the water, his face was all messed up. And people can tell you all they want about them beating the boy up, his face was this, that, and the other, but the reasons that boy's face was messed up was because when that gin wheel hit that water, his head was tied up so tight to it 'til his head just went right down in there and messed his face up.

If that little white boy, Robert Hodges, when he saw those feet sticking up, all he had to do was take a rope and tie it to them feet and put them right back down in the water and get on his boat and come on out. But he don't know too much about segregation and discrimination and how big this case is, so why in the hell is this Nigger's feet in the water? Come on down here, y'all, here's a Nigger in the water!

CH: *He obviously knew enough about it; he was seventeen years old. But the problem is, he didn't look at it as a crime.*

RM: *No, he ain't looking at it, he don't know how big it's gonna be! So now we go down here and get him and finally got him. And they dig a hole and put him in the ground.*

So the next thing, well, let's bury it right quick, so they dug a hole, by that time, the Sheriff and Crosby Smith were riding all through the country (in Mississippi), hunting [for Till's body]. When they found it, that's all he had a chance to do, was grab some more clothes and throw them in the bag and come on here [to Chicago] just like he was. But Crosby got there just in time, just before they covered the body up. So if they would have gotten a chance to cover it up, they wouldn't have let anybody dig it up. He got there just in time to keep them from covering it up, so that created another stink.

So when he took it over to the white undertaker, to embalm the body, take all that water out of it. He had to promise that man that he wasn't going to let nobody open that box. The man told him, the way this thing is messed up, you can't take this body out of here. He made a vow that he wouldn't let anybody open that box. But when that box came here [to Chicago], that was the shape it was in.

But, when he gets here, it's a different story. He was supposed to deliver that body to his mother, and he did. So when it got to this mother, the body still had that thing on it, but the mother was determined to see it. And when she opened that box, that opened up another can of worms, and the case got big. So they don't know what to say now. They said, "That was the wrong Nigger."

CH: *And it wasn't a black. In fact, someone intimated it wasn't a black person.*

RM: *Yeah, the old coroner that signed the death certificate said he couldn't tell whether it was a Nigger or a white man. Said the body was so decomposed, you couldn't tell what it was. So why did he sign the death certificate? Why did you send him to a black undertaker if you didn't know who it was? It's against the law to send a white man to a black undertaker, or send a black man to a white undertaker.*

But anyway, wouldn't no lie stick up, no lie they told would stick up. So the Till case got bigger and bigger. And it finally busted. People began to find out who the boy was, and where he came from and all the other ramifications. And time brought it down way in October before it really subsided.

But then, even now, you got to go back. You still wasn't free. You still didn't have the right to vote, and you didn't have the right to vote from 1955, in 1965 when Johnson signed the Voting Rights bill, now the people was still scared to vote.

CH: *But it takes something, as Gus Savage once said, to jolt the sleeping giant. To have an innocent child like this completely mutilated, and then to show it to the world. This is what happened; it angered people so much, it became the talk of the nation. Everybody talked about it. I was very young at the time it happened, but everywhere you went, you heard people talking about that fourteen-year-old kid who was killed in Mississippi, and you did not sleep after that.*

We're supposed to have the sense to know what's dangerous to our lives. The adults. But to pick an innocent child, who knows nothing of segregation and the taboo of the white woman; a child from Chicago would not necessarily be cognizant of that. Ann Moody talks about that in her autobiography, Coming of Age in Mississippi. In a conversation between her high school classmates, the boy was saying, "He probably didn't even know that she was white because what did that mean up North to a fourteen-year-old; they went to school with them, so it was no big issue." So it was not necessarily taboo as much as it was in the South.

RM: *There comes a time when everything must come to an end. I don't care how long a tree's been standing, eventually Mother Nature and Father Time will bring it down. Same way with a system. I talked to a young lady who came here from New York. She wanted to interview me about the struggle in labor unions, and I was telling her that all you have to do to people is keep pressing them. If you really want to get a good whipping, you just pick you out a person that you can whip, and you know you can whip 'em. You whip 'em every time you see 'em. And one day you'll be done just like Frederick Douglass did that boss he had, Covey. Whipped him until he called him "Mister." And he didn't tell nobody about it. And he didn't get lynched for that, either. Covey didn't tell nobody that Frederick Douglass whipped him.*

It's the same way with a system. A system can only last so long. This system here in Chicago right now is getting the biggest shock it's ever had in the history of Chicago with a black mayor downtown. And all he done, and he done the right thing: slow walking. He didn't try to outrun them. Slow walking, and you can take 'em one at a time. Once you learn. Some people are gifted for certain things. I'm not gifted for certain things, but some things I can do better than others. Some things I can do better than anybody else. Some things I can't do. But once you get the right man in to do the right thing, all you got to do then is just wait on him.

I had a great lesson from a little old black-and-tan dog we used to have. A dog, she was a rabbit dog. And she knew the characteristics of a rabbit. And everybody come, old Joe, old Robert, old Minnie, and old Betty, and all the dogs gonna run, and they gonna get down there, and they gonna go jump a rabbit. And we couldn't make old Queen run in that gang for nothing. We used to whip her to make her run in that gang; she'd never run in that gang. She'd always go in the opposite direction. But she always caught the rabbit. And she caught rabbits until she was so old she lost all her front teeth and she couldn't hold a rabbit. Sometimes we would hear her down there scuffling with the rabbit, we'd go down there, and we'd kill the rabbit. She caught rabbits until she was too old to hold them.

You learn the characteristics of what you're going after. You learn the characteristics of it, and it's easy. And one more thing about this struggle. You can't give it up. You can't stop. It's got to be a continuous struggle.

One more animal we had was very educational. He raised all of us. A little old bob-tailed gray mule. And he wouldn't wait for you to start to fighting with him; he would start to fighting you. He would attack you, and make you so mad 'til you'd want to kill him. The first thing that he would start to do would be reach for your line, and he betted on that tail; he had a little short tail and he was strong. Once he caught your line with that tail, then you negotiated with him. And he didn't stop to wait for you to whip him, he'd always make you whip him, make you try to whip him. If you wanted to go down the road and you wanted to go fast and he didn't want to, then you didn't go! You went his way, because the first thing he would do is to start feeling for your line. Once he got your line and drew it up under his tail, you negotiated with him. Because he got to them White folks' house, anybody's house, he's taking right off into their yard, right off into their house; it didn't make him any difference.

The struggle don't stop. Frederick Douglass told you that years ago, "Without struggle, there will be no success." And eternal struggle is the key to success. Eternal struggle. If I hadn't been fighting, like that picture you see there; that was a labor picture there, those girls right there. That was all done at the same time, then I went around through the plant and took up Red Cross, and those was the girls that were making their contributions. But we wanted that picture taken because he was selling Red Cross, and he wanted to see what kind of joint committee we could get. And after we got that, they told me to go through the plant and I went all over through the plant.

But that's part of the struggle. You don't bend and bow to nobody; you teach them to respect you. First of all, you respect them, and then you demand respect from them. And that's the way we got that set up, and that relation lasted until the last one of all of the workers that were in that plant retired. I don't know now, because the company sold out several times.

But that's part of the struggle. And getting back to the Emmett Till case, it's just like anything else, it had to come to an end. Something had to happen to bring it to an end. What was it that happened? Was it her child, or whose child was it? But that didn't give them the right to vote. That only stirred them up. The only thing that gave them the right to vote was when Johnson signed that Voting Rights bill.

CH: *Do you feel that the dominant culture or any black organization might have been aware of the power that the display of the body could impact on society? Because I really think that from that day on, things kept escalating until 1965 when President Johnson signed the Voting Rights Bill. Just like you had thousands and thousands of people who viewed that body during that four-day display on Labor Day weekend. People came from all over the world, all over the States particularly, to see this body.*

In fact, Jet magazine or the more recent one that came out thirty years later, snapshots of all those people who came by to view this body. And Mamie Bradley was going to these various places, under the auspices of the NAACP to talk about the Emmett Till murder case. And something happened?

RM: *Out of all of the struggles there has been, there had to be some radicals in the start of the struggle. You have to understand, number one, the NAACP is the biggest organization that we had. The organization that they belonged to, these religious people (there were a lot of them), all they were going to do was pray and sing and cry. They weren't going to get out here and get in no fight.*

The NAACP, it was in October before Roy Wilkins was ever accepted as executive director. All this other stuff was done by these little chapters. Every little city had a chapter. Now there is a director over so many chapters; that's how Billy Jones was able to get us; he was director over so many chapters in this southern Illinois and Missouri thing. That's why he had us scheduled, not Roy Wilkins.

All these people that had her scheduled on the west coast were under a director. And every one of them was broke. So we want anything to try to get some money. Now there was quite a bit of discussion about this money business. That chapter was not going to let you come there in their thing and make all that money and carry it away with you. They weren't going to do that; they were going to give you a certain portion of it, and they weren't giving her enough. And I think I pointed out to you that Dr. Howard, before he went to speak, first thing he told 'em, "I'm going to pay them out of this money to fight segregation in the South." So that money went to his little organization down there, earmarked. He couldn't get it out himself. They had to have two or three people to get it out.

So there was no organization willing to roll up their sleeves and go into this fight. It had to be a spontaneous thing. And then there had to be some radicals to grab it and run with it. Had to be.

Like I told you about Bill Abbott. Bill Abbott was fighting Dawson here; he was fighting AFL-CIO, and he was fighting the Cook County Industrial Union Council, grabbing for anything he could, pow! So he grabbed it, and this was something he could work with. So it wasn't easy for him to grab it and tear into Walter Reuther and holler, "You ought to do something about this case." It was easy for Boyd Wilson to go in to Dave McDonald and say, "We want to do something about it." And that's how Dave McDonald sent a telegram to the governor of Mississippi. That's why we had a special prosecutor to prosecute this case. He did a wonderful job, in fact, I never listened to a sermon like that in my life—like that man put up in that courtroom. But the odds were against him; he was beat before he got there because the people had not violated any law.

It didn't make any difference what you said. No matter what kind of fight you put up, what the NAACP or nobody else said, churches or nobody else. Out of all those preachers that were running around foaming at the mouth, there were only three people that were left here because they was killing Niggers, and they were putting them in jail, and they were fining them all over, every one that would come down there.

So we went down there on a plane, and we deplaned in Memphis. And we drove all the way from Memphis down there in an automobile, drove right up to the door. So it had to be something that they didn't expect; they had been expecting a trainload of Niggers to come down there and call themselves trying to take over Mississippi when they didn't have the right to vote in the first place.

They didn't expect me to come down there, I'm just a local union leader, and I lost my local the next day; they were so mad at me for going down there. They voted me out of office.

CH: *Who did?*

RM: *My local union. But somebody's got to carry the battle. Now to open that case up, it took some radicals like Bill Abner, like George Wilson, crazy like myself, crazy like a lot more people. Then everybody got in the thing. Didn't nobody get in there when they heard about the Reverend Lee. Rev. Lee called himself a child of God, a righteous man. "I believe in God! But I'm going down there and I'm going to register to vote." But he didn't have the right to vote. He can go down there and vote now because he's got the right to vote.*

I got pictures over there right now of a boy they just hung down there in Alabama last year in 1985. It was the Ku Kluxers; there's an organization down there right now that's training for guerilla warfare all through Alabama. So that's the struggle. But if you've got the right to do a thing, then you can do it. People had a right to kill that boy, they had a right to kill Rev. Lee; they had a right to kill Lamar Smith, they had a right to kill Medgar Evers. They had a right to do that under their laws. And that's the thing that the NAACP has been doing for years and years. When they go down there, "We're going to protest, we're going to protest" and do all that protesting and everything, and when they come out, they have not violated a law. There's a thing right over that will tell you that the government could not come into that case. Why? Because they had not violated the law!

We're messed up, up here [pointing to the head] right now. We're beginning to resolve ourselves right now. Just yesterday, they changed the boulevard Warren Boulevard to Nancy Jefferson Boulevard, trying to make the west side the best side. Looks like that should have been done with the stroke of one pen, shouldn't it?

You got land out here growing weeds clear out over your head, and we're too lazy to go out there and cultivate it. But you know, if we could go out there and cultivate that land, we could. But you know, I don't blame them because this government thinks that they can feed all these people and they're not working. I remember a time when they didn't give nothing but hard tax and corn bread, fatback and corn bread. But now they give steaks, pork chops, chickens. But one thing is he can't keep on feeding these people and they're not working. So you just let 'em keep on eating until they hit rock bottom.

CH: *You know, I did a perusal of several history books on the Civil Rights Movement. I'm still concerned as to how Emmett Till got skipped in the history books. And when I say skipped, how it was so deemphasized when it was such an issue. There were the newspapers, the TV. This information saturated the media. The Civil Rights Movement, according to historians, started with Rosa Parks. I know there was a whole lot, and nobody's going to forget the bus boycott, and that was a big issue, and King came in on that, and Gus Savage talks about it in the recent issue of* Jet *magazine that came out on the Emmett Till case. He mentioned the fact that there is only one statue of Emmett Till, and that is the statue in Denver, and it actually is a statue of King with Emmett Till in the shadow, sort of like*

under him. I'm wondering; I'm really curious as to why they have not explored the Emmett Till case because it was such a big thing when it happened.
It was to me, as big and as much publicized certainly as the Montgomery march.

RM: *Did you ever see anybody get a big barrel of soap suds, and the more water you pour in there the more suds you get, and all of a sudden you take a gallon of kerosene and throw in there, and all of the soap suds just die? Did you ever see that happen? If you don't mind, I'll refresh your memory. When we went to Washington, D.C., if you can remember we said we would stay over another day, one day to view Washington, so we did. So during our trip, we had a nice big steak dinner. We left there, and Ethel Payne, who was writing for the Chicago Defender at that time, was covering us. We went to the Capitol steps, and we took a picture on the capitol steps where there were two columns. The first column in the Chicago Defender that morning was open at the top; the second column was this picture that we made on the capitol steps. But right on the first column was the first time that this Louis Till had ever been revealed, because she was trying to get some report on Emmett Till.*

She sent it to Symington from Missouri, who kept a record of all soldiers that died, regardless of how they died. This boy was executed in Italy; and they put that picture, with the picture we had, on the front page of the Chicago Defender, and they put this boy Louis Till in the first column. And they told the whole story about what happened to him in Italy in 1945.

And this she had never heard of. She had never heard what really happened to him.

CH: *So are you saying, Mr. Mooty, that when she read the paper, that was her first time knowing it too, because she hadn't been able to secure any information?*

RM: *She said that was the first time that it had ever been revealed to her how her husband got killed, and why he was killed. All she had heard was that he died in service. Sent it to Symington, and didn't release it until that Monday morning.*

CH: *Mamie Bradley had all of this to deal with, the brutal slaying of her son. And then after, for at least ten years, trying to find out why her husband had died, to find out that he had died a very ignoble death! And to expose this to the world before they even consulted her.*

RM: *The only thing that I can do is give facts, and that is exactly what happened in that day, that Monday that we stayed over. So we left there at four o'clock Monday evening coming back to Chicago.*

CH: *You have quite a few clippings here of the Till Case. I never saw this one; this is the* <u>*Chicago Sun-Times,*</u> *September 3rd, 1955, which is right after the body arrived here I would imagine.*

RM: *Well, I couldn't do nothing more because I did talk to the Reverend Isaiah; and I wasn't closely acquainted with him, but, with the type of man that he was, he had a broad view of what happened. So when I came to him, and he sat and listened to what I was telling him about the opportunity we had, this would be the greatest opportunity if we could just display the body. And we did do something that they didn't expect us to do. They didn't expect that box to be opened, because they had an order on there, and if you ever talk to a Mr. A. A. Rayner, he will tell you that they had orders not to open that box. And when they found out that the box was open, they raised a boat load of sand, because they interviewed me.*

When we got to that courthouse, we got the opportunity to leave on the recess to the lunch room, whatever lunch room they had. So a lady was walking behind me, and she said, "Is you Mr. Rayfield Mooty?" And I said, "Yes I am. Who are you?" She said, "I heard what you told them white folks over that radio." So she must have been listening, too, you know. But they didn't let me say very much, you know; they cut it off and maybe it was a good thing they did because my anger was ... So they were very concerned that we had opened that box.

Thousands of people came. Couldn't even come down the sidewalk. I don't think there's been a funeral in Chicago as big as that funeral was. Mayor Daley didn't have that big a funeral.

I predicted that they would put this on the screen—they had to put it on the screen. They have reproduced everything that has happened in America, and I've been to movies for many years, and I've studied that. Some of it is real, some of it is imaginative, but I knew they had to put this on the screen; they couldn't dodge this. I knew that if we lived long enough ... We talked about this on the way down to Washington, and we talked about this on the way back.

CH: *With the Reverend Smallgood Williams?*

RM: *Smallgood Williams, yeah. They had a big arena where they had it at. They had two meetings that same day. They had a meeting that started at four o'clock, and it was over at eight, and they had one that started at eight and was off whenever they got through with it.*

So we were in the hands of decent people. We couldn't carry nobody down there that had any more respect than they had for him. Rev. Smallgood Williams was a notable man in Washington, and he was a big man in Washington, and he got a lot of publicity and did a wonderful job because he had so many people there. The fire department wouldn't let them hold any more in the church. I just happened to be in there, I just happened to be involved in it, and that's how I know it from inside out.

So I was glad that we lived long enough to tell it.

8
His Cousins Remember

Personal Interview with Relatives in Argo, Illinois, on July 19, 1986

CH: *Just identify yourself in any way that you want.*

WHEELER PARKER: *I live in Argo, Illinois. I've been here since 1947.*

CH: *And your relation to Emmett Till?*

WP: *Emmett Till's great-aunt married my grandfather.*

SIMEON WRIGHT: *I'm from Greenwood. I've been in Illinois since 1955, right after the murder trial. Emmett Till was my second cousin. His mother and I are first cousins.*

CH: *And Mr. Mooty is Emmett's second cousin by marriage?*

RAYFIELD MOOTY: *Yes, Emmett Till's grandmother married my uncle, my mother's brother, in later years, and that's how I happened to be involved in the Till mur-*

der. When the case broke it seemed like everybody was at a loss to find someone to spearhead the case. With the little experience I had had over the years, in things of this kind, that's why I became involved in it. The first day it happened, my uncle came and got me himself.

CH: *Mr. Parker, could you give us an account of the incident as you recall it. At the time, were you living in Mississippi, or were you there? What can you tell us?*

WP: *Emmett Till was living in Argo, and he moved to Chicago, and my grandfather came here for a funeral. Then he took Emmett Till and me back to Mississippi with him on vacation. So we left together going to Mississippi in 1955, along with another lady, who is since deceased. This incident that came up happened one Wednesday evening. And as I recall, we were there at the store, and I was in the store first. Then Till came in, and I went outside. Till came out, and a lady came out. She was going to her car.*

CH: *Was this lady black or white?*

WP: *White. This is Bryant. I think the whistle was before she went to the car. Anyway they said she's going to get her pistol. I can't remember which happened first—the whistle or she said she's going to get her pistol. So in the meantime, we all got scared.*

CH: *What you're saying is that Emmett Till whistled at the lady. Okay, then something apparently happened.*

WP: *The pistol thing came up, so we all started running to the car. There were about seven or eight of us in one car. So we all jumped in the car because we thought something was going to happen. It was about dark on a Wednesday evening. And we started down this Darfield Road going toward my grandfather's house. It was a rock road, so it was dusty. And this car was following us. So we thought the people were behind us to catch us. My uncle, Maurice, stopped the car, and he jumped out of the car—we all jumped out of the car and ran on through the cotton field. The car passed on by so we realized then that no one was following us because of that incident. Till begged us not to tell my grandfather. I said, I won't tell. So we didn't tell. And there was a girl there. Her name was Ruth Crawford—she's still there I understand—and she told us, "You all are going to get some more from this."*

CH: *She's black? Is she about your age?*

WP: *Yes, she was a little younger than me, I'm forty-seven now.*

CH: *So, she's a little older than Emmett Till. Were you and Emmett close to the same age?*

WP: *Two years apart. He was fourteen, and I was sixteen. So time went on, and I forgot about it, you know. It was Wednesday, Thursday, Friday. Saturday we went to town. Then early Sunday morning some people come knocking on the door. I heard them talking to my grandfather. They were at the door. I woke up, and I became alarmed. I became really afraid for us in there, that he was going to kill us. So they were saying they want the "fat boy" from Chicago. My grandfather not knowing what was happening, when they got to the door, they had a pistol and a flashlight. So grandfather not knowing what bedroom he was in—the house was a big house—what you call a landowner's house. So he didn't know what room he was in, so they came to the room I was in first. My uncle, and I, and Maurice was in that room, he wasn't there. So he proceeded to the next room where Curtis, who is now with the police at the Chicago police department, and my other uncle, Robert. Then they proceeded to the next room, which Simeon and Till was in next to my grandfather's room. So they were over there talking to him, and he was saying, "Yes" and "Naw" like that [not "Yes, sir," and "No, sir" as a Nigger should, in the South], so they didn't like it, and they started cursing him.*

CH: *This was Emmett?*

WP: *Yes, Emmett was saying, "Yes" and "No." They didn't appreciate that so they were cursing. I remember them telling my grandfather—my grandmother said something, but I can't remember what happened—things was happening so fast. I think she went out the back door or something. Anyway, I heard them tell my grandmother or grandfather that if he wasn't the one, they would bring him back. Then they left out of the house with Till. After that my grandfather took my grandmother to her brother's house.*

CH: *Was this the same night? Did he leave immediately after that? Or did he think that he was actually coming back?*

WP: *Oh this is the same morning, within minutes—it wasn't an hour—after they took Till.*

CH: *They went over to other relatives?*

WP: *To her brother's house.*

CH: *To tell what had happened?*

WP: *I don't know. He took her over there to stay over there. She wanted to go over there. I think she had gone next door to get some help. Some white people lived next door. There was no help there.*

CH: *But everybody was pretty scared?*

WP: *Well, everybody didn't wake up. I woke up, Simeon woke up, and, of course, my grandfather and grandmother. But the rest of them didn't wake up.*

CH: *Who else was in the house?*

WP: *My two uncles, Maurice and Robert, and Curtis, my cousin who is a couple years older. He was eighteen at the time.*

CH: *How did Emmett react to this abduction?*

WP: *Nonchalant.*

CH: *He was not terrified, or anything?*

WP: *I couldn't see him. Simeon was in there with him. From hearing, you couldn't tell that he was upset. I guess it was kind of a tense moment for him.*

CH: *Simeon, you were actually in the room with Emmett, right? And you were in the store with Till?*

SW: *Right. I went in [to the store] right behind Till. To make sure that he didn't get out of line. I was waiting.*

CH: *You were from that area?*

SW: *Right, I lived there. I knew. He went into the store, and he bought some candy and whatnot. And we all came out. And she came out of the store.*

CH: *You recall his whistle?*

SW: *It was outside. After he came out of the store. She was going toward her car. He did whistle. And after that, we all got scared. We ran, jumped in the car, went down Darfield Road, I think we lived about three miles from Money. We thought someone was following us, so we stopped the car, everybody jumped out and ran down into the cotton field. The car passed on by. Emmett, he begged us not to tell Dad.*

CH: *Now your relation to old man Moses …*

SW: *That's my dad.*

CH: *What's the difference between your age and Emmett's age?*

SW: *Two years younger than Emmett, I was twelve at the time. We didn't say nothing. Nothing happened, Thursday, Friday, we went over to town Saturday, got home after twelve that night. The next thing I knew I heard a lot of talking, I didn't know what it was. I thought maybe it was my uncle. I thought somebody had come to take Emmett home. I opened my eyes, and I saw these two men. This one man had a pistol in his hand. He told me to lay back down, to go back to sleep. I think he struck Emmett one time.*

CH: *In the house?*

SW: *Right. He got up and put his clothes on. After that he didn't say anything. By this time my mother offered them money. They hesitated a little bit, but they just took him on out.*

CH: *She tried to bribe them out of whatever they were doing? Did Emmett appear to you afraid? Both of you heard a commotion before they got to your bedroom. Of course, as you said, because you were from Money you knew what type of people you were dealing with. Emmett apparently did not have the same type of apprehension or fear that you would have.*

SW: *No.*

CH: *So do you think that he in any way demonstrated fear at all?*

SW: *He didn't appear afraid. He just put his clothes on and went on out with them.*

CH: *He probably never imagined what was going to happen.*

SW: *Probably had no idea. He probably thought they was just going to whip him or something like that. I guess we all were waiting for them to bring him back. It was a long night.*

CH: *That was Saturday night, Sunday morning? After he didn't come back Sunday, you knew something had happened? You were still afraid? Everybody was still waiting?*

SW: *We were still waiting, but we were getting a little tense about it.*

CH: *What day did the body show up?*

WP: *It was a Wednesday. I left that same morning going to another spot in Mississippi where I caught the first train out.*

CH: *Was this Sunday?*

WP: *Actually I went over early Monday morning, 4:30. I was heading home. I was from Argo. Till used to live here in Argo. Then he moved to Chicago.*

CH: *And you said you were going to another part of Mississippi?*

SW: *Yes, I went to my uncle's house.*

CH: *You were afraid, is that why you left?*

SW: *I was afraid when they came in the room. I was literally shaking. They came with a pistol. I believe Milam had the pistol. The tall guy had the pistol. Well, I just knew because before I went down there, they told me what could happen. That they will kill you. But Till, he had no way of knowing what they would do to him because he was not raised or born here. He and I weren't old enough to recognize discrimination as it was. But I was from Mississippi.*

CH: *At what age did you move from Chicago?*

WP: *I was about seven. My mother told me plainly what could happen. So the moment I heard them out there, I said "They're going to kill us." I thought about it. I started praying to God, I said, "Lord, if you let me live, I'll straighten my life up." That was my attitude at that time. I didn't experience nothing but fear, even after that. I never felt any sorrow or sadness because I didn't accept, well it was like it didn't happen to me. The only thing I experienced in the whole thing was fear. I don't know why, but at the funeral I felt no remorse, no hatred, no sadness.*

CH: *You were engulfed by just fear?*

WP: *After that passed, for years, even until now. I could feel probably more remorse about it now than I could at that time. Because for years always, in my mind, I said I'm going to see him again. I never accepted it. That's probably the best way to put it. I saw him dead, in the casket, I knew they had taken him, but it was like a nightmare that happened.*

CH: *So how long did you stay in Mississippi?*

SW: *After this incident? About six weeks. Because right after we had him to trial, he was let go—we started packing.*

CH: *You were afraid to stay?*

SW: *You knew they got away with that, they could come back and kill all of us and still get away with it. We didn't want to take that chance.*

CH: *What do you think about the attitude of the people there—black and white?*

SW: *Most of the blacks was afraid, they didn't want us to go to the trial. They didn't want us to leave the house. They didn't want us to even stay in the house. So being at night, my brother and I we'd go to the neighbors … But my Ma left the same night, and she never came back. She came on up here to Chicago.*

CH: *She wasn't there during the trial, was she? Well, what about the whites, what was their attitude?*

SW: *Well, I guess some would come down to the house at night and try and scare Daddy. There were whites around where we lived there. See down there, there was really no contact, that much. There were too many. It was like going to one, I'm not sure if you're familiar with how you used to have clean houses out there. Then if you got the boss mad … so as far as out in the country, you didn't come into contact with whites. It was only when you went into town that you really came into contact with whites.*

CH: *I read a lot of things in reference to this case, and they said that many blacks stopped going to the store. They mentioned that a lot of whites were disenchanted with what had happened to the point where they felt that it was a bad taste for them, too.*

SW: *They were probably talking about whites, there weren't hardly any whites in Money. Most of the whites in Money didn't like Bryant anyway. They didn't like him because, I saw with my own eyes, he made one man close his store.*

WP: *Bryant did?*

SW: *Yes, I guess he spoke toward the store for something, and he did. Bryant made him close it. So he can get his business.*

SW: *His brother was more of a (political?) power than he was?*

WP: *Are you talking about Bryant or Milam?*

CH: *Bryant is the youngest one?*

SW: *He's the youngest one. He's the one who owned the store. We knew Bryant. We didn't know Milam.*

RM: *Let me ask one question. I can remember a little boy in that courtyard going to the trial. And I have always pictured that being you.*

SW: *It was.*

RM: *In the courtyard it didn't get in the courtroom. But I remember seeing a little young boy out in the yard. And I've always pictured that being you. But I remember seeing, and they said that you were Mr. Moses' son, baby boy.*

SW: *They kept me in the witness room most of the time.*

RM: *Did they ever call you to the witness stand?*

SW: *They never called me. I was supposed to identify Emmett's ...*

RM: *They called Willie Reed. They called Mandy Bradley. They didn't call Milam. Willie Reed testified. I think we got lots out of Willie Reed's testimony.*

CH: *How did they beat the kid in that row?*

RM: *... When we storied that case up here, I was wanting to instigate it. We had labor leaders, blacks in the labor movement, that had pretty good influence with the top echelon of people in the international union. Like Bill Albert in the UAW. So all those people appealed to their international heads. To jump into this case. I had a report from a lawyer in Greenwood, Mississippi, when I become president of a local union here all the lawyers were looking for cases, so he jumped on me. So I told him I got a problem here. He said, "I ain't got time to be bothered with you." He had a lawyer in Greenwood, Mississippi, named Petite. He told Petite to call me. Petite called me, and I told him. And he told me, he said, that breed right in that neighborhood will do anything. I hope that you don't get disillusioned by what I'm telling you, but that group right in there will do anything. So don't be surprised if you don't hear until the file plate. So it didn't make no difference what the people did, they go to court, and what I'm figuring to say now, they had all of their Walter Reuther, Dave McDonald, Senator Douglas, all of the people that had any authority, appeal to the governor of Mississippi to send a special prosecutor in. You can't have a special prosecutor. If you read close enough about the case, it was a special prosecutor. But there wasn't nothing that he could do. Because you got to get the jury from the county. You wouldn't find not one that wasn't dogs with the same damn breed. They was all dogs with the same breed.*

CH: *That was a docufilm that Mr. Moody gave to me a couple of weeks ago, that they did thirty years after, on CBS TV. There was a white guy on there—there was actually a recapitulation of the trial, and when the attorney went to give the closing remarks, he stated (this is not verbatim) that I don't think not one of you Anglo-Saxons, will find these boys guilty. I'm sure you'll bring back a "not guilty." They had said even prior to the trial that no white man would ever be convicted, in Tallahatchie County or in the state of Mississippi, for killing a black guy. That would not happen. So that was the whole thing.*

RM: *A lot of people were disturbed about it. Like, why did they do this, why did they do that? When that case was handed to the jury, Congressman Diggs and his group, we all got up, and we got in Dr. Howard's car, and we left. So she was asking, "How you think the trial going to come out?" And he told her, "There ain't going to be no trial. You don't have enough evidence." And when we weigh the evidence, I think I've got the evidence documented. With the evidence they had, they were home free. But now you got some type of a right. They didn't have a right. When President Johnson signed a voting right bill, then you had a right. You don't have to be out here getting beat up by dogs, and being stoned by rocks. All you do is just ease up to the pole, ease up to each other, and do just like we did Henrihan. When Henrihan killed them boys over there, Mark Clark, and them boys shot 'em in the back. Every little nigger ran out; he would be so drunk because he didn't know his heel from his head, but when he had his ballot, and all of them went in there together. When you get mobbed right around Henrihan, you ain't hearing no more from Henrihan. There wasn't no fighting, no biting, no scratching, no nothing. Did Jane B. the same way. So that's why you don't have to be bothered with that man. Ten days after Rutherford B. Hayes was elected he started to pulling the troops out of the South. And in twenty days he pulled them all out. And in the next year, he put a bill in the Congress—that it was against the law to have federal troops in there to protect the niggers, and they shot niggers at the polls just like you was shooting rabbits.*

CH: *And tell us what happened to Lamar Smith. The Reverend Lee was killed in July, two weeks before Emmett Till. So you can imagine the type of the hostility and anger that was already there. Really they killed Mack Parker, a month or so later?*

RM: *Yeah, that was a little after that.*

CH: *As Sheriff Strider, the man on the 60-minute docufilm statement, "We never had no problems with our Niggers, until they went up North, or some out of the North came."*

RM: *They were scared. I remember the time I was down South cutting rot away—all the way from Alabama clear across Georgia. We'd step into camp, white man come through there, bam! Hitting on that telephone pole making everybody go to bed, 9:30. Better go to bed. Wouldn't have been nobody on the street, come by and hit on that telephone pole to let you know it's time to go to bed. These things that happened in later years; they were just products. If you were going down the road and you met a white man, you better pull over to the side of the road and wait, not give him half of the road, give him all of the road. There's no law to stop them from beating you up out there in the road. So you boys came along just at a time where those things went on. They was scared. That's the reason there was peace. Dr. King said it was a negative peace, not a positive peace. But deep down in, every nigger at heart, he was still mad. He was hurt, but he was scared too. But you know, even at that, they was scared to vote. Jesse Jackson stood up more people down there in this last election, and when he started to stirring them up, every Democrat in this country went Republican, and people were hollering about Reagan right now. All the people that cast an electoral vote, they cast them for Reagan. There were eight Democrats running, and they couldn't carry a state apiece. So what you think? They ain't got no good blood for you right now. That makes no difference about what they did way back then. They so hot in Chicago, right now, they don't know what in the world to do because they got a black mayor down there.*

WP: *They ain't changed. Laws just changed. After the Emmett Till Case, blacks, well, like the fear starting leaving, said, they're going to kill us anyway. When they found out that the casket was open here, they was in trouble. They know they was in trouble. So they wanted to find out, why, who? And I'm the guy that opened it. When they started to interviewing me like we're interviewing now, I started using so much bad language, heck they just cut me off. This Mamie got $15 from a little Sunday School way down in Georgia, telegrammed to her to that courthouse. It said, "We didn't have but a little bit of money, but we sending you what we got. We just left Sunday School, but we was so glad when we saw you on television." Everybody saw us getting out of that car. And then them* *kids way down in Georgia were sitting there with their eyes fastened on that television. And they sent her $15. I will never forget it. They said, "We were so glad when we saw you come to that trial." It took them a long time to get up and get them to voting. A long time.*

SW: *They didn't want the body to get out of Mississippi because we was getting ready to bury him down there. We had dug the grave. The only someone to stop him was Curtis Jones. He called back to Chicago. They didn't want the body to get back to Chicago.*

RM: *It was too messed up, they didn't want nobody to see that.*

SW: *We found out later that whites owned that funeral home.*

CH: *I think we got the main facts. Thank you so much for your cooperation.*

9
Mamie, 1988

Interviews with Mamie Bradley, on January 6 and March 24, 1988, in Chicago, Illinois

CH: *Today, we have an interview with Mr. and Mrs. Mobley in their home in Chicago. I would like to have Mr. Mobley, if he can, give just a few moments before he leaves to share with us some of his reflections on Emmett.*

GENE MOBLEY: *I always called Emmett "BoBo." He was such a wonderful youngster. He used to take my hats and clothes to the cleaners and leave notes for me, especially when he was going out in Argo to play ball. He always said that he would like to be a pitcher in baseball someday. He used to play all types of positions, but mainly pitching.*

CH: *I think you commented that he was your buddy.*

GM: *Oh yes, he was my buddy, because anything I would tell him to do for me, he would always do it and leave me a note telling me the results.*

CH: *Mrs. Mobley, how, if at all, do you feel that your son's death affected the Modern Civil Rights Movement of the fifties and the sixties?*

MAMIE BRADLEY-MOBLEY: *Emmett was killed in August 1955. We know, in fact, that his death was a turning point in the Movement; we know that.*

CH: *When you say "we" who are you specifically referring to?*

MBM: *I mean all of the people, the writers, people who publish magazines, anybody who was in a position of authority of any kind.*

CH: *Do you think that the knowledge of his death, which, of course, is a reminder of the assault on black people, and also the black child, could motivate today's society to push for racial parity as it did then? We're still looking for racial equality, parity, and I'm wondering if you think that reflecting on, or just the knowledge of, what happened to Till might possibly intensify our insistence upon political, economic, social parity in this country.*

MBM: *By all means, yes I do. In fact, that is the main part of my work in life right now is keeping Emmett's memory alive and letting boys and girls know the price that has been paid, letting them know that freedom is not really free; we have to work for it. I have found that even through my teaching, and through my work now, an extension of my teaching now that as I make children aware of what was given for them to enjoy now, it really makes an impact on their lives. We started off by talking about whether Emmett's death, the knowledge of Emmett's sacrifice could turn people around, even respark the movement today. By all means it can. This is because of the work that I have done with the children, and I let them know that I'm teaching history every step I make. I'm trying to let them know mainly that you've got to get something in your kids. And if you were to see some of the report cards you would swear that they've made them up themselves.*

CH: *That's going to give them a sense of pride, I'm sure. You are a teacher by profession now. What was your profession at the time of Emmett's death?*

MBM: *I was working for the Federal Government. I was at the United States Air Force at the time, and I was in charge of the secret and confidential files.*

CH: *Were you a member at that time of any labor union?*

MBM: No.

CH: *There has been conflict of information concerning Emmett's death, which basically needs to be resolved. It's an ugly question, but it has to be answered at some point. Some say that he was castrated—different things like that—and I was wondering if you knew whether or not he was castrated?*

MBM: *Yes, I know. And the answer is, no, he was not. I know so well.*

CH: *Some say that you did look at the body.*

MBM: *Beginning at the toe all the way up to the hair. Yes ma'am. When I insisted that I wanted to look into the casket to see what was in the casket, I don't know that I wanted to see or to verify Emmett's body for fear that someone would doubt it later on. I just had this compulsion that I had to know that was Emmett. And for no reason other than I had to know. Not would it come up that she didn't bury her son, or that was another body, I just had the overwhelming desire that I had to know who was in the casket. And when Mr. Rayner asked me after I had looked and after I had been so shocked by what I had seen, he asked me, "What do you want me to do?" I said, "Let as many people look at the body as want to see it." He said, "Do you want me to fix it up?" I said, "No, let the people see what I've seen." Nobody had to persuade me to let the people look at Emmett. I needed somebody to help me look at that. I couldn't, I knew there was no way I could ever describe to anybody what I had seen. So it was important that somebody else see it. Then if we got a chance to talk about it, they would know what I was talking about. The Mississippi seal was on the casket.*

CH: *And the seal said, "Do not open"?*

MBM: *Mr. Rayner had gotten instructions from somebody, I don't know who, but he relayed these instructions to me that I could not open the box because of the seal. Now Emmett was actually, well, I don't know. When I saw Emmett the first time, he was laying out on a big table. I saw the great big box. But I didn't see what was inside the box. I could smell what was inside the box. I only saw this great, huge wooden box that contained something. Mr. Rayner had told me about the seal. I never saw the seal, but when I saw Emmett, he was out on (I think my aunt called it a cooling board) whatever it is, but that's where he was with all of this white stuff over his body, which someone said was lime or something. Well, whatever it was, he was covered, and I couldn't see. I told Mr. Rayner that if you can't open it, you give me a hammer, I can open it. And I was positive it was going to be opened, I mean it had to come open. Nobody was talking to me, my own father wasn't talking to me. I mean it seemed to me that everybody was in a state of suspended animation. Everybody was just frozen. The only dialogue I remember went on between old man Rayner and myself. And when I told him, "Do you have a hammer? I'll open it myself." That's when Mr. Rayner (he was uptight and I remember when his shoulders kind of slumped) he said, "You go home, and when you come back, I'll have it open." That's when he joined me. I remember when he joined me. I went home, and when I got back, sure enough, Emmett was laid out, but as I said, he was all covered. I said, "Well, I can't tell who that is." He sent me back into the waiting room into the front of the parlor. And they took hoses and washed him off. He called me back again. And oh, God. That's when I took one overall view, and then I had to start at the feet, and I told Gene, "Go home and get me some pictures." And we have had all those pictures made that you saw for Christmas. First time I'd ever done that, and I took the picture, it was a picture of him in the hat, and then it might have been the other one of him standing with the tie on. And with those two pictures I just did an item-by-item analysis starting all the way down to the toe, and I checked him all the way up to his head.*

CH: *What about Mr. Mooty?*

MBM: *We were just like two poles, just like the negative and the positive end of a pole suddenly drawn together. I mean he joined me then never to be separated. Mr. Mooty. He stuck right there.*

CH: *Do you remember when the photograph of Till was taken standing next to the television?*

MBM: *I certainly do. This was what is so unusual. We didn't take pictures back in 1955. We didn't have picture money. But I go to work with a fellow, and I was talking about this exceptional Christmas that we were building up to. Because I was really excited about it. I said there's just one thing that would make our Christmas complete. I wish I could have some photographs. And he said, "I take pictures." I said, "You do?" He said, "I'll come and take your pictures for you." Well, I kind of backed down because I didn't really have money for pictures, but he kind of pushed it, and we didn't even talk about money, and I had just decided well I've gone all out this far, I'll get the money some kind of way. He came during the holidays. He took pictures of Bo in his coat, in his new hat that Gene had given him, the tie. He took pictures of the family that lived in the basement and all of their children. All the gifts that Bo had bought. I had given Bo about $100 to spend on nothing but gifts, and honey $100 was our whole Christmas back in 1955. But I think when I figured up what I had spent, I had gone about $500 in debt. And that was really unusual. But this fellow, can't think of his name, but I remember he owned a big Packard automobile, and he took pictures awhile, and when I finally timidly asked him, "What do I owe you?" "You don't owe me nothing." I nearly fainted. But that was one of the unusual things about it all. And when I called my mother, I said, "Mom, we've never had a Christmas like this one and we're* *never going to have another one like it." Because, among other things I had bought a Christmas tree with the long needles, and until then we had always bought the short-needle trees. And that was really a departure to get those big needles. I remember relating to her the story of the king who called on his wise men and told I want you to tell me something I've never heard before. And as these men continue to fail, the king gave them a death sentence. So one of the court judges came forth and he said, "Oh, king, I would like to speak to you." And the King, with his authoritative voice, he said, "Speak, knave." And he said, "Oh, King, I wish to tell you that this too shall pass." And then he went on to explain to the king what he meant. The king agreed that he had never heard anything like it before. And this knave was elevated to the status of a wise man. And I was telling mother that this too, shall pass. We have never been on this level before, we're never going to reach this level again, because I'm going to have better sense than to go out and spend all this money that I spent this Christmas—not knowing that that was the last one.*

CH: *And that was the last picture you have of Till alive?*

MBM: *I can't think of any other pictures we had made after that? I don't believe I owned a camera. I don't think I did. But those pictures—that's the only Christmas that I know of that I ever had pictures made. Too many unusual things happened then.*

CH: *What was Huie's (William Bradford Huie) reference to the photograph of the white girl?*

MBM: *This wallet that I had bought him contained the picture of a movie star. They all did. His favorite of the time was Hedy Lamar and Dorothy Lamour. I am almost positive that this picture was Hedy Lamar. But it was either one or the two of them that was into his wallet. You know when we would buy a wallet, the boys particularly would go through the wallet looking at the pictures until they found one they wanted, the one that contained the movie star that was their favorite at the time. And that was the picture that was in his wallet. That's the irony of the whole thing. The school that Emmett was going to then, if there was a white girl in the school, I doubt it. But that was an all black school, out of Champaigne. All black. Now in Argo, Illinois, the schools were mixed, but Emmett had been away from Argo several years. Those pictures then came out then were the big printouts where he had all the kids on one big picture—not individuals. That's something they started doing after I started teaching in 1960.*

CH: *So he couldn't have possibly had an individual picture of any white girl?*

MBM: *No. And I'm looking at the parallels. Yes. How he didn't say a mumbling word. Under that kind of stress, Emmett would have had a hard time trying to talk. Even I would have had a hard time, and I don't have the speech impediment that Emmett had.*

CH: *How supportive was the NAACP, and how supportive was the labor union in terms of how they brought the case to the public's attention? I understand you did several speaking engagements under the auspices, particularly, of the NAACP, and I think you spoke out for various labor unions nationwide. How supportive were they in bringing this case to the public's attention?*

MBM: *All the labor unions were just fantastic. I can't think of anything that the labor unions did that I would have done differently. I didn't know anything about labor unions to begin with. I mean my dealings with labor unions, I just didn't know what they were. It just happened that Rayfield Mooty (you interviewed him already, I think you said) was with the labor movement. I didn't even know that. I mean you're talking about someone who was naive—I was very, very sheltered, I guess. There was just a lot I didn't know about. Did you go to the town of Argo? Well, that little town was just like another world. It is far more sophisticated now, but when I lived in Argo back in 1928, I believe until 1950, everybody knew everybody.*

The labor unions as I had said were just fantastic. Now, I have no quarrel with the NAACP either. In fact, I solicited the protection of the NAACP because there were many organizations asking me to come, come, come, and I didn't know one from the other one. People had heard of communists, but I didn't know what a communist was. I mean I didn't know who the communists were. I didn't know which organization was this, or that, or the other. Rayfield Mooty had told me, "now you be aware of this one because they are a little bit pink," and I actually thought they were pink. And, oh Lord, I don't know how I could have been so dumb, but that's how inexperienced I was. And I had to finally ask him what he meant because all of those people looked the same color as we were looking or either they were white. Nobody was looking pink to me. He looked at me as if, are you for real? That is somebody who has dealings with the Communist Party. And they are dabbling over there, and they are supposedly straight, but they have connections. So he made me understand what it meant. I realized that when a particular group called me, I couldn't screen these people, so that's when I put myself under the supervision of the NAACP here in Chicago.

Then I went to New York and talked to Roy Wilkins. I met him in person, and he hesitated to deal with me because he said they've had so many unhappy experiences with other people who have come seeking their help, and then they had turned on them and whatnot. But he finally did say that they would arrange my tours, and we reached an agreement, and we got along quite well until the trip to California came up. Now when the California trip came up, I just could not make it on the honorarium that they were allotting me; I just could not make it. It would have caused me to come out of pocket, and I didn't have anything in my pocket. I mean I just didn't have anything in my pocket, because in getting Emmett's body out of Mississippi, that just strained us financially.

CH: *In reference to the dispute with the NAACP, you said specifically what happened?*

MBM: *When I was supposed to go to the West Coast and do a two-week tour, they were going to pay my expenses, and I know they were going to give me $1,500. I can't remember the exact amount. In the meantime, I had taken on my father to travel with me because, going places alone, I just couldn't handle my luggage, and the emotional experience. It was too much for me all alone. I was paying my father $100 a week because he was off his job. And in addition to this I was going to* *have to pay his fare and take care of all the rest of his expenses, because the NAACP, according to Roy Wilkins, would not assume any other expense other than my own. When the lady who was my secretary figured it out, she said, "You cannot possibly go on this trip because you don't have enough money. You actually do not have the dollars and cents to support this tour. And you will have to have at least $5,000 to keep up your household expenses and to pay me and pay your dad. She said that's the cheapest you can go for a two-week period. And when I talked to Roy Wilkins and told him this, he became very distraught. Then I was called from the West Coast by one of the leaders, and he was in total agreement that $5,000 was little enough to ask. I think we came down to about $3,500 after talking back to Roy Wilkins again. I settled for $3,500, so that I didn't come out in the hole. At least I might have had a couple of hundreds left. Roy Wilkins just put his foot down, and he said he would not do it, and he accused me of capitalizing on my son's death and broke the relationship, and that was the end.*

I'm sure that you know, and everybody else knows who has ever dealt in these kinds of cases, that the money that was supposed to come to me, $9 out of $10 was diverted. I mean I never saw it. I read in Jet magazine how one man built him a home and bought him a car and so forth, I believe that was some big amount that came from some organization and in a few weeks he was broke. I don't know how he got the check signed; I don't know nothing.

CH: *He wasn't connected with Till, was he?*

MBM: *Yes. So all kinds of things happened back there. And I would receive mail that was wide open—when it came to my mail box, the letters had already been opened. And I'm sure there were many that I didn't receive at all. Except for the money that the people brought to me directly and gave to me in my hand, most of it I didn't get. Even when the people were viewing Emmett's body at 40th and State at church, my present pastor was one of the people on duty, and he said people were dropping money in a number three washtub (that's a big washtub), and when I told him how much money I got from it, he just wanted to cry. He said, "Oh, my God, no, that shouldn't be. There should have been twenty times that much." Money just disappeared.*

CH: *Were there any groups specifically involved in trying to bring the people who were responsible for your child's murder to justice, beyond mere lip service. For example, were there any investigations or anything of that sort?*

MBM: *Not to my knowledge. I thought that my appearances under the guidance of the NAACP was going to provide me with a lawyer and funds to go to Mississippi when the time came. And then when I made this request, I found that they fought on a different level where they challenged Supreme Court decisions and whatnot. But that was not the way I had understood it.*

CH: *Have any of the family members of Bryant expressed remorse during the time or in years to come of the deed?*

MBM: *No. I've had no direct contact with any of them.*

CH: *Your son's death, many people feel, served to sensationalize blatant racial brutality. What is your reaction to this statement?*

MBM: *Well, I think people got a chance to actually look and see what was happening. I think until then it was almost as if there was a cover or a blanket over what was happening in certain southern states, and America just had the cover pulled off of her, and everybody could see what was going on. The world looked in on the United States.*

CH: *So it wasn't sensationalized, it was actualized. As Mr. Mobley recalls, Emmett expressed an interest in playing professional baseball. Did he express an interest in any other particular profession? He was fourteen at the time, so perhaps junior high, high school, old enough to perhaps think of something else.*

MBM: *Well, he always wanted to build his grandmother a church. Yes, he wanted to build—my mother was a church lover. And Emmett said he was going to build his grandmother her own church. He always heard her complaining about something that wasn't going the way it should have been going. You know how everybody just does not have the same vision. And my mother, if there was ever a visionary, it was my mother. She was a woman with a vision. She's been dead since November 1981.*

CH: *Do you have the same minister now that you had at the time of Till's murder? I think it was Rev. Ford?*

MBM: *No, because I've been with this church since 1973.*

CH: *Rev. Ford was your Reverend at the time, right?*

MBM: *No, Bishop Ford was not actually my Reverend at the time. I was still connected with the Argo church with Elder Goodwin. That was actually my pastor at that time. I wasn't going to church as regularly as Emmett would go. Emmett would go every Sunday. I'll tell you what had happened. I'd started working for the United States Air Force, and we were working sometimes seven days a week. We were working long hours and my church-going was sort of giving way to my work at that particular time.*

CH: *Was it Bishop Roberts who presided?*

MBM: *Yes, that was my mother's pastor. Bishop Ford preached the funeral. Bishop Roberts was the host pastor, and he emceed the funeral.*

CH: *I see. I interviewed Bishop Roberts and his wife at their home. Publicly you have been very forgiving, basically in reference to your son's death, but I was wondering if you perhaps harbor (and, of course, justifiably so if you do) any inner resentment toward the murderers, and perhaps even whites in general?*

MBM: *To tell you the truth, Clenora, it was almost as if I had a heart transplant at the time. One of the experiences I had was that if I were to go around harboring hate, that hate would eventually destroy me. And it was just as if the whole thing was just lifted. Toward these people, I had no feelings whatsoever. I went completely into neutral. I do not hate them; I have on occasion felt sorry for them, because I know that if they could have undone it, that that was one tar baby they touched they wished they had never touched. And have you seen "Fatal Attraction"?*

CH: *No, I haven't, but I intend to see it.*

MBM: *See it. Because I feel that they have found themselves in the same position that the fellow in this movie found himself, and if he could have done it over, you better believe he would have not let himself go in the direction he went, because they are yet paying. And you see, I'm not paying. I haven't done anything to them. Ever so often I get revelations, or dreams, or whatever you want to call them. But it is as if the Lord is reassuring me that I have nothing to harbor, to feel guilty about. I have no guilt; they have the guilt. For me to just put them aside. Leave them to Him, He will handle them. There's nothing I can do about them anyway. My job is to do exactly what I am doing. And in doing what I'm doing, I'm molding character. If you would go to our church, I could sit and point out half the young people, young adults, who were former Emmett Till Players. They are ministers, they are deacons, they are ushers, they are choir directors, they are musicians, they are choir members, they are missionaries. I mean everybody almost who is doing something worthwhile in the church came through Sister Mobley. And how it happened so fast, I can't understand it, except that my first group of children in 1973 (I activated the first group in 1974), they were sixteen. They were kind of up like that, but it only took them two to three years, and they were ready to get married. And I am now working with some of their children, and that's the most unique feeling.*

CH: *Do you think that the legacy of Till has been treated properly?*

MBM: *No. Because I've seen things and I know, I'm asking myself, my book has not been finished. I know that I was disappointed with the first draft, and I really had to do a whole lot of praying, and I have allowed myself to not get back to it. But I think after talking to you today, I will be more motivated to go ahead and get on with the business. But some of the things that I've seen, Emmett was standing on the corner chewing gum, swinging a chain like they did back in the forties—you don't know the Zoot Suit group?—and whistling at the girls as they go by. And you see, had that been Emmett, Milam and Bryant would never have gotten a chance to get a hold to Emmett, because Emmett would not have lived to get to Mississippi. I would have taken care of it! Emmett was—well, I just really cannot describe him. I realize that as time passes—I know all about the halo effect. I studied about that. I know that things get sweeter as time goes by. But I think about that kid and I think about the responsibilities that I put on his shoulders, and Gene told you he wrote notes, you know. He would do a job, and he would tell Gene, I went to the cleaners, I went to the laundry, and I did so-and-so, and so I was not able to get so-and-so done, and then he would have the date on there, and he would have the time on there. I mean these are things I taught him to do. He was very efficient, because even when I take notes, so often I will put the time on there. I was looking to see if I had put any time on any of yours; it looks like I didn't, I don't know why.*

CH: *I think it's timeless.*

MBM: *Usually, if somebody calls and I will put 8:30 a.m. and the particular date and stuff like that, and this is what Emmett would do so often, especially in his notes to Gene. When I was working those terrible hours (I mean I was working until it was just ridiculous), Emmett told me one day, "Mama, if you can go out and make the money, I'll take care of the house." And I accepted that. I mean if you're going to take care of the house, I began to outline what taking care of the house was.*

CH: *You were not married at this particular time?*

MBM: *My husband and I had separated; I was separated from Bradley at the time, yes. It was just the two of us, yes. The things I would give him to do—and he was thirteen! And you know, you don't get anything out of these teenagers. I mean, they sit in front of the TV, and eat, and invite their friends up to eat and drink pop, but my rules were nobody in the house when I'm not here. And you don't lay on my telephone when I'm not here. And you do this and that, and if you got all of that done by the time I got back, you have had a good day's work. Emmett and I had been reading a comic strip together, and I don't know if there was Captain Jammer Kids or one of those spoofs, but they had swept some dirt under a rug and put the rug down over it. I told Emmett, "When I catch you sweeping dirt under my rug, you would eat the dirt." I said, "That's the day you'll bite the dirt—get it?" You know, after he died, I was sleeping in my front room; the way the house was built, you entered from the side. I made where you entered my living room, and made that room up there my bedroom. I looked under my rug, and I saw this lump! That little rascal had been sweeping dirt under that rug. He didn't do that until I had told him what I would do to him if he did. I know he was disappointed I didn't find it, but it was right under the edge of the bed.*

CH: *In fact, he probably thought you were going to find it.*

MBM: *I was supposed to find it.*

CH: *It was planted there for you.*

MBM: *I was so dead tired when I would come home from work. When I would go to bed, he would sit right by that phone, and if that phone would ring, I mean it didn't get to ring a whole ring, he got it off the hook. And he would let them know, "Mom is asleep, I'll have her call when she wakes up. But I can't wake her up now." And very, very, very protective.*

CH: *What do you think should be done for the Till legacy to be better treated? It definitely has not been treated properly. It has not been exposed properly. As you have said, there are a lot of false statements in reference to his character, his mannerism—what do you think basically could redirect the legacy of Till?*

MBM: *Well, I would certainly like to see a memorial to my son in the city of Chicago, in his home, in his native city. That would certainly be a start. And then, I think a school should have been named after Emmett, the Emmett Till School; he certainly deserved a school named after him. And I think somebody—whoever is in charge of the history books—I think they should have certainly taken a little time to do a little research. You know, not just take the word of the people. I know that off the surface if you went to Mississippi and asked them questions, I know what answers you would get. I know that every black man in the state of Mississippi has raped a white woman, or wanted to, so far as a white man is concerned. I know that. Yes. Nine times out of ten, he's done it! And I can even remember little experiences I had on some of my visits there, and I was a girl—a little twelve-year-old girl—and yet I was unable to connect that to Emmett's visit to the South.*

CH: *You've spoken often of Dr. King, and you have the Till Players recite his "I Have A Dream" speech. I'm wondering if you've ever spoken to Rosa Parks or Martin Luther King in reference to the Till case then and its impact on them?*

MBM: *No, I've never had the pleasure of meeting Mrs. Parks. We passed as shadows in the night last July. We were both in Huntsville, Alabama. I was there on a Tuesday, and she was going to be there the next day, I believe. We were there with one of the colleges, and they were showing* Eyes on the Prize*. They showed the first half of the first tape, the part that featured me and the child and everything. And then it went into the Montgomery bus boycott, so they were going to have her the next day, and she was going to talk to the students about that part of it. But I couldn't stay because the next day was the beginning of my pastor's fourteenth anniversary, and I was on that committee, so we went to dinner Monday, I flew to Birmingham early Tuesday morning, and spoke Tuesday, and flew out of there Wednesday morning, and attended church Wednesday evening. I was tired! I understand we're somewhat in the same family. My mother has a first cousin, and I* *think that my first cousin's husband and Rosa are sister and brother.*

CH: *As I reflect on Rosa Parks and Martin Luther King, Rosa Parks took her heroic stand just three months after Emmett Till was killed, and it was my conjecture that she may very well have had that on her mind at the time. I think it was something that people had gotten fed up with. My impression, of course, is that it was the impetus for the Civil Rights Movement, and that in fact she probably had this very heavy on her mind at the time, and that was her private reaction, too, given the opportunity. I intend to speak to her if I can get an audience with her, and I was wondering if you had any important talk with her or King.*

MBM: *No, my mother talked to Dr. King right around the corner. He was at Mahalliah Jackson's house, and my mother went in and talked to him, and they talked about Emmett. But I never had the pleasure of meeting him. Now I was in Georgia, and I did meet with Dr. King's two daughters. They had me come and bring some of the Emmett Till Players a couple of years ago.*

CH: *Did your mother relate any of the conversation she had with King on Till?*

MBM: *Oh, yes. He said it had a very decided impact on his life, in helping him decide which way he was going.*

CH: *Actually when you talked to many people who were active, and civil rights advocates will say in retrospect that that particular incident played a major role in their lives.*

MBM: *That's right. And so many people left the South, and every time we do a program, so many people come up to me, and they let me know that when that happened my family left the South. There was a great migration taking place at that particular time.*

CH: *We spoke earlier, Mr. Mooty and I. He seems to be in a lot of the photographs. I was wondering what do you feel his role was in the Till murder case?*

MBM: *Well Mr. Moody was sort of like the one who was steering me which way to go because he was quite active in the labor movement; he knew the politicians. I didn't know a politician. I was brought up in Argo, Illinois. I didn't even know how to come to Chicago. I mean, it had to be in the fifties before I learned how to travel from Argo to Chicago by public transportation. I could drive, but public transportation—that was another story. I was twenty-five years old when I got my first job with the Federal Government, and my mother had to take me downtown everyday and pick me up every night from 1 North LaSalle on public transportation. And the day she told me, "I will not be picking you up tonight," she scared me half to death. It had never dawned on me that she was going to tell me I had to do it myself.*

CH: *Were you an only child?*

MBM: *Yes.*

CH: *And Emmett was an only child?*

MBM: *And he was an only child.*

CH: *Had you ever thought of having kids after that, or had it really soured you? Sometimes you have a fear after something like that, that if it happens again, I couldn't do it, I couldn't go through it, you know.*

MBM: *I wanted four children. And I went to the doctor, and the doctor said there is no reason I couldn't. That was the only pregnancy, I never knew anything in the early forties about contraceptives. Not in Argo, I don't know what Chicago knew! But in Argo, we were in a world apart. I knew nothing to do. But I had that one pregnancy. And my mother had two. But the first baby was a miscarriage, and she got me safely here, and that was the end. And she knew less than I knew. She had the one sister, Elizabeth, the one that my son was visiting, who must have had twelve or thirteen children. Not all of them survived. I think she actually had six that lived, and then she had other sisters and brothers who had none. So, that was a strange family. I think there were six older sisters and brothers, and my mother had one, another brother had two, Aunt Lizzie had a gob of them, then my Uncle Crosby fathered two, then the other two had none. Papa Mose came for whatever reason he came, and he took Parker and Bo back with him.*

CH: *And he was to go there for a week or so?*

MBM: *He was going to be gone maybe a week to ten days. Actually Emmett and I were planning a vacation. And when Papa Mose came, and Emmett found out that the other boys were going to be with Papa Mose, then he switched his plans. That really shook me up a lot because I was getting ready as fast as I could to take off for Detroit, then we were going to go to Omaha, Nebraska—my first vacation. The first one.*

The thing that has struck me through all of this is how it just keeps coming up again. People are actually saying, "Why don't you stop this thing?" And I looked at them in amazement. I said, "Do you really think I could do all this? Do you really think I am this powerful?" People would call me from all over the world. They would be crying so until I became the consoler. There was this Mrs. Phillips from somewhere in California. Oh, that woman, that woman. I guess for about five years that woman cried over the telephone, and it was me trying to dry her tears. And all of a sudden, I stopped hearing from Mrs. Phillips. She even came here, and when she came, I was out of town. Mother had a chance to meet her. Mother just moved in my house—she had to move in and take my house over for almost the period that I was going through school. Because between going to school, I would take off on a junket, and then I would have to come back, and everywhere I went I took those books with me.

CH: *Where did you go to school?*

MBM: *I went to Chicago Teacher College. Started out at the top of the bottom third.*

CH: *Were you in school part-time when Till was …*

MBM: *No, it was after that. It was all I could do to keep up with the United States Air Force. Those people were working me night and day. I was just about ready to retire, and then all of a sudden the work didn't slack off, I had taken off because I was getting ready to go on my vacation. I started working for the Federal Government in 1943.*

CH: *So this was your first vacation?*

MBM: *I had never in my life taken a vacation before. In our salary bracket, you didn't take vacations. If we went down South, that was our vacation. We went to visit my mama's sister or something like that. That was the highlight of a vacation. But to plan to go north and then to go west? I was the first one in my family that I know of, outside of my Aunt Mamie, who had taken a vacation. And I was taking a month off, and I had been home about four days, and that's when Emmett twisted my arm and Mama's arm, and we let him go South with Papa Mose.*

CH: *So you really didn't want him to go?*

MBM: *No, no, we didn't want him to go. He was going with me. And we were going to have a ball. What with driving; and I bought a 1955 Plymouth, and Gene had told Emmett he was going to let him drive on the highway.*

CH: *So, the three of you were going to go?*

MBM: *The three of us were going to go, yes. Gene was trying to get his foot in the door. He was just kind of a spoiled boy. Every time Gene would tell Bo that he wanted to marry me, Bo would tell him, "Not yet. We're not ready yet." And finally Gene just pinned him down. He said, "What is the problem?" He admitted that I might do some things—might warrant a beating—but he really didn't care to have anybody beating me. That would mean, you see, that Emmett would have to get in the act. Gene would beat me, and Emmett would have to beat Gene. And he really wasn't for all of that activity. Oh, Gene tried his best. He said, "I wouldn't hit you, I wouldn't do that." You know every so often, he'll bring that up. He says, "You know, I wonder if Bo sees us together, and does he see how nice I treat you? I told him I wasn't going to beat you, but I will admit you need it!"*

CH: *You said you worked for the United States Air Force. Now Emmett's father was a serviceman?*

MBM: *Yes.*

CH: *I'm reflecting on the story of his death that came out and obviously for the purpose of trying to discredit Emmett. I think that Ethel Payne did a beautiful story, and Attorney Huff made it very clear that this was their motive. Of course, they were effective, because after that the jury did hand down an exoneration in reference to the kidnapping for the murders. I'm wondering how your employers reacted to you after the Till incident and the exposure of that information on your husband, whether it was true or not, the whole picture, if it had any effect on your relationship with your employer or fellow employees?*

MBM: *I never returned to that job. But I had made many friends on the job. In fact, I was part of a bridge club at the time. And you would not even guess that they had read anything that would discredit Louis or be a reflection on me. It's amazing, the standing I had, the fact that I was a black girl, I was in charge of the secret and confidential files. At the time, you see, that just wasn't. We had these little filing jobs and the little clerk typist jobs, but to actually go into ... I'll never forget, I was reading this stuff, and it didn't mean anything to me. I remember black-eyed Susan and all that stuff, but to me I considered a black-eyed Susan a flower. But I knew that I could not talk about it because I'd been told that I could not talk about it. I was in what you might call an enviable position. Because, except for the officer in charge, I was the only one who knew the combination to the safe that the files were kept in. Even my immediate supervisor did not know. Every thirty, forty, or fifty days they'd change the combination, and then I'd have to learn it all over again, and only the OIC and myself would know. But the people that knew me, it made no difference in our relationship whatsoever. After all, true or not true, the charges they made against Louis, that would not have anything to do with me. But the sad part about that was they didn't even bother to tell me what had happened.*

CH: *That was amazing, you just found it in the paper.*

MBM: *They just told me, "This is to inform you that your husband, Louis Till, died" and they gave me the date, and whatever that town was in Italy, and that was that. When I started making inquiry, they let me know that all of this is confidential, and they wouldn't give me any details.*

CH: *So you had no idea?*

MBM: *I had no idea. They let me know that there was no compensation forthcoming, so I ended up with no husband and no compensation.*

CH: *Eisenhower was in charge at that time, and I understand that he signed the authorization of the execution.*

I have the newspaper article with your pointing at the capitol and saying, "Maybe I can get justice here." It might have been within days that Eisenhower had that heart attack.

MBM: *You see, I sent a telegram to him asking for help, because I needed a whole lot of help. Instead of getting a response from the president, I read in the newspapers that the president had a heart attack and was in some hospital, Bethesda Naval, I imagine.*

CH: *Did he have time to respond to your letter prior to the heart attack?*

MBM: *Oh sure. It looks like he read the telegram, and they decided "We better put you in the hospital right away." How long does it take a telegram? One going to the president is almost going to get there instantly, right? I don't know how fast it got into his hands, but like I sent the telegram today, the president went into the hospital the next day. Within twenty-four hours or less.*

CH: *So they placed him in there, but do you think he actually did have a heart attack?*

MBM: *I don't believe.*

CH: *That hasn't been established, but they say he had a heart attack. It was timely, wasn't it?*

MBM: *But you see, I learned something else about Eisenhower, too. The fellows who come back from over there, I've heard all the nightmarish things that went on, how the fellows would come out of the bed. They would have to fall out, and the women that go through the line pointing, "this one." And some of them said, "I know that one. He sleeps right next to me; he hasn't moved all night long." They'd never see that one again.*

CH: *Oh, my Lord. See that's what I'm talking about—how this information has been fed to people—it continues to be fed to people. There is a white feminist, I think Susan Brownmiller in her book Against Our Will: Men, Women and Rape, who bases this theory that Till was a potential rapist.*

MBM: *I wished she could have seen him shouting around in the church in Argo, Illinois, a little saved boy.*

CH: *He was a kid, and a kid could be mischievous. He was just fourteen years old.*

MBM: *He was, he was, and he had a sense of humor. We played like kids. You wouldn't know who the mama was, who the child was. I mean we got along fabulously well. Then when I did have to play the heavy, when I did have to beat up on him, he'd call my mama and tell her, "I think you ought to come over here and talk to Mama." Because I'd lay him away. But that was very, very seldom. Usually that would be about something he hadn't done right in school that I thought he should have done better. And I'd get uptight about that. Other than that I didn't worry about, I just didn't get conduct reports like this. I remember after I got promoted on my job, he did a little show-out in school, and I got in my car and came over there, and he never showed out in school anymore. Because I did, too. It was like they sent him to the principal. He is now the alderman in our area. After Mayor Washington's death, our Alderman Sawyer became the acting mayor. His right-hand man, Robinson, was Emmett's principal, and now Robinson is the alderman; he took over for Sawyer, and Sawyer is now the mayor. I saw him just the other day because I'm appreciating that—to have some recognition here in the city. Also I'm pushing to get the Emmett Till Players into the city council. I'd like for them to perform; there are a few that are good enough to perform. And they don't have to be that good. The fact that the kids have the nerve to walk to a mike and attack the mike; I feel this is worthwhile. I have twenty kids. They would eat a mike alive. I mean all the way from age five up.*

CH: *Why do you think Bryant and Milam were so adamant, beyond the fact that Emmett whistled?*

MBM: *They said that Milam asked Emmett, "Are you as good as I am?" Either when he was in the truck or in the barn. And Emmett continued to answer the affirmative, "Yes, I am as good as you are." And Milam said that's what he couldn't stand. He just had to kill him. It was so incredible that these two men thought that he couldn't affirm his humanity. It was like three-fifths human had become five-fifths human.*

CH: *Well, that's an easy gesture of confidence that I'm talking about in the face of adversity. It's so natural for him to be himself. Any other private emotions or private facts you'd like to share that we've not heard in reference to Till? Refutations of any information they put out on him that you'd like to share? Any false statements that you can think of that need to be readdressed at this point?*

MBM: *As I said, I haven't read too many things about Emmett, and that kind of bothers me. Better something false than nothing at all. Emmett was the turning point, regardless to what anybody might say, Emmett was the turning point.*

CH: *Have you been back to Mississippi, particularly Money or Sumner, since Emmett's death?*

MBM: *I have been back to Sumner several times. I don't recall that I've been to Money since I was twelve years old. I don't even know that I've even been to Money. I don't know how long my uncle lived there. I remember when I visited them as a child. I never visited them as an adult.*

CH: *When you went to Sumner, Mississippi, when you went down for the trial, did you run into any repercussions, any hostility from the people, or fear expressed on the part of blacks, that you were able to remember? Was it known that you were a visitor there?*

MBM: *It was not known that I was a visitor there except among a few of my uncle's good friends. He would not advertise my coming, and he was very discreet. But my uncle took me to the courthouse, showed me around town, and things like that.*

CH: *It's been quite a while since you've last seen your uncle?*

MBM: *I saw him in November 1986.*

CH: *I'm looking at a photograph of Simeon, Maurice, and Mose Wright. It's in a 1955* Jet *magazine with an ar-*

ticle about Emmett Till. I have been able to interview Simeon Wright, who was twelve at the time that Emmett was abducted. But I have not been able to get any information on Maurice Wright, who was sixteen and two years older than Emmett. What happened to him?

MBM: *We don't know. Maurice hasn't been able to get himself together since Emmett's death. The last I heard of him, he was in Phoenix, Arizona. Since then, other members said they've heard of him being in some place in California. But he seems to be a man on the run.*

CH: *When did you last hear that he was in Phoenix?*

MBM: *Oh, goodness, that had to be about ten years ago. And the last I heard of him, period, was perhaps five years ago. I don't know if anyone has heard from him since then.*

CH: *Was Maurice one of the boys who was with Emmett at the time that the incident occurred?*

MBM: *I understand that Maurice was the driver of the car.*

CH: *I'm reflecting on your mother's quote the day that he was abducted, and I quote: "It was so beautiful that I'm going to put this up carefully. This could be his obituary." What does she mean by that?*

MBM: *Aunt Lizzie had written a letter. In her letter she was saying what a beautiful son we had raised. And she went on to tell us how, when the boys would get up in the morning and have breakfast, they would depart for the field immediately with Papa Mose. But BoBo wouldn't go until the last dish was washed. And then his next job would be to start up the wash machine, because he washed every day. All those boys there, it was necessary to wash. She didn't know Bo knew how to wash—Emmett knew how to wash. But Emmett did the laundry. Then they would go to the garden and pick the food, the veggies for the lunch, dinner meal. And when that meal was ready and in the pot, then Emmett went to the field, but not until. And she thought that was the greatest thing she'd ever heard of.*

10
Conclusion—The Truth of Till

To try to silence all the fuss o'er you
Is nothing more than base futility.
It's true it's taken over thirty years,
But that does not mean truth does not exist.

The truth is, Emmett, You ignited fear
And rage and shame and pure impatience.
The truth is, Bo, you sparked the crucial movement,
Birthing the signing of the Civil Rights Bill.

You could have done and will do still much more
To redirect man's gut response to man.
Because your impact lingers yet with us,
I'm confident the truth of Till will reign.

Clenora Hudson—December 1987

I was a sheltered ten-year-old, an innocent and naive Memphis girl, when Emmett was killed. Unearthing the truth of this incident is critical for me, both as a scholar and as an individual, because I cannot profess to be an objective observer. Emmett and I had much in common: we were kids; we were black; we were living human beings. Unearthing the truth is a difficult task because there is a dearth of information on this incident and because the experience of re-evoking it is so painful.

The snatching of a child has to be the most horrific of human crimes. The fear is that this could happen to each and every one of us, just as the systematic slaughtering of blacks during slavery was a formidable reality. The Till incident and the fear of its recurrence is an unnatural ugly thread, permanently woven into American culture and the emotions of countless American people. The power of these realities is so real, so devastating, so overwhelmingly compelling that the impact lingers eternally.

Till's murder is one of the most critical factors of the modern Civil Rights Movement; it is more plausible as instigator than the Parks incident. When a child is robbed of life, leaving behind utter devastation, one impulsively and unhesitatingly reacts. This is what happened when Till was snatched. Americans, and African-Americans in particular, reacted. Their response was immediate, and it was unquestionably direct. African-Americans had suffered for over three centuries, but the Till incident, "the straw that broke the camel's back," demanded immediate change. As if it was not enough that the safety of blacks in general was at a risk in America, more unacceptable was that a child, the symbol of innocence, was brutalized. That was all it really took for African-Americans to say, "Enough."

The identity of the source of the power behind the modern Civil Rights Movement has too long been concealed, perhaps because it became a moral critique of American culture. It was an embarrassment to white America, which boasts that it is "the land of the free, the home of the brave." The infamous Till incident makes a mockery of the symbol of American freedom, with its towering statue of liberty—not so much that the incident occurred alone, but, more important, because the guilty were exonerated of their deed in the mock trials. Obviously, the Till lynching ignited the Movement, but it was an embarrassing and hideous event. American society has deemed Rosa Parks and the Montgomery bus boycott more suitable as the beginning of the Civil Rights Movement.

During the mid-fifties, African-Americans were at a zenith: the 1954 United States Supreme Court decision, *Brown versus Board of Education,* voter registration drives, the Emmett Till murder case, the Montgomery bus boycott, and the desegregation of the Little Rock public schools. African-Americans were boldly demanding their human rights. Unfortunately, the spirit of that era was aborted; the need to revive it is demonstrated in the status of race relations in America today. It is crucial that African-Americans today pick up where they started immediately after Till's lynching, with the fervor, the level of awareness of our status, and the realization of the need to forge a fair course and place for black people in this country. African-Americans need to reclaim the direction of their people, articulate the demands, design a strategy, and execute the necessary action so that truth, justice, and parity for black people will be realized. Blacks need to pick up the torch that was launched during the Till incident and carry it to the end. That is one effective way that we can realize our ultimate goals and objectives for real freedom.

The Till incident was a watershed in American history. For the first time, the whole world, in unmistakable measure, was able to see what Jim Crow in America was like. As Till's mother herself asserts:

> *I think people got a chance to actually look and see what was happening. I think until then it was almost as if there was a cover or blanket over what was hap-*

> *pening in certain southern states, and America just had the cover pulled off of her and everybody could see what was going on. The world looked in on the United States.*

Prior to Till, there were lynchings and other incidents of racial discrimination and degradation; but this incident was the first case where clearly Jim Crow was looked at for what it really was. One must remember that it was difficult to attack Jim Crow because it was a way of life, not merely a group of laws. Being uppity is not in the law; Till did not break a law. He became a victim of both a vicious insidious act of violence and the criminal justice system with its sanctioning of such an atrocity. African-Americans, in turn, became secondary victims, primarily because of the incessant terror imposed on their lives. In Jim Crow, whites made blacks accept segregation, legalizing it; and Emmett Till's style became his demise.

While many have avoided the Till murder case, understanding and dealing with it is critical to ameliorating American racism. Through this act, one is able to understand why an oppressor needs an oppressed, and why it is imperative that the oppressed participate in affecting radical change in present human relations. This case must be properly addressed and placed in the perspective of American race relations and modern-day social movements. Thus, the world cannot afford to forget the Emmett Till murder case. Although it has been underplayed, it has not been laid to rest; for it just keeps coming up, again and again. People have not forgotten Emmett Till. Nor can his murder be forgotten. People cannot and will not let it die.

Epilogue

On July 25, 1991, the day that would have been the late Emmett "Bobo" Louis Till's fiftieth birthday, hundreds assembled at the corner of 71st Street and Oglesby Avenue in Chicago to memorialize the young victim of a racial atrocity and to witness the ceremonious renaming of 71st Street—Emmett Till Road—symbolizing the undaunting struggle against racism and for civil rights for Africans everywhere. Among the witnesses of this historical occasion were Emmett Till's mother, Mamie Till Mobley, and her husband, Gene Mobley; the mother of the Modern Civil Rights Movement, Rosa Parks; the mayor of Chicago, Richard M. Daley; and the former mayor of Chicago Eugene Sawyer. During the day-long commemoration, there were a number of speakers, myself included, attesting to the fact that their politicization commenced with the brutal lynching of this fourteen-year-old Chicago youth, whose life and death must never be forgotten.

Appendix 1

Documents of the Murder Trial

THE STATE OF MISSISSIPPI,
TALLAHATCHIE COUNTY.
SECOND CIRCUIT COURT DISTRICT

In the Circuit Court in and for said District of said County, at the September Term thereof, in the year of our Lord, 1955, the Grand Jurors of the State of Mississippi, taken from the body of good and lawful men of the District and County aforesaid, duly elected, empaneled, sworn and charged, at the term aforesaid, of the court aforesaid, to inquire in and for the body of the District and County aforesaid, in the name and by the authority of the State of Mississippi, upon their oaths, present that

Roy Bryant and J. W. Milam

late of the District and County aforesaid, on the 5th day of September, in the year of our Lord, 1955, in the District and County aforesaid and within jurisdiction of this court,

did wilfully, unlawfully, feloniously, and of their malice aforethought kill and murder Emmett Till, a human being

against the peace and dignity of the State of Mississippi.

Gerald Chatham
District Attorney

No. 1960

THE STATE OF MISSISSIPPI
SECOND JUDICIAL DISTRICT
OF TALLAHATCHIE COUNTY
CIRCUIT COURT

STATE OF MISSISSIPPI

vs.

J. W. Milam
Roy Bryant

A TRUE BILL

Jerry Falls
Foreman of Grand Jury

WITNESSES

George Smith, J. E. Cothran
J. C. Strider, Mose Wright,
Simmy Wright, Dr. L. B.
Otkin, Chick Nelson,
Garland Melton -

Filed and Capias issued on this 6
day of Sept., A. D. 1955
C. W. Nicholas Cox
Circuit Court Clerk

THE STATE OF MISSISSIPPI,
SECOND JUDICIAL DISTRICT
TALLAHATCHIE COUNTY

TO THE SHERIFF OF ~~SAID~~ LEFLORE COUNTY, GREETING: You are hereby commanded to summon George Smith, J. E. Cothran, Mose Wright, Sonny Wright, Simeon Wright, Maurice Wright, Mose Wright's wife, Dr. L. B. Otken, Chick Wilson, Garland Melton, H. C. Strider

if to be found in your County, to be and personally appear before the Circuit Court of the Second District of the County of Tallahatchie, in said State, at the Court House in the Town of Sumner, Mississippi on the 9th day of September 1955 at 9:00 o'clock A. M., and there testify on behalf of Defendants

(at whose instance this writ is issued) in a certain case pending in said Court, wherein the State of Mississippi is Plaintiff and J. W. Milam and Roy Bryant are Defendants and that they in nowise fail to appear under the penalty prescribed by the statute; and have there then this writ.

Given under my hand and Seal of said Court, and issued this the 6th day of September, 1955

Charlie Cox, Clerk
By Mrs. D. R. Rogers, D. C.

THE STATE OF MISSISSIPPI,
TALLAHATCHIE COUNTY. } Second Judicial District,

TO THE SHERIFF OF SAID COUNTY, GREETING: You are hereby commanded to summon

Charles Fred Mims
W. E. Hodge
Robert Hodge

if to be found in your County, to be and personally appear before the Circuit Court of the Second District of the County of Tallahatchie, in said State, at the Court House in the Town of Sumner, Mississippi on the Instanter 194...., at .... o'clock, ...M., and there testify on behalf of State (at whose instance this writ is issued) in a certain case pending in said Court, wherein the State of Mississippi is Plaintiff, and Bryant and Milam .... is Defendant, and that ..... he..... in no wise fail to appear under the penalty prescribed by the statute; and have there then this writ.

Given under my hand and Seal of said Court, and issued this the 19 day of Sept, 1955

Charles Cox, Clerk
H H Wimbly, D. C.

HE STATE OF MISSISSIPPI,
ALLAHATCHIE COUNTY. } Second Judicial District,

THE SHERIFF OF SAID COUNTY, GREETING: You are hereby commanded to summon

Mamie Bradley

o be found in your County, to be and personally appear before the Circuit Court of the Second District of the County of ahatchie, in said State, at the Court House in the Town of Sumner, Mississippi on the 20 day of Sept 55 Instanter, at .... o'clock, ...M., and there testify on behalf of State

whose instance this writ is issued, in a certain case pending in said Court, wherein the State of Mississippi is Plaintiff, J. W. Milam & Roy Bryant

.... is Defendant, and that s he...... in no wise fail to appear under the penalty prescribed by the sta-; and have there then this writ.

Given under my hand and Seal of said Court, and issued this the 20 day of Sept. 1955

Charlie Cox, Clerk

........, D. C.

THE STATE OF MISSISSIPPI,
TALLAHATCHIE COUNTY. } Second Judicial District,

TO THE SHERIFF OF SAID COUNTY, GREETING: You are hereby commanded to summon Johnnie Jennings. Mamie Bradley. Mrs J. W. Melam. Mrs Roy Bryant. Mrs Eula Bryant Chester A Miller. Charles Fred Mims W. E. Hodges. Robert Hodges

if to be found in your County, to be and personally appear before the Circuit Court of the Second District of the County of Tallahatchie, in said State, at the Court House in the Town of Sumner, Mississippi on the 20 day of Sept 1955, at Instanter o'clock, ...M., and there testify on behalf of Defendants (at whose instance this writ is issued) in a certain case pending in said Court, wherein the State of Mississippi is Plaintiff, and J. W. Melam & Roy Bryant ......is Defendant, and that they in no wise fail to appear under the penalty prescribed by the statute; and have there then this writ.

Given under my hand and Seal of said Court, and issued this the 20 day of Sept 1955

C. Curtis Cox, Clerk

................................, D. C.

STATE OF MISSISSIPPI

VS.

J. W. MILAM and ROY BRYANT

Instruction No. 1 for Defendants

The court instructs the jury to find the defendants, Roy Bryant and J. W. Milam, not guilty.

Refused

Refused & filed. Sept 23 1955 [illegible] Clerk

STATE OF MISSISSIPPI

VS.

J. W. MILAM and ROY BRYANT

Instruction No. 2 for Defendants

The court instructs the jury to find the defendant, Roy Bryant, not guilty.

Refused

Refused / Filed Sept 23 1955 / Charlie Cox clerk

STATE OF MISSISSIPPI

VS.

J. W. MILAM AND ROY BRYANT

Instruction No. 3 for Defendants

The court instructs the jury to find the defendant, J. W. Milam, not guilty.

Refused

STATE OF MISSISSIPPI

VS.

J. W. MILAM and ROY BRYANT

Instruction No. 4 for Defendants

The Court instructs the Jury for the Defendants that although you may believe from the evidence, beyond every reasonable doubt, that the Defendants did kill and murder Emmett Till, the person described in the indictment in this cause, and the person whose body was taken from Tallahatchie River, as shown in this cause; but unless you further believe from the evidence, beyond every reasonable doubt, that the said Emmett Till was killed and murdered by the Defendants in the Second Judicial District of Tallahatchie County, Mississippi, then, in such event, you would not be authorized under the law to return a verdict of guilty in this cause.

Refused

Refused & filed Sept 23, 1955
Charley Cox Clerk

STATE OF MISSISSIPPI

VS.

J. W. MILAM and ROY BRYANT

Instruction No. 5 for Defendants

The court instructs the jury for the defendants that the defendants at the outset of the trial are presumed to be entirely innocent of the whole charge against them and every part thereof, and that this presumption attends them through out the trial of the case, and the court further charges you that they are not required to prove themselves innocent, but that the burden is upon the State to prove them guilty beyond every reasonable doubt, and the court instructs you that if from the evidence or want of evidence it should appear that the defendants are even probably innocent, it is your duty to acquit them.

Refused

Refused & Filed Sept 23 1955
Charles Cox Clerk

STATE OF MISSISSIPPI

VS.

J. W. MILAM and ROY BRYANT

INSTRUCTION NO. 6 FOR DEFENDANTS

The Court instructs the Jury for the Defendants that the body taken from Tallahatchie River as testified to in this cause, as a matter of law, is not shown to be that of Emmett Till, the person described in the indictment in this cause.

Refused

STATE OF MISSISSIPPI

VS.

J. W. MILAM and ROY BRYANT

INSTRUCTION NO. 7 FOR DEFENDANTS

The Court instructs the Jury that any statement against interest made by either of the Defendants, out of the presence and hearing of his Co-Defendant, is not admissible against such Defendant who was not present when such statement, if any, was made.

Refused

State of Mississippi

Vs Nolle Prosequi

J. W. Milam and Roy Bryant

This day this cause came on to be heard, came the District Attorney for the State and moved that this cause be Nolle Prosequi. And the Court considering the same finds that this motion should be and the Court hereby sustains the said motion. It is therefore ordered by the Court that this cause be and it is hereby Nolle Prosequi. And it is furthere ordered by the Court that the Sheriff of Tallahatchie County, Mississippi, deliver to the Sheriff of Leflore County, Mississippi. the said defendants, J. W.Milam and Roy Bryant.

So ordered and adjudged this the 23rd day of September, 1955.

____

Circuit Judge

We the Jury find
the Defendants
"Not Guilty"

State of Mississipp

Vs   Trial and Verdict of Jury

Roy Bryant and J. W. Milam

This day the trial of this cause continued to be heard with all concerned present as of the day before and with the defense continuing its presentation of evidence to the Jury by its Witnesses until the counsel for defendants announced that they RESTS, after which the District Attorney announced that the State RESTS. And this cause continuing to be heard this day with the jury hearing the arguments of counsel for both the State of Mississippi and the defendants and receiving the instructions of the Court, the said jury retired to consider of their verdict and having duly considered the same returned into open Court in the presence of the Defendants and their counsel and the District Attorney and Special Prosecuting Attorney for the State this their Verdict to-wit: "We the jury find the Defendants "Not Guilty". It is therefore considered by the Court and so ordered and adjudged that the Defendants, Roy Bryant and J. W. Milam, be and they are hereby discharged from this cause and that they go hence without day.

So ordered and adjudged this the 23rd day of September, 1955

____

Circuit Judge

Minutes of Circuit Court, Tallahatchie County,

23rd DAY September TERM OF 2nd Judicial District 1955

1959 State of Mississippi ()

Vs () Trial and Verdict of Jury

Roy Bryant and J. W. Milam ()

This day the trial of this cause continued to be heard with all concerned present as of the day before and with the defense continuing its presentation of evidence to the Jury by its Witnesses until the counsel for the defendants announced that the they RESTS, after which the District Attorney announced that the State RESTS. And this cause continuing to be heard this day with the Jury hearing the arguments of counsel for both the State of Mississippi and the defendants and receiving the instructions of the Court; the said Jury retired to consider of their Verdict and having duly considered the same returned into open Court in the presence of the Defendants and their counsel and the District Attorney and the Special Prosecuting attorney for the State this their Verdict to-wit: we the jury find the Defendants "Not Guilty". It is therefore considered by the Court and so ordered and adjudged that the Defendants, Roy Bryant and J. W. Milam, be and they are hereby discharged from this cause and that they go hence without day.

So ordered and adjudged this the 23rd day of September, 1955.

Curtis M. Swango Jr.
Circuit Judge

CERTIFYING STAMP

I hereby certify that the foregoing is a true copy of the original thereof now in my office.

Attest: P. O. Eastridge
Paul O. Eastridge, Circuit Clerk
By [signature]

1960 State of Mississippi ()

Vs () Nolle Prosequi

J. W. Milam and Roy Bryant ()

This day this cause came on to be heard, came the District Attorney for the State and moved that this cause be Nolle Proseque. And the Court considering the same finds that this motion should be and the Court hereby sustains the said motion. It is therefore ordered by the Court that this cause be and it is hereby Nolle Prosequi. And it is further ordered by the Court that the Sheriff of Tallahatchie County, Mississippi, deliver to the Sheriff of Leflore County, Mississippi, the said defendants, J. W. Milam and Roy Bryant.

So ordered and adjudged this the 23rd day of September, 1955

Curtis M. Swango Jr.
Circuit Judge

Appendix 2

Official Letters/Telegrams

ESTERN UNION

W. P. MARSHALL, PRESIDENT

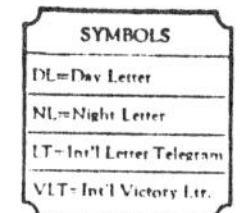
SYMBOLS
DL=Day Letter
NL=Night Letter
LT=Int'l Letter Telegram
VLT=Int'l Victory Ltr.

The filing time shown in ... on telegrams and day letters is STANDARD TIME at point of origin. Time of receipt is STANDARD TIME at point of destination

NA770

LONG NL PD=WUX NEW YORK NY 23=

RAYFIELD MOOTY=

5438 SOUTH LA SALLE ST CHGO=

SEP 23 PM 5 52

WOULD APPRECIATE DEEPLY YOUR ACCEPTANCE OF INVITATION OF NEW YORK DIVISION OF THE BROTHERHOOD OF SLEEPING CAR PORTERS TO ATTEND AND SPEAK AT MASS MEETING OCCASION TO PROTEST AND ORGANIZE NEW YORK PUBLIC OPINION AGAINST THE BRUTAL LYNCHING OF YOUR NEPHEW IN MISSISSIPPI. THIS MEETING FIRST ORGANIZED EFFORT IN NEW YORK ON THIS UNFORTUNATE INCIDENT TO TAKE PLACE THIS SUNDAY, SEPTEMBER 25, AT WILLIAMS INSTITUTIONAL C. M. E. CHURCH LOCATED 2225 SEVENTH AVENUE, NEW YORK, CITY. TIME IS 2:30 PM THE ORGANIZATION'S INTERNATIONAL PRESIDENT, MR. A. PHILIP RANDOLPH, WILL BE CHAIRMAN AND SPEAKERS WILL INCLUDE SOME OF NEW YORK'S DISTINGUISHED CITIZENS, WHITE AND COLORED. WE WOULD ALSO DEEPLY BE VERY HAPPY TO HAVE MRS. MAMIE BRADLEY. I HAVE TALKED TO OUR MUTUAL FRIEND, BOYD WILSON, OF YOUR UNION. THE BROTHERHOOD OF SLEEIING CAR PORTERS WILL BE HAPPY TO PAY ALL EXPENSES FOR YOU AND MRS. BRADLEY IF IT IS POSSIBLE FOR YOU TO ACCEPT THIS INVITATION. KINDLY WIRE OR TELEPHONE ME COLLECT AT MONUMENT 2-5079=

THEODORE BROWN, DIRECTOR OF RESEARCH AND PUBLICITY BROTHERHOOD OF SLEEPING CAR PORTERS 217 WEST 125TH STREET SUITE 301 NEW YORK 27 NEW YORK=..

WEST SIDE UNIT
OF THE CHICAGO BRANCH

NATIONAL ASSOCIATION
FOR THE
ADVANCEMENT OF COLORED PEOPLE

1427 SOUTH SPAULDING AVENUE, CHICAGO 23

EXECUTIVE OFFICERS:

JOSEPH H. AUSTIN
PRESIDENT
CRAWFORD 7-4928

DIANNE JONES
SECRETARY
ROCKWELL 2-6906

MATTIE KELLY MOORE
1ST VICE-PRESIDENT

CARTER D. JONES
2ND VICE-PRESIDENT

BETHEL JONES
CORRESPONDING SECRETARY

FREDERICK SUMMERS
TREASURER

COMMITTEE CHAIRMEN:

GERTRUDE WHITNEY
BERTHA MCKINNEY
EDUCATION CO-CHAIRMEN

EFFIE PEARSON
MEMBERSHIP

CARTER D. JONES
HOUSING

CLIFFORD ESTERS
JOSEPH MCKINNEY
LABOR CO-CHAIRMEN

EMORY ANDREW TATE
MARK JONES
LEGAL REDRESS
CO-CHAIRMEN

JOHN M. RAGLAND
LEGISLATIVE

HELEN BURLESON
ENTERTAINMENT

WEST SIDE BOARD MEMBERS
OF THE CHICAGO BRANCH:

DR. A. M. MERCER
JOSEPH MCKINNEY
REV. J. ARCHIE HARGRAVES
FAITH RICH
GEORGE MCCRAE
JOSEPH H. AUSTIN

CORA PATTON ANDREWS
PRESIDENT, CHICAGO BRANCH

Friday, September 23, 1955

Rayfield Mooty
1627 S. Central Park
Chicago, Illinois

Dear Sir:

We would be honored to have you as a guest on the platform at our Mass Rally on Sunday, October 2, 1955, 3:00 P.M. at Stone Temple Baptist Church, 36 22 W. Douglas Blvd., to protest the lynching to Emmett Till.

Sincerely yours,

Joseph Austin

Joseph Austin.

NATIONAL OFFICERS
President
ARTHUR B. SPINGARN
Chairman of the Board
DR. CHANNING H. TOBIAS
Secretary
WALTER WHITE
Administrator
ROY WILKINS
Special Counsel
THURGOOD MARSHALL

NATIONAL ASSOCIATION FOR THE ADVANCEMENT OF COLORED PEOPLE
NATIONAL OFFICE 20 WEST 40th STREET NEW YORK 18, N.Y.
GRAND RAPIDS, MICH. BRANCH MICHIGAN AT MONROE AVENUE
Official Organ: THE CRISIS

GRAND RAPIDS BRANCH OFFICERS
President
ALPHONSE LEWIS, JR.
Vice-President
LOREE GLOVER
Secretary
MRS. SADIE BARHAM
718 Lafayette, S. E.
Assistant Secretary
MRS. MATTIE L. RODGERS
Treasurer
MRS. CARRIE HUSTON

October 31, 1955

Mr. Rayfield Moody
C/o Mrs. Mamie Bradley
6527 St. Lawrence
Chicago, Illinois

Dear Sir:

Please acknowledge our thanks for the fine down-to-earth message that you brought to our mass meeting on Friday, October 21, 1955. I truly hope that Mrs. Bradley's bravery through her long suffering will not be forgotten by this or any other community in this nation.

I trust the message that Mrs. Bradley and you bring will be long remembered.

Very truly yours,

Alphonse Lewis, Jr., President
Grand Rapids Branch, N.A.A.C.P.

AL:ero

HELP US WIN UNQUALIFIED EQUALITY OF OPPORTUNITY FOR ALL AMERICANS . . .

Memorandum: September 27, 1955

To: Mr. David J. McDonald
Mr. I. W. Abel

From: Boyd L. Wilson

Re: Labor Meeting Regarding the Louis E. Till Case

Monsignor Cornelius J. Drew, pastor, St. Charles Roman Catholic Church, before an impressive crowd of ten thousand people in New York City last Sunday, made an impassioned plea that the decent, right-thinking people of the United States rise up and make a repetition of the Till case impossible in America.

He was joined by A. Philip Randolph, president, Brotherhood of Sleeping Car Porters; Roy Wilkins, executive director, NAACP, and City Councilman Earl Brown, before a rally sponsored by trade unions and instigated by the Brotherhood of Sleeping Car Porters, AFL.

I was asked to participate, primarily because Till's grandfather is a member of the Steelworkers' Union and his uncle, Rayfield Mooty, is president of Local Union 3911, Chicago, Illinois

Resolutions were adopted calling upon Governor Hugh White of Mississippi, and the United States Department of Justice to investigate and establish the whereabouts of two missing witnesses. Likewise, to establish, beyond the shadow of a doubt, as to the identity of the body discovered in the river, if indeed it was not that of Till.

The murder of fourteen year old Till was the third known killing of Negroes in Mississippi in recent weeks, for crimes no more serious than exercising the right of vote, or advocating compliance with the Supreme Court decision regarding integration of schools.

The Till case has been a rallying point for liberal movements and peoples within the United States in recent weeks, and it has been my considered judgment that it is to the best interests of the Steelworkers' Union to carry its share of the responsibility and to do what it can to further the cause of justice of all people.

I trust that it will be in accordance with your wishes, since I have been asked, should a national committee of labor and other people be formed, that I be permitted to serve on such committee.

United Steelworkers of America

1500 COMMONWEALTH BUILDING

Pittsburgh 22, Pa.

September 28, 1955

Mr. Rayfield Mooty
5438 S. LaSalle Street
Chicago 9, Illinois

Dear Mooty:

Reliable information from New York supports the suspicion that the meeting now being arranged for that city, October 2nd, involves some questionable possibilities.

You probably noticed a number of telegrams received at last Sunday's meetings. You will recall none of them were read. The reason was some of these wires were from known communists. We could not properly read some of these telegrams and not read others without having demands made for reading all of them, hence rather than read communists demands for action, none of the wires were made public.

I am reliably informed that next Sunday's meetings will provide an opportunity for these communists telegrams to be read, thereby furnishing an opportunity for communists to be identified with our movement. I fear this will tend to kill the support and give hundreds of liberal people an excuse to refuse to support our demand for redress in the brutal murder of an innocent boy in the State of Mississippi.

This is for your information which I trust you will give due and proper consideration.

With warm personal regards.

Fraternally,

Boyd L. Wilson

BLW:gy

P.S. Enclosed is copy of memo OK'D by our International President, David J. McDonald.

Appendix 3

Voices from Outside the Story

TALMADGE ANDERSON: black professor and chief editor of *The Western Journal for Black Studies;* Fort Bragg, North Carolina—

That was a period in my life when I was relatively young, in my twenties. The Emmett Till lynching brought me to a realization of what America was really like. Before then, I had known that black people were under foot in the American society. After Till, it brought to me the focus of what the inhumanity of racism was/is. For all blacks at that particular age and time, it brought to us a realization of how brutal and atrocious racism is. I think it shook blacks in America. Without Emmett Till, King would not have been successful. The lynching and brutal slaying of Till mirrored the whole struggle; it was in the minds of all folks during the King era. It was the new electronic communication media era when all could see. I'm sure that more brutal atrocities happened before Till but there was no way to know about them. They happened in isolation. Till was real; you could see it on TV, over the wire. It just happened at the right time. It was the nucleus, the impetus of the Movement, not the Rosa Parks incident. People had decided that we had better get up from here and fight, do something.

MOLEFE ASANTE: black director of Africana Studies at Temple University; Valdosta, Georgia—

The Emmett Till case was the most awesome event that occurred in my childhood because it revealed to me in the most profound manner how fragile I was as a black boy in America. The impact made me aware for the first time of all that my grandfather Moses and my father, Authur, had told me about black manhood being at risk in America. It came together with the most deafening sound of despair. My life's pilgrimage, in many respects, has been to seek liberation from the moment of Till's death.

MILDRED BARKSDALE: black retired academic dean of the University of Illinois; Atlanta, Georgia—
I remember the Tallahatchie Bridge and this little boy who whistled at a white woman in the candy store, if, in fact, he did and the total lack of regard for human life. If you did feel like somebody, you certainly didn't after Till. You can be as intelligent as you want to be and you can be intimidated by white people. Living in that time, it was not that unusual. This child comes down to visit his uncle and couldn't imagine what could happen. He thought he was free. It's the kind of thing that you just had to relate to. This was a rude; here we were in 1955 trying to emancipate ourselves of what we did not achieve in 1865. You suddenly realize that you haven't come very far in human relations from the early part of the century when lynchings were widespread.

RICHARD BARKSDALE: black Professor Emeritus of English at University of Illinois-Champaign (now deceased); Boston, MA—
It had a very severe emotional effect because it reinforced all of the southern rituals—a young black boy whistling at a white woman and, of course, that takes you back to slavery. The Till case is a reminder of the southern way of life—racial violence.

GEORGE BARLOW: black national poet; Richmond, California—
The Emmett Till lynching, from the time it happened in my early childhood to the present, hasn't lost its horror. Every time I think about it, I think of photographs, like in Richard Wright's Twelve Million Black Voices *with photos of lynchings, those seen in* Places in the Heart. *It makes me ask what I don't hear anybody else asking and that is where are all those people, those citizens who participated in those "festival" events. The common American myth is that this is a handful of drunken rednecks, but the real horror is that these people were "normal citi-*

zens." I think it is the deepest, darkest taboo in our country's past and present. Just the idea of what happened! You multiply that by I don't know how many people that died that way and you're really confronting this country at it's worst. When I hear about the Nazis and the atrocities in the camp, Pogrom and the wholesale slaughter of Native Americans, it always gets me back to the lynchings of black men and women and white sympathizers.

ARTHENIA BATES-MILLIGAN: black author and Professor Emeritus at Southern University; Sumter, South Carolina—
I was teaching at Mississippi Valley State University (then called Mississippi Vocational College) in Itta Bena at the time of the incident. There was an old mill at the edge of the campus and they took the wheel from the campus to weigh him [Till] down. Reporters were here from everywhere, London, everywhere trying to get the story. I remember some saying that this isn't anything new; it happens all the time. But it was so tragic. At that time, things were very tedious: They had a hit list. Medgar Evers was doing a lot of things there. I wanted to do something, but I was so full of terror. It was only after I was away from Mississippi that I was able to put this case in perspective, that I could realize the sadness and the tragedy of it all. One of my student's grandmother had said to him, "Boy, you bett not whistle no mo." That was so sad to me; a boy could not even whistle for fear that it may get to the wrong ears. I kept thinking how sad that was. It made me think of my brother who always loved to whistle. That was an expression of joy. Then I reflected back on Till and wrote the short story "Lost Note."

NOAH BOND: black retired Memphis public school teacher; Memphis, Tennessee—
The main thing is the impact of the rural South over the changing thought patterns in the fifties. There was this terrible resis-

tance of white southerners to realizing the humanity of blacks, an assault on the initial changing attitudes blacks were manifesting in the Deep South. Their attitudes were brought about out of World Wars I and II, attitudes which affected the blacks who were living in the South. Whites wanted to maintain the tradition. As a result, when the alleged flirtation was to have taken place, here was a nigger with "uppity ideas." After that there was the immobilization against even wishing to break down the tradition. That was something that stayed with me. The result of what happened affected me to being extremely active in civil rights. It made me determined to be involved in the NAACP, any way I could involve myself to improve the race relations in Memphis. It changed my attitude to the point that I got a true picture of what basically white people think. From then on, I was able to detect the tonal quality of the denial of my humanity. The whites of that time tried to find excuses. T.V. had just come to Memphis, and the Till incident stayed in the news about a month. They tried to discredit his mother. From that experience, I got a total different picture of what it was going to be like to break down the mental attitudes. I was fired seven times for my stands for civil rights issues. Had it not been for the Till situation, I would not have been able to cope with it. I think about that even now. It's always there.

SHANI BROOKS: black University of Iowa Medical Social Worker; Memphis, Tennessee—
I was angry, angry to the point of being obsessed with it and hatred because I felt that he was a child caught up in white America's hatred for black people. Emmett Till was a victim of white pathology. What it validated for me in terms of white people's relating to black people as human beings was somewhat of an illusion because white people will have to be forced to do that because I don't think that they have the innate capacity to acknowledge them or even treat people as human beings when they belong to a different race. I think that's because white people are

caught up in that whole special type of white socialization, thinking, even as little children, that they are the best, the center of the universe, that they determine if anyone else is good or bad, pretty or ugly. In other words, they use themselves as a measurement for all other people. If you don't measure up to what they believe or determine as right or good or bad, they either destroy you or control you, one or the other. Even those who claim that they have never been taught racism by their parents in words, they've been taught in deed, reactions, and behaviors toward people of color. Till to me is the epitome of America's justice when we finally reach the court room and all of the white men got off scot-free, didn't even get chastised, just walked off free as if they were innocent babes.

BILLIE CAMPBELL: black child welfare specialist; Chicago, Illinois—
I think that it was a classic case of injustice, but that was the mentality of the rednecks during that period—thinking that any white woman was too good for the attentions of any black man. I think that in some instances it may have done some good. For example, some whites saw the injustices which made them come out of the wood works to fight for civil rights. I think a lot of those bizarre cases where people could see the injustices, could see the cruelty, where they didn't have to dig out and think it through, raised the consciousness. It was obvious; they could see it. It struck me as a cruel thing but it raised the national consciousness as to the injustices to the black race.

WILFRED CARTEY: distinguished black professor of African World Literature at City College of the City University of New York (now deceased)—
The Till incident happened when I came to this country at first as a Fulbright graduate student at Columbia. I encountered total racism. The case catalyzed me, the sense of deep anguish. I felt that the Civil Rights struggle really began then. When the Till

case broke, I could have committed murder; my body almost betrayed me. I started running down South right away. I started going South for freedom marches even before they started. That whole Emmett Till story and that time lies on the conscience of this country. Emmett Till is symbol, reality, fact. He epitomizes the viciousness of this country.

THEO JAMES CARVER: black Sears employee; Brunswick, Georgia—
During the time when I was coming up, there were many lynchings of young black men who had been accused of saying sexual words to white women, like "Baby you look fine and sweet." This was back there in the fifties in Brunswick, Georgia. Mama always said that you never mess with a white woman anyway, 'cause you get yourself in trouble or killed for nothing and a white woman ain't worth it. 'Course a white woman is known for flirting all the time but you just ignore her, keep on about your business.

ALVIN CHAMBLISS: black civil rights attorney; Columbia, Mississippi—
I was with my grandmother in Columbia, Mississippi (my mother was still in New Orleans) and she was very strong in the movement. Her position was "Don't say anything to white folks, and especially white women. The Lord will avenge this horrible incident." I later found out that she was actively involved although she would stop us from talking about our rights because she was trying to protect us from a hostile environment of white folks. I thought that she was afraid of white folks. But I came to find out later that she was not only not afraid of them but insisted on her rights. Till, Charles Mack Parker (lynched in Pearl River County in Popularville, Mississippi), Verner Damer (lynched in Hattiesburg, Mississippi), Noah (a black man who was light-skinned and apparently had been wronged in some manner and decided to fight back; he took a rifle and killed sev-

eral whites and got away. When he was caught, he was placed in an asylum. We all saw him as a hero, like John Brown—all of these lynching motivated me to being a civil rights attorney, committing me to a life-time struggle for black people.

JOHN HENRIK CLARKE: black Professor Emeritus of African World History at Hunter College, City University of New York; New York City—
The Till incident was the direct line between the confrontation between the blacks and the whites, the raw show of the deficiency of Southern manhood. People confront us because they do not have the courage to confront themselves. If the southern white looked at himself, he would see that the northern financier is his real enemy. It's like they are saying, "You'll be the agrarian; we'll be the industrialist." We become the scapegoat of scapegoats.

MARIAN COLEMAN: black public school teacher; Cheraw, South Carolina—
That thing scared the hell out of me because I thought that any boy that looked at a white woman could be killed the same way Emmett Till was killed. It was just a frightening situation to imagine that your friends could get killed. It wasn't for a very long time that I realized that it was just a brutal murder and that the same crime would probably not be duplicated on whites for the same reasons they gave us.

EVELYN CONNERS: white retired licensed practical nurse; Iowa City, Iowa—
They said he [Till] was an "uppity nigger" from up North. That's what we read in the Cedar Rapids News Gazette *or the* Iowa City Press Citizen, *one or the other. It got quite a bit of coverage in Iowa. I can remember talking to a friend and she said, "Why did he go down there?" I got so angry with her. Why can't he go down there; he had relatives there, didn't he? They*

didn't want a northerner down there, black or white, because they would go back North and tell about it, which they thought would start some sort of repercussion. You just don't know how a jury can come back with an acquittal. I really think this should be tried even today, by the United States Court of Law because he was tried then by the State Court of Mississippi.

JAMES CROFT: black Mississippian who ran for judge; Sumner, Mississippi—
It was hush, hush. Really, seriously, that's basically what it was like. You actually didn't learn too much about it until you began to grow up and read about it and different things like that even though it happened just right below you. I lived in Webbs, just nine, ten, or twelve miles actually from where it happened so you didn't know very much about it. You know it was basically fear. The person that was sheriff at the time, his son is about to be sheriff again. So you can see how much progress we've made, not very much.

DOUG DAVIDSON: black sociologist at City College of New York; Vandalia, Michigan—
The most frightening thing about the Till incident was that it could have been me. We had cousins from St. Louis and Chicago and they came every summer and when we moved up North, we did the same thing, going to visit our grandmother. The reason we had to leave in '54 was because my older brother and some of his friends had beaten up some white boys and we left under a sort of emergency. It could have been me, my brothers, my uncles. And then when I went to Toogaloo in '61, Mack Charles Parker was fished out of one of those rivers in the Delta. Anger, too. I was one of those who, after that, wanted to get a gun. I'd always thought that was the only way we'd get respect from them; if they killed one of us, we'd have to take one of them. "An eye for an eye." Like my grandmama said; that's what the Bible said.

HAZEL DIXON: black LeMoyne-Owen College teacher; Memphis, Tennessee—
Emmett was only fourteen. He was down to stay with his grandpeople. He did not know anything about "yes mam" and "yes sir." He spoke to the white woman wrong in her mind; that's all he knew to say. He did not understand the tradition of the South, and she told the other people that the boy had molested her. The baby did not know what molestation was. He did not know it was wrong to not be subservient. That boy was lynched, killed right there where I was brought up. He had a different accent, and they decided to destroy him, and they did. They thought that here was a northern boy that tried to be aggressive. Rednecks always think that you want their women. The thing that was so sad to me was that Till was trying to deal with race prejudice that he didn't know nothing about. The outcome, however, was that everyone decided to not have anything to do with them. The wife was ostracized. They were not able to live in Mississippi society anymore. They lived in ostracism.

ALMA DORSEY: black cosmetologist; New Orleans, Louisiana—
It was the most horrible thing I had ever heard of. It was devastating and it just made you cry. I cried for the family, I cried for him; it was just a horrible feeling all around. I still have papers I saved on him. I don't know if anything ever affected me as this did. The child was so young and innocent. Right now, when you think about it, it just brings tears to your eyes.

ANNETTE DUNZO: black Howard University professor; Memphis, Tennessee—
I was very shocked and frightened as a pre-teenager. I knew him as about the same age I was; it was similar to having it happen to a friend of mine. I was additionally shocked by the pictures I saw. To this day it has left a bitter taste in my mouth. Whenever

I go through Mississippi, I have a lingering memory of that kind of terror that befalls blacks in a black/white situation.

MARY FLEMMINGS: black resident of Greenwood, Mississippi; Chicago, Illinois—
I was in my forties and was living in Chicago. When they said that he gave a wolf whistle, it was said that it wasn't true. They got him out from his grandpa's house and put sankers [weights] on him and killed him. I was very, very upset, sure was. It stayed with me a long time. Still with me.

ADDISON GAYLE: renowned black literary critic (now deceased); New York City—
To me, it was a metaphor for this country. I wasn't surprise that it happened because that is the way America was and is. As terrible as it was, it was a more honest act than those perpetrated by more "respectable" racists, such as those presently seen in the Reagan Administration.

KATHY GIBSON: black college professor; New York City—
I remember it was really something vivid. There were a lot of rallies in New York. Either my mother took me or I just went. I couldn't believe that anybody could get killed for whistling, or whistling at any body at all. I remember being more shocked than angry. Whistling—that's regular, that's minor. I remember reading about people getting killed or put in jail for so-called infractions, some violation of some man-made law. But whistling did not fit into any category or regulation. To whistle was such a natural thing that it was shocking that anyone could be killed for it.

LUCY GRIGSBY: black Professor Emeritus at Atlanta University; Atlanta, Georgia—
Some of the newspapers called it eyeball rape. I thought it was one of the more outlandish situations involving blacks and whites. Here is this kid whom nobody accused of actual, physical rape. He looked at a white woman and lost his life. The absurdity of race relations in the United States at that time was dramatically set forth by the accusation against this kid who eventually lost his life. But the thing goes beyond race relations. To me it's more of that perception of one category of people (white folks or black folks). Those white folks had no sense of the humanity of black folks, which is a comment on human relations. The teaching was that many black persons were taught as a child not to look directly at white people. And especially black men were taught not to look at white women. Here was a kid from the North who was not taught that.

MARY HARRIS: black retired laundry worker; Gary, Indiana—
I thought it was terrible. Just because he whistled at the lady, they killed him. I was just real angry. People talked about it a lot here in Gary, on the job at the hospital and around.

ROBERT HARRIS: black retired steel mill worker; Gary, Indiana—
I can say one thing—it was one of the most brutal things I've ever heard of. It took a long time for people to get over it. One of the guys who killed Till moved to Gary, Indiana that next year and opened up a store in black Oaks on the corner of 25 and Burr and blacks got in the wind of it and he had to let it go. It was one of the awesomeness things I ever heard of.

RICHARD HATCHER: black former mayor of Gary, Indiana; Michigan City, Indiana—
It was very frightening, very intimidating to think that white people were capable of doing that to a young black boy. It made me very angry and bitter towards white people. That's how I felt at that particular time.

KING HENRY: black retired federal employee (now deceased); St. Louis, Missouri—
When this news first hit in this particular area, a crisis orientated community, they [blacks] came out of the shell and cooperated. It takes a tragedy to arouse them. Most of the people got very upset about it. They had planned a meeting at the Masonic Hall, one of the largest places owned by blacks. I had never seen a crowd so large. The place was just packed. Some of the relatives from Chicago were the main speakers. Afterwards they starting to collecting money for legal expenses to try to bring about justice. The people gave very generously and they collected bushels of money. A lot of churches collected money also. When I went back to work, I detected some negative reactions from the black workers. I noticed productivity among black workers went down. It also affected race relations among blacks and whites. It promoted sloppy workmanship among blacks who normally took pride in their jobs. It promoted job absenteeism. Also there was a destruction of white property in some of the areas where people were not very affluent. There was a disrespect for authority on the job and where policemen were concerned. It also provoked a tax on white people who were in the neighborhood who were not aware of this meeting that took place. His age was what really got next to the people, the tender age of fourteen.

RICHARD HILL: black contractor; Oxford, Mississippi—
At that particular time, I think I was traumatized; he was close to my own age. The same time that happened, I had a friend who was a white girl who picked cotton along with me. And after the

incident, my people became frightened for me because she was a white girl, and she liked me and indicated that. That could be one of my reasons for getting the hell out of the South.

DALE M. HILLER: white chemist; Wilmington, Delaware—
It seemed to me that it was just part of the continuity, that we fight wars about these things and it all boils down to not being able to treat people as human being. Those guys who killed Till didn't know him and they didn't even care who he was. He was a reflection of their fears, their insecurities. But hardly any of those people know anything about Emmett Till. That's evil.

ENDESHA IDA MAE HOLLAND: black professor at the University of New York at Buffalo and Playwright; Greenwood, Mississippi—
We all were stunned in the Delta when we heard about Emmett Till. I remember my mother in 1955 when she told my brothers, Bud and Simon, Jr., "Y'all hide, y'all hide." And she said to them, "Now you see why I been telling y'all don't be looking up in no white women's faces 'cause you see what happened to the boy from Chicago." One of the funeral men was there when they actually pulled him out (a lot of folks were there from my home town). He said, "As long as I've been embalming bodies, I ain't never throwed up before, until I saw that boy from Chicago's body."

ROSIE HOLLY: black retired school teacher and spiritual advisor; Memphis, Tennessee—
I felt it was very distressing, and it was a time when everything was so frightening. You had read about things like that, and now you knew that it could happen. I thought he [Till] was an "unlearned" person from the North, who did not show good judgment. His attitude didn't help him, I don't believe. I think that the whites who did it were animals, with the type of pit bull

dog attack mentality, trained to attack blacks. Just because this boy whistled, they thought he deserved to die.

JUANITA HUDSON: black entrepreneur; Memphis, Tennessee—
I remember it vaguely. It was frightening and it was also sad to know that people could be that cruel and get away with it. I felt that it was totally unnecessary and it was an injustice. It made me feel that white people were just sick. It was a big write-up about it in the newspapers and people were really up-set about it. I can still see his face. He had an honest face, an easy-going face. When you think about, it seems like yesterday.

TOMMIE LEE. HUDSON: black contractor (now deceased); Memphis, Tennessee—
My trying to reflect on something like that during that time, with my present frame of reference and mind, is something entirely different. It puts fire in you. I was angry about Caucasians doing that, angry about anything they did to blacks like that. You know when something like that happens something ain't right. Seeing everyone else being afraid of them, what else is there for you to do.?. You had to be a special individual to come up like that.

LENA JAMES: black machine operator; Memphis, Tennessee—
I was a child, the same age as Till. He was black like me. I remember how I cried. I thought it was the most hideous thing I'd ever heard of. He had gone away to have a good time and had gone where he had never been before. I thought how unnatural it was for him to be in a place where people were so cruel and prejudiced and bitter against black people and he was from up North, naive. I never understood that kind of hatred because I never spent that much time around white people as a child. I knew we looked different but I thought that people were people

and that hearts were the same universally. All the other hangings didn't faze me as a child because I was a child and lived a child's existence. But when this happened, this was another child and naturally this got my attention. I couldn't see where a child could cause such an impact on a community just because he was black. That was the reason, the only reason and that he whistled at a white woman. I followed all the news, the pictures, all of it. When they brought him up from the waters and how he looked, that was always imbedded in my memory. They showed everything and they told everything. The story was so gross, every detail. The press played such an important part in showing how he looked before and after. I had such a relationship with that whole thing. I tried to play myself in the role as the mother and how she must have felt when she received the news, blaming herself for even allowing him to go in such a prejudiced world that he was not ever familiar with. I'm sure he didn't have the fortitude to know what his action could cost him. Then my heart went out to the great uncle for how he would feel and how he would have to face that child's mother. And the hurt would always be there. Oh, I'm sure there was a lot of blaming going on there. Then I remember, oh so well, the bitterness that sprung up in me towards the woman herself. I remember how I felt thinking that she would have to live with this for the rest of her life. It caused me to be so bitter against white people in general for a long time in my own life and it had such an impact on me that I never wanted to be a part of Mississippi. I shuddered at the word Mississippi because it brought back so many bad memories. Nobody ever said that he had whistled before, at her or anybody else for that matter. It only happened one time, at least recorded, with him and he lost his life.

JOYCE M. JOHNSON: black Chicago investment broker (now deceased); East Chicago, Indiana—
I felt that we were powerless to do anything. I felt sad for his [Till's] mother. I think that I felt a little disheartened that, if the

flirting part was correct, many blacks would always have that tendency to be attracted to other people more than to our own self or to our own people. It is very devastating. We are not yet at the point where we are reminding ourselves of that event; we have a tendency to go on and repeat our mistakes because of our tendency to want to forget and that is not the best posture for our people. We do not need to forget. Some of our youngsters do not know anything about it and that is unfortunate.

CHINWA KENJYATTA: black fashion designer; Seaford, Delaware—
It was the worst case I'd ever heard of. It was just horrifying to know that people lived like that and humans treated each other like that. We were having race problems in Delaware, and I'll never forget, my whole class was upset about it. It was the first time that our school had addressed such an issue and I was going to a black school. It hit home with me, what this whole racial thing was about. Even my children today, at ten and twelve, asked me about it; they wanted to know everything I knew about the Till case.

OLA KENNEDY: black mid-western labor-union activist; Gary, Indiana—
For me it was such a horrible thing. I felt sad, mad. I think that that turned people on to the fact they had to really start thinking and doing something about civil rights. The hurt and the shock of it went so deep that I think that it moved me more to wanting to be committed to the struggle to change the unjust situation more so than the Rosa Parks' refusal to move because that had really happened before. Maybe it did not receive the same notoriety. I think that people around you, even the whites, would look at you sort of different. My supervisor was in a sort of trance, the expression on his face. They knew what the burden was like and it really was a burden. I felt angry and hurt, a mixture of the two. I think really the climax, if there was any doubt in your

mind, was when the body was brought back to Chicago. That really did it. I think it really affected people. Everybody was really sincere at that time. It kind of really shook you up so that you really wanted to do something. That lit a fire that probably made others not able to take what they were able to take in the past. The Emmett Till death really started the fire that really made us know that we had to make changes.

JAMES SCOTT KING: black chairman of the department of English at Delaware State College; Marion, South Carolina—
I remember their mentioning it in school; we were told that there was a lesson to be learned and that we should avoid encounters with white girls. The term "reckless eye-balling" came up as a sort of joke among black boys. This incident served as a kind of general warning that we were still in the South and that we still had to be careful in all of our actions and that the same thing could happen in Marion, South Carolina that happened in Mississippi.

SANDY KRAVITZ: white fashion designer; New York City—
My immediate reaction was that they were just looking for an excuse to kill a black. Anything would have triggered the reaction to kill. I don't think that it had anything to do with what they said. It was no different from the Germans, the Nazis, no reason except inbred hatred—a pretty damn feeble excuse for killing unless you just want to kill. My opinion was that he just had to be there; that was all that was needed. He was a victim. Who would know what really happened. It was a made up reason, a false reason, no reality. They just wanted a scapegoat for their own inadequacy. Just like South Africa. Blaming the victim—that's what it is.

CHARLOTTE KUH: white economist; Chicago, Illinois—
I was eleven and lived north of Chicago. That was a real big thing. What it did to us as northern liberals was it really brought home that the South was a dangerous place filled with red necks, really violent, irrational people. To an eleven-year-old, a fourteen-year-old wasn't that different and we knew kids that whistled. It was a terrible shocking thing. For a lot of people, that was a central event. My mother was from Georgia. After that when we would go to Savannah, it made me very leery of strangers down there, that kind of feeling that any southern person was capable of this sort of violence. It made people of the North feel self righteous and there wasn't any justification for northerners to feel superior and feel that it was them and not us also. I remember that picture and the picture of the crowd. I think it was in the Sun Times *because we didn't take* Jet *in my household. I'm really glad that someone is doing a study on this.*

KATIE THOMPSON LACKY: black head nurse at Mississippi Valley State University; Itta Bena, Mississippi—
When it happened, we just got furious. We were just about angry with every white person in the South. We were just angry and hurt. I just wondered and I said now, I wouldn't let no child go out of my house with a white man, knowing that he might beat my child up or whatever. He'd have to kill me; he'd have to take me on out with him. And we were just angry to the point where as it was so tense at the hospital. We just couldn't work well and this was all that we could think about is what happened to the child. And the grandfather, of course, during those days, they were afraid of their boss man. And these people owned the plantation out there what came to pick him up. And then after they took him away, they didn't know what had happened to him. The grandfather reported it and the next three or four days they found the body floating on the water. I just can't tell you how we felt. We were just hurt and stunned. We didn't even feel like communicating with the white people we were working for.

It was to that point. And, of course, a lot of them expressed how they felt and how angry they were that this happened. Because things were really supposed to be getting a little bit better. This was the beginning of it [the Movement] I believe. The half brother helped to do this the murder], Milan. He has a store right there on the corner here in Itta Bena. And so it could have been possible [getting the cotton gin fan used to weigh Till down in the river] cause at that time, the school was rather young because the school was opened in '51. And they probably had a lot of old materials and stuff around on the campus. They probably saw this and maybe got it. But believe me, they have suffered.

JOYCE A. LADNER: black sociologist; Hattiesburg, Mississippi—
I remember Emmett Till; I was eleven or twelve then. I still remember the picture of him in Jet, his face grotesque, disfigured. His mother refused to have his face reconstructed during the embalming; she wanted to show to society his face. What I remember most was each day running literally three blocks to the store to get the Hattiesburg American *newspaper. My sister and I would lie on our stomachs on the floor and read the articles. I remember crying over it, and the tremendous fear. I think that it was one of the greatest influences that ultimately led me to becoming a scholar, a sociologist. It was impossible for me to become a dispassionate observer. I am more of an active observer, dealing with policy implication and finding solution to the problems. I don't deal with a lot of abstract ideals in and within themselves, and quite by choice. I was able to identify with Till because he was my age. I had never heard of a child out of a racial incident being killed before Till. Back then, I was used to people living a long time. And he wasn't from here; he was an outside child, and killed. It's like saying you're not safe. I felt very vulnerable. I shared it with some of my friends. I had always looked at northerners as less vulnerable, being able to go back home. I felt that this could happen to my brother, my father.*

Since I was a girl, I was maybe not as open to being murdered, but I felt that something could happen to me like being raped or some other terrible thing. I felt powerless, but optimistic that justice would prevail. I have felt then that the government in Washington would come in and give us justice, because we couldn't get it from white Mississippians. I felt that it wouldn't happen again, but it did happen, again and again. I also felt very, very sorry for him. What do they call us in the South? Tender hearted. I felt the pain he felt as much as you could feel it. Empathy. I felt sorry for his mother and his uncle with whom he was staying, for their loss and their pain and sorrow. My mother had a friend who was a root doctor, not a psychic, but who sold natural medicine. We called him "Cuz." During that time in the fifties, the NAACP was underground in my area and Cuz was an acknowledged NAACP member. To be an undercover NAACP member was really something to be proud of then. He subscribed to Jet Magazine, Ebony, and other black magazines and would bring those papers to our house and my sister, Dorie, and I would read these events, which were not recorded in the local papers. The white papers were so censored. We got our accurate information from rumors and black presses. It was like bringing information into a wilderness. It showed what we could not have access to in our own state. It was the first time we knew that a child was murdered. They were usually men. It took the opposition of whites to another level. A very important thing is that it followed the Supreme Court decision in 1954. It's like the whites said that they don't care what rights we were given. And they went overboard in the other direction. It was perhaps a flagrant act, giving whites more rights. It served as a grave incident that showed people how intractable a problem could be and how difficult a solution would be. So when the spark came in Mississippi to sit in the public library, for example, people who participated had been incensed by the Till incident and were just waiting for the spark to come. The Till incident was the catalyst.

CHERYL LEGGON: black educator; Ohio—
I just remember that it was just horrifying. Although my family is from Louisiana, I never went South until I was twenty-two. I was terrified of the South; I thought I would get lynched. We used to get Jet Magazine every week and I remember the pictures. I remember not being able to understand why being accused of whistling at a woman would be a capital crime, for which he was not even tried in court. It was a sort of "vigilante justice" (townspeople would take justice in their own hands). It wasn't even that. In fact, there was no conscious deliberation, weighing of facts, consideration of justice. There wasn't anything just about it. You literally take the law in your own hands and it can be abused. The problem with taking the law in your own hands is that you think that you are above law or that you can define it. And I don't even think that they considered him human. It was a gut reaction, what the whole lynch-mob psychology was about—the unbridled, the base emotions without any social or moral element. The reason I got into sociology was to get answers to these sort of issues, which were social rather than psychological.

MINNIE WALKER LOGAN: black public high school counselor; Memphis, Tennessee—
My first response when I heard it was anger because of what had happened. I was hurt because a young person's life had been taken. He had not been given a chance or opportunity to prove that he was guilty or innocent or anything. I also felt when I finally could calm down that I had to do whatever I could to keep those things from happening again. Whether small or large, I felt that I had to do something for my race. Those feelings have still not left today. I still have that sad feeling when I think about it even today; we will never know what he could have become because his life was taken so early.

CHRISTINE MALDONADO: black medical professional (now deceased); Evanston, Illinois—
The boy was really from Chicago, and his parents were originally from Mississippi. He had gone there to visit. At first the papers in Evanston, Illinois, where I was living, was pretending that it was an accident. They were trying to cover it up. But so many people knew something about it, and they could not cover it up any more. My feelings at that particular time was wondering why people go to that kind of place for vacation when there are so many other places to go. I had gone to Mississippi in 1944, and I visited that place. I got frightened and was apprehensive about going down there. During that time, Governor Bilbo was having blacks, who were coming back from World War II with a different attitude, executed in the open, right there in the square in Holly Springs, Mississippi. They were being hard on people returning. This really frightened me. For that reason, I thought it was a horrible place, and I would never go back there. I could never understand why people go to that place.

EMOGENE McCATHEN: black counselor for the Atlanta public school system; Pass Christian, Mississippi—
Living in Mississippi, I felt that that was sad that something like that had to happen to an innocent black child. I remember Mama and Daddy talking about it; they never dwelt on it that much, perhaps because the crime was so terrible. They didn't really want to discuss it with their children and I can understand that. It was such a hideous crime. I was only nine then.

CLYDE McGLAUN: black semi-retired housekeeper; Memphis, Tennessee—
I thought that it was a low-down trick for a boy that age; and they do that sort of thing today. They didn't allow him a chance. Meanness and low-downness, that's all it was.

CAMILLA MILAM: black Iowa cosmetologist; Chicago, Illinois—
It was a shame, a terrible tragedy. And I really don't think justice was done. It was bad because he was just a young person who had just begun life. Whatever white person did it should be hung. I was really angry about that. It was a shame for a thing like that to even go on, and they know about it.

ELZA H. MINOR: black American businessman; Richmond, California—
I was born and raised in New Jersey. My mother was a teacher and she told me that race was just on more obstacle to overcome. I had had no serious confrontations with racism. When the headlines hit about Emmett Till and I read the events that led up to his murder, I realized that I was reading about someone the same age as I was, who evidently represented a threat to white maleness to the extent that they felt that they needed to murder him. That shocked me into the reality that my blackness was more than just a barrier to overcome. This made me reexamine all of my relationships with white people.

MARIA K. MOOTRY: black educator; Chicago, Illinois—
The first thing I remember was standing in line and the line snaked for blocks just like with Harold Washington's funeral. We stood in line for at least two hours, everybody waiting, patient, to see the body of Emmett Till with their own eyes. I was eleven when we went to see Till. We had just moved to Chicago form the South (Nashville, Tennessee) in August, my introduction to Chicago. Our cousins had bragged about Chicago and we were excited. That week I got there, Till was killed. I remember his face; it was greenish. White people were saying that this was not an eleven-year-old kid; he looked like an old man. He had gone down south. People always talked about going down south. What a horrible thing it was, killed for looking or whistling at a

white woman. I'll never forget it—all those people brought together by the death of a child.

MENSA MOOTY: black retired labor-union activist; Chicago, Illinois (wife of Rayfield and second cousin by marriage of Emmett Till)—
I prayed, Father please, just stick a foot up and let 'em see his foot 'cause they want him found. Killing that child, he begging 'em not to kill him, crying for his mama. And that's the way they found him, too, that foot sticking up.

H.E. NEWSUM: black professor and social critic; Memphis, Tennessee—
What I remember is negative, but you have to understand the thinking of a young black child in the fifties before the black consciousness movement in the sixties took place. I remember thinking that the Jet Magazine story that my parents were talking about was so distasteful, the actual picture of Till and all of the water damage. I remember wondering why Jet published such a distasteful thing. I was also angered by what happened to Till. Anger and emotions that adults around me exerted influenced my thinking about white on black violence. It was my first introduction to white on black violence. Before that I had no real concept of the violence that existed between white folks and black folks. It was actually the Till incident that made me realize that it was a hostile and antagonistic relationship between the races. And the most memorable thing about it was the feeling as a young boy that I was unsafe and that white women were taboo.

ERMA O'HARA: black Dallas public school teacher; Jackson, Mississippi—
Living in Mississippi, I had experienced some harsh treatments from whites myself and thinking of my personal experiences and what had happened to him terrified me. Then I noticed that in the black community there were feelings of courage and strength

and togetherness that really encouraged me at that young age. And somehow I was able to cope with that fear because I felt so secure in that community, with my black relatives and friends and teachers and church folks. I shall never forget.

MARY COHRAN PEARSON: black retired cosmetologist; Memphis, Tennessee—
Everybody was upset; I know that. I really can't remember the details. The boy was all swollen up, they say, looked like an old man. Those folks killed that poor little boy 'cause he whistled at a white woman, they say. Pitiful.

MATTHEW PEARSON: black retired railroad worker; Memphis, Tennessee—
I can't remember exactly. I know he got killed in Money, Mississippi, didn't he? I heard about it. They say he whistled at a white woman and they did him worst than they would do a dog. It was really bad, really wrong. And they threw him in some river and tied a weight around his neck. That was terrible. That's all I can say.

OJIDA PENN: black musicologist; Montgomery, Alabama—
I remember hearing about Emmett Till in Mississippi; I was twelve then and remember thinking that these white people are really evil. More than anything else it showed me how evil and little they regarded black life. What? He was killed for that. Damn! This was after the Brown vs. Board of Education, *which was a signal that thing were all right, and you sort of let your guards down thinking that integration was just around the corner. All you had to do was let the word out. But when Till was killed, that made me reconsider where we were. Till sort of shocked me out of that momentary complacency into which I had lapsed.*

DORIS POWELL: black LeFlore county (Mississippi) hospital clerk; Greenwood, Mississippi—
It was a shock that anyone would be so cold-hearted to do a thing like that. The only emotion that I can remember was just fear. I was very young, ten years old and it's difficult for a kid to understand why anyone could do such a thing so cruel. Who would they chose to lynch next? That was the question. The kid hadn't really done anything. They say that he whistled at a white woman. White people used that as a measure to keep blacks in line, to keep the fear in black people to keep them humble. I think that it was fear tactic, lynchings and what have you. If you decide to do anything on your own, you'd be next.

JEWELL PRESTAGE: black political scientist; Houston, Texas—
By that particular period, a lynching was not an everyday occurrence, even in Texas where I was teaching at the time (Texas Southern University). I remember discussing it with several people from Mississippi and getting their reaction to it. It was a shock but I think the thing that stood out in my mind was the story in <u>Look Magazine</u> *about the follow-up of the case. One White person who lived in that area in Mississippi said that he did not want too much to do with those people who killed Till because he felt that if they got away with killing a Black, they could get away with killing White people. They were fed up with that kind of behavior on the part of Whites in that area and really started to regard these people as a lower element in society. That was the only ray of hope that came out of the whole incident. It was such a terrible incident. The follow-up story indicated that the accused were ostracized by the rest of the community. I was angry because you know that the administration of justice would result in the accused party being exonerated. The other thing about this particular case was that the people were not killing the healthy adult, but a handicapped child. So it seemed to be in the final analysis so senseless—whistling at a*

grown woman and the fact that he did not attempt to do her any harm. This is also a reflection of the insecurity of the male of the "master" race. More revealing is that it says something about the White southern male's attitude toward his woman. He regards her as a pawn, defenseless, unable to deal with the real world, as his personal property. It is also an indication of the fear he had that his woman would be attracted to a Black man.

EVELYN REAVES: black acting dean with a Gary Public School; St. Louis, Missouri—
I was terrified when I first heard it. I was a child myself and was appalled that someone could do that to a child. I thought it was a heinous crime. I found myself looking at the picture of his swollen head in Jet over and over again. It was a topic of conversation among my friends and me for months; we talked of nothing else. I thought those people who lynched him were the scum of the earth and I was afraid that they were going to be feted as heroes in their community for having rid themselves of what they perceived as a "crazy nigger" from up North. I was very pleased with the fact that these people were later ostracized by many of their own peers.

ARKELA REVELS: black storyteller and community activist; Detroit, Michigan—
It was 1955, four days after my fifteenth birthday. I remember that it came on one of the black radio stations. Because blacks in Detroit were in very concentrated areas in the city (all over), and because of the cohesiveness of various southerners that had migrated to Detroit ever since the Great Migration after World War I, the news just traveled very fast. The response was outrage that he was missing, number one. Then it was the period of days when they were looking for him. And after that, the shock that they found him in the river. Immediately I recall hearing about the scheduled funeral in Chicago. Within a few weeks, we were getting messages from our black newspapers and black

churches that they were going to hold rallies so that people could get the true story about what had happened. Then I remember that the rumors were that they had castrated him and done other mutilating things to the young man's body. Finally the Jet Magazine picture came out, right after the funeral, instant reporting. They were there like Johnny-on-the-spot to report the news to the nation and to black people. We have to appreciate the diligence of our black news media, such as Jet and the Michigan Chronicle. I recall being very appalled at the happenings in this case. I was following it. I heard about the rally at New Bethel Baptist Church, headed by the Rev. C. L. Franklin (Aretha Franklin's father). He had been announcing the rally, the purpose and was providing leadership at a very crucial time. At the rally they had speakers; the mother of Emmett Till was there and people had the opportunity to meet her, which gave people a more realistic identification with this case. People wanted to contribute either time or money to draw attention and awareness, creating enough friction that the whole city of Detroit was very much riled up to the point that masses of people that had never formally been really active (they had been passive protesters) protested. Although I was only fifteen, the horror of the incident was such that the arousal of people in Detroit included young people like myself. I rose up for the occasion and was in attendance at New Bethel Baptist Church for the rally to hear and see for myself and share the pain of his mother. I also remember the outpouring of donations, regardless of the negative rumors that were going around that she was trying to gain sympathy from people and that she would not use the money for the intended purpose. In other words, there was skepticism but people poured out money still. The place was packed and I think that probably other places where she was to appear attracted the same heart-felt kinds of people. It affected my life and I have a pain every time I recall the picture in the Jet Magazine or hear the name Emmett Till. It became indelible in my mind. So that even today, when I hear his name, it conjures the picture in Jet with him fixed up for the funeral, his body swollen, looking like an old man.

JANIE RHYNE: white retired psychologist; Marianna, Florida—
I had studied psychology at that time and it was just beyond my comprehension that people who call themselves human could do that. I still have the same feelings now. I feel that they demonstrated primitive emotions. These people who killed him were not evolved humans; they were less than human. It has something to do with the brain or development, which has to do with rearing, too. The horrible thing is that people like that will usually find a minority or someone who is different, and act out their emotions without any sense of decency or human passion. In this particular case, Till was a perfect victim—a stranger and black. Till was not only black but was from a different culture; he behaved differently from the fourteen-year-old Mississippi black boy. What was natural in his behavior in Chicago, they used to put into action their own perverted animal instincts (the limbic system, our emotional process) as if the human higher awareness simply wasn't functioning. They turned that off or blocked it out, that which makes us human. The most horrible of all was that they could do this to Till because he was black, which kept them from seeing him as a human being. The other horrible thing was that people with any reasonable intelligence or awareness could think and act as if black people are not human. As far as I know, these people did not think this thing out; they did not use their Cortex (the rational brain, the process of knowing, recognizing). They cut off all thinking and reacted to their emotions and instincts. I don't suppose anybody truly understands it; I certainly don't.

BOB RUDMAN: white Professor Emeritus of molecular biology; Philadelphia, Pennsylvania—
The Till murder happened very early in the Civil Rights Movement, after the Supreme Court decision in the Brown versus Topeka, Kansas Board of Education. I remember that I was very upset about it but not surprised about it, as I had come to expect that sort of thing in Mississippi, much to my regret. I vaguely remember some meetings. It happened before the real unfolding of the Civil Rights Movement. Actually in the updating of the movement, he [Till] still is not reflected.

CROSBY SMITH: black great-uncle of Till who escorted Till's body back to Chicago; Sumner, Mississippi—
When it happened to him down here where I was at, they happened to get a hold to me and had me look for him. I put out looking for him, a hard three days. So finally we heard where he was at, in a river down near Money. And that's where they got him at and got the body and I got him away from here and got him up North. I was down here and went down to the grave site where they had the grave at and they were getting ready to bury him, but my sister hadn't got there. She was up there at my house and I was down there. Her name was Lizzy; she's dead now. [When they abducted Till], she had to stay in there (the bed room) from the time they got there 'cause they didn't want her to stay there and watch the bed, wouldn't let her get out. One stayed there and watched her and wouldn't let her out. He went on back in there and showed where he was sleeping, showed 'em the bed he was sleeping in. They hired a sheriff from here who carried me down there and we rushed on out there, got out there just in time to keep them from putting the dirt on him. They were waiting on Lizzy to come so she could be there. But for some cause they got tied up over here and they had it all tied up. They were all sitting down waiting. It was a lot of them down there, colored people, but none of our folks there. Quite a few Wrights there. I was told not to catch the train right at once.

When the train got there, I was down the hill and when the porter throwed his hand up, I run up and showed him the ticket and he drove me on up there. When we got to Chicago, there was strict orders not to open that box. But those undertakers tore that box all to pieces.

LULA SMITH: black, wife of Crosby Smith, great-aunt of Till; Money, Mississippi—
The white people, they were all sorry that it happened 'cause it give Mississippi such a hard name when it went out that a child, a minor was killed and murdered like they did, so brutal. It was a hard time. I was very sorry 'cause that was the only child Mamie had. To be mobbed up like that. The little child came down here on a visit.

GUS SMITH: black attorney; Detroit, Michigan—
When I saw that photo in Jet, I couldn't imagine a more gruesome thing. All that to that kid for whistling at a white woman. I believe I was ten or eleven years old when I saw the gruesome photo of the remains of Emmett Till while viewing the latest issue of Jet Magazine. I had heard earlier accounts of his alleged abduction and the attention that was focused on the search for him. My thoughts drifted to stories of a similar fate that had befallen a grandfather I never knew. Grandfather Caesar, they said, was retrieved for the Mississippi river some days after his reported mysterious disappearance. The shock of Till's photo made me wonder whether my grandfather, too, had met such a gruesome end. That photo has fixated in me an image I can't erase from my mind.

JAMES STEWART: Vice Provost and former Director of Black Studies at Pennsylvania State University; Cleveland, Ohio—
In 1955 I was about eight and really not conscious about the level of open hostility and violence practiced against blacks in

Mississippi because my parents had long ago left Mississippi during the Great Depression. But I overheard their conversations about the Till case and picked up a few things that led me to ask them some questions about my history. One of the questions I asked them was were my ancestors slaves prior to the Till case. I had been sheltered from the most horrified aspects of the history of blacks. But the Till case and my visit to Mississippi a couple of years later were probable the pivotal points of moving me toward active involvement in the freedom struggle in my later years.

CURTIS STRONG: black labor-union activist; Gary, Indiana—
I was a union representative at the time. The Till incident was one of those repulsive, revolting type of things. It almost turned you against a whole class of people. It made you think of the ego and the arrogance of the southern white. At that time, I wasn't too far removed from living and going to school to all whites and subject to a lot of discrimination. Although the Civil Rights Movement was not in full bloom until later on, we knew then that something had to be done. And you wanted to do something but did not know what to do. The revolution hadn't caught fire yet. I think it was leading towards it. Till did more to galvanize blacks since the day of Marcus Garvey. Frankly, I think this did more to rekindle it. The Movement is up and down and always has been. I think this was one of the incidents that sparked it more so than the bus boycott.

CHARLES TEAMER: black gas worker; Memphis, Tennessee—
The name Emmett Till is like relating to my brother. I guess tragedy has a way of imbedding itself in your memory. A lot of times insignificant individuals, except for circumstances they get caught up in, get lost in history. Most mass movements are triggered by incidents of violence (police brutality, lynching).

One event could start a riot, a series of violent acts against a people. Mass uprisings come as a result of these violent acts against our people. Emmett Till is a perfect example. And Mississippi is on the cutting edge of revolutionary struggle of our people. The people there have faced the brunt, the people have made their leaders. They are working people who have, out of necessity, to protect themselves, which is essential in any struggle. Till came at a breaking point when people were biding their time until they could strike out. Our history is at the mercy of capitalistic interpretation. The power of truth is timeless and the history of our people is the salvation of our people.

JAMES THOMAS: black lawyer; late thirties; Tallahassee, Florida—
Basically my comments reflect the perceptions of a young black child growing up in a southern city, realizing something seriously wrong had occurred. At this time in childhood when one so young does not recognize one's mortality, I could sense something had occurred that had a chilling and paralyzing affect on those adults around me (parents and other relatives). The atmosphere was filled with a sense of powerlessness—don't do this or that because even the lives of black children were worthless.

SILAS THOMAS: black retired Memphis meat-packing worker (deceased); Memphis, Tennessee—
I feel that he was mobbed. I felt that he wasn't did fair. They tell me the people, especially blacks, down there wouldn't work. They couldn't get no cotton picked, no work done there. That was some of the background of King. He didn't do nothing but whistle at a white woman. But they paid for it; they lost their crops 'cause black people wouldn't work for 'em. The blacks on our job booed at him, the brother of the one that killed Till. They come to waking up after that, the murder. That's what started the ball to rolling. That Till case started it. Something else might have kept it going but that boy started it. They couldn't hire

them [the blacks] for no amount of money. One of the black workers said that before this thing is over with, blacks and whites will all be as one.

CAROLYN BANKS THOMPSON: black public school teacher (deceased); Chicago, Illinois—
I was in Chicago then; I remember my parents talking about how inhumane this was. It was hard to believe that we were in the twentieth century and this could happen. As a child, unless it is happening in your own little sphere of life, it really doesn't impact on you. But later as a teenager, in retrospect, I asked myself what kind of sub-human would perpetrate this kind of atrocity upon another person. It's hard to think that a civilized twentieth century man could do such to another human being. It really hit my mother because my own father had been lynched and burned alive in Arkansas because they [whites] wanted his land and that was their way of taking it; he refused to sell. The rationale they used to justify my father's death was that he whistled at a white woman. As a result of the similarities, my mother was more horrified and appalled. It was like pouring salt on an open wound. My father had been killed only two years before [1953] and my mother hastily remarried (about a year later) so that we could move to Chicago.

IRENE THOMPSON: black political activist and public school teacher; Memphis, Tennessee—
It was singularly the most grotesque event in my life. It came to full fruition in the death of Emmett Till. I was just coming out of college, full of dreams of freedom and awareness of life and still in the "I pledge allegiance to the flag … with liberty and justice for all" stage. All wrapped up and then flung right down in my guts. It was an age of awakening, the catalyst for the thirst for freedom, the catalyst that precipitated the yearning for real freedom, the right to stand up and say, "I am and I am going to be." This was the thing that led me into the sixties. The

death of Emmett Till catapulted us into the Civil Rights Movement.

ORVILLE TOWNSEND: black specialist in vocational rehabilitation and adjunct university instructor; East St. Louis, Illinois—
I was young, and I was angry because it was a clear indication that hate can drive people. The thing that bothered me most was that I feel that fellow had been dealt a very unjust and unfair hand because he was a black youth that was raised up North. When they allowed him to travel South, nobody conditioned him or explained to him that there was a hell of a difference down South. There was a time when, as a black people, we were at a disadvantage, with second-class citizenship. But at least northern bigots wore false faces and had limitations placed on them by the law. When this young man went South, he went into an environment where the majority felt negative toward blacks. In most cases, those white people were the law. So when Emmett crossed the Mason-Dixon Line, it was like he was in a different ballpark. His existence as a black person lost its significance. Basically when he was confronted and he did not yield as the southern blacks did, then he created an atmosphere of hatred; he added rage. Initially when they confronted him, he was not aware of the true danger he was in. By the time events had progressed to the point when he was aware, he had already presented an image of a black person they were not ready to accept. In short, I think that what he said to them in action was that he was their equal as a human being. When you take bigotry, hatred, and rage, and put them together, then it's not difficult to create a situation where people will exceed the limits they began with. I don't think they intended to kill him initially. You had a northern black who went South and did something that blacks were not allowed to do. And when confronted, he refused to conform.

ELEANOR TRAYLOR: black cultural critic and professor of English, Montgomery College, Thomasville, Georgia—
I was terrified; it evoked in me the image of a lynching I had almost seen when I was three years old growing up in Thomasville, Georgia.

WALTER WILLIAMS: black author and professor of Economics; Philadelphia, Pennsylvania—
The Till incident struck me as something offensive. It galvanized black people to focus their outrage against those kinds of injustices. One thing it did to me; it did lead me to punch one of those rebels in the face when I was stationed in Fort Jackson, Florida in 1959; I was twenty-three. One guy in my union, a real red neck, said to me, "I'm from Parkersville; that's where we lynched Emmett Till. It led to a fight, but then it wasn't really a fight. I punched him hard in the face. I had been sent to the South from Philadelphia without being educated about the nature of Southern life style.

CHARLETTA WRIGHT: black co-head nurse at Mississippi Valley State University; Greenwood, Mississippi—
We were angry, we were mad. And it sort of carved a different feeling. As a matter of fact, my aunt, Charlene, and I were youngsters, too. At the time, we sort of began to hate white people because of how the trial came out and every thing like that. We felt that he was a child just like us. It wasn't fair the way the trial came out. So everyone started turning the people down, these people that killed the child. Then they had to move from Money. The whites didn't accept them either into their area. They went to Clarksdale. They refused them. The people, white and black, did not want them in their town because they killed a young person for no reason at all, just because he whistled. Our parents were very protective of us, [especially] my brother, because of this. A lot of times we couldn't go different places because of the fact the parents feared the safety of their children.

Probably that caused a lot of emotions, blacks to have a lot of hostility against in them. It did, it really affected them. I think they looked at Emmett as color. They dealt more with the word color. I think the white man is on an ego trip. He is. You have to be to some sort of trip in order to murder a child. And you have to not love humans yourself. I'm sure he's protective of his own children. Everybody has feeling of their children. Let me tell you this, the reason they [blacks] participated in the murder was that these black people that assisted, two other black men who helped carry this body and put it in the river, had no choice. The man told them he would cut off their food. They were living like on a plantation and they had no food to eat and they kind of lived under this white man. He issued them money for paying gas. You just ought to see it, the area around here. Mississippi has not changed in a hundred years in some areas. All you have to do is travel around. Mississippi has not changed. It's changed on the surface but still you find people subjected to I pay your bills, you do what I say. These black men didn't have no choice. They didn't kill the child, but they assisted.

EDWARD YOUNG: black retired labor-union worker; Chicago, Illinois—
I was working in the Reynold's Aluminum Plant in Chicago. The first thing that crossed my mind when this happened was the Birmingham, Alabama incident similar to the Till case, which this guy was beat up and killed by a couple of white policemen. The reason why he was killed was that he was supposing to whistle at a white girl. In fact, they cut off his penis and put it in his mouth; they beat him unmercifully. He reminded me of Emmett Till cause he was light with curly hair. Naturally, I felt awfully bad, wondering what's gonna happen next, until we do something about it. My reaction was more of a mixed emotion. I hope that the truth is finally coming to light.

UNIDENTIFIED BLACK WOMAN: Greenwood, Mississippi, who did not want to be identified—
Well naturally I felt sad, even if he had of been white, I'd of felt sad. But I was really sorry just the way it happened. That's what hurt. He wasn't nothing but a baby. Every once in a while, your memory goes back to it.

UNIDENTIFIED WHITE MAN: Greenwood, Mississippi, —
I'd rather not identify myself because I've been here all my life, born and raised here. Now, I'm gonna give you an honest opinion, OK? To say that I'm not prejudiced would be a lie 'cause I am. I think anybody says they're not, be they black or white, they not telling the truth 'cause I believe all us are prejudiced to a degree. We were born and raised in this society. As I recall, Emmett was accused of making forward motions, let's say, passes, at a white woman and this is what incited it. 'Course from this on is just hearsay of accounts of what happened 'cause I wasn't anyway that closely associated with any of the people that were involved. I'm trying to be honest without hurting anybody's feeling. Really and truly, the way we grew up around in this neighborhood, this was a no-no back then. Everybody thought that this was just unheard of, this was something that didn't happen—making passes at a white woman. This just wasn't done. It was just something that you [black] didn't do so therefore you thought that anything that happened was justifiable. Really, in the Christian society, it is hard for Christian people to accept this kind of action regardless of the motivation. And if you're gonna think "that vengeance is mine saith the Lord," then you're gonna have to let the Lord take the vengeance. This is what this boils down to. This was taking revenge for an act and the Southern Belt, let's be honest about it, is a Baptist Belt. This is a very religious section. It was morally wrong.

Appendix 4

Mamie, South Bend, Indiana, 1955

MAMIE BRADLEY-MOBLEY: I would like to extend my *appreciation to all of you for coming out tonight, to hear what has happened and to find out what you can do about what has happened. I would like to thank the youth group. How impressed I am by the beautiful job that they are doing here. You young musicians and you young children everywhere. Surely the things that we do here tonight is going to make the way for a better tomorrow. And only the foundation that we lie here that they can build upon. So its up to us, to us grown-ups, to get together and build a foundation for them to build a future upon.*

At this particular time, I would like to introduce to you a gentleman who has stood by during this entire ordeal. We called him the very first day that we found out that Emmett had been kidnapped. He, like so many others, stood by and given of himself and his time very unselfishly. Mr. Mooty and my father went with me to Mississippi to face the trial, or at least a mock trial of Emmett Louis Till's murder. I would like to introduce you to Mr. Rayfield Mooty. He will speak to you for a few minutes, allowing my mother a chance to come.

RAYFIELD MOOTY: *Mr. Chairman, honored guests, first of all, I'd like to extend you my appreciation for the warm invitation you have extended to Mrs. Bradley in bringing her up to your city. I know that you have been waiting quite patiently to hear what's happened in the case in Mississippi. And she just mentioned to you that we have been going so fast since this incident occurred, so we haven't had time to hardly catch our breaths. I'm not going to tell you the mother's reaction, she will explain that to you herself. I am only going to brief you on some of these things that occurred in this case, and before I leave here I hope to be able to tell you what you can do to see that this doesn't happen again in America. Especially this same kind of event. Because I know that you are interested in hearing her story, but also you should be just as much concerned knowing where in this program do you fit. And when you learn what part you have to play in this program, the rest of it will be up to you. There isn't anything that we can do for Emmett Till. Emmett Till is dead and buried. But direct something we can do to see that the rest of the Emmett Till's don't meet with the same fate.*

As Mrs. Bradley pointed out to you, I came into this case, the first day this thing happened. We went all the way through, all the way through, even down into the depths of Mississippi to where the trial was. I want to stop for a minute here to talk about what happened when Emmett's body arrived in Chicago.

This was one of the most trying times that I have ever witnessed. When we looked and found out this casket had come into Chicago, we met it, and we had no idea, no idea of imagination, what that casket held until we followed it to the undertaker's shop. When he got there, the undertaker was looking at the body, he pleaded with his mother to not look at what was in that box. She had made up her mind definitely before, when she first heard that her child had been murdered, it made no difference what it looked like, she would have to see it. When she gave that determined stand and I took it upon myself to lead her to that casket to see what was in there. Some of you saw the pictures, but you didn't see the real thing. I saw it. And when I looked into that casket and she looked into that casket, we stood side-by-side along with her father. Something happened to her. If you would have been there it would have happened to you too. Something happened to me so severe until I can't explain what it was, but there's one thing that keeps ringing in my mind, that this has got to be the last time this kind of a thing happens in America. I don't know what I'm going to do to see to it, I don't think I can handle this whole job by myself. I think it's going to take everybody in America to see that this doesn't happen again.

A lot of things started rolling in my mind. How could I rile up the people of America to know what has happened? Oftentimes (this is not the only murder that has happened in the South, it's not the only link) it just appeared to me that if a hundred thousand people, if a million people could see that body, that it would be enough to keep you up late at night. It would be enough to start you to thinking. When you start to thinking, then you are going to start acting. Because when a normal person is born they are born with five senses. But by the time they reach twenty-one years of age they should be able to develop two more senses. You are born able to taste, to touch, to hear, to see, and to smell. But when you get twenty-one years old, you have to be able to think and then you ought to be able to act. Because when you get about then, they put a ballot in your hand. They don't put it in there until you are old enough to think and act. So that should give you possession of seven senses …

MBM: *You probably have heard snatches of the speeches that we have been making through the country. I don't know how you reacted to them, perhaps you're wondering how I'm standing up here doing it. Well, I'm wondering the same thing, but I haven't really had time to sit down and analyze what was going on. It just seemed that I was caught up in a whirlwind and there was only one thing to do and that was to go and do the best that I could. In doing so, the NAACP had me to come to their New York office, they have sat down and talked to me, they have started to arrange these tours for me, which has really and truly taken a great burden off of my mind. In all of the turmoil, upset, and the daze of what had happened, it was just almost impossible to make a telephone call.*

Back on August 28 when the call first came to the house that Emmett Till had been taken from my uncle's house, I had had no way of knowing or preparing myself for what was fixing to happen. I really didn't know what to do. The first thing that I did was to call my mother, because that is where I had been taking all of my burdens all of my life. When I called her, she said, "Sister, you come right over." And I think that I broke just about every speed record in the city of Chicago getting over to her house. I certainly ignored stop signs and red lights, I just had to depend on the horn to clear the way. For some reason, there wasn't a policeman on the street that morning. I only saw one car and no one was in it. I had decided if anybody did stop me I was going to tell them that I didn't have time to argue—just clear the way to 1626 West Fourteenth Place and I'll talk to you when I get there. But as God would have it, there was nobody to interfere with me that morning and the street was just about deserted.

Then I walked in mother's house, and I just knew that I was going to go in there and throw this burden all on her shoulders and sit down there and see what she was going to do. But as God would have it, when I walked in her door, I found out that she was in worse shape than I was. And for the first time in my life, I was going to have to stand up and take care of my own problems, because there wasn't a soul there who could do it for me.

We had made numerous telephone calls. The first thing we did was to call Michael Crosby down in the state of Mississippi who had lived down there for nine years. We had been wondering for nine years why Crosby went to Mississippi. He had a home in Argo, he had the use of my mother's car, and he ate all of his biscuits and cakes over at our house, so we really didn't see why he wanted to go to Mississippi. But God sent him down there nine years ago and prepared him—helped him to go among the people to be uncle, to be strong, to be a man, to be man enough to get Emmett Till's body out of the state of Mississippi. Out of our family there must be hundreds and perhaps even up to a thousand, but that was the only man in this entire family that could have done the work necessary to get Emmett Till back to Chicago. At last, we know why Crosby went South.

When we started making calls to Mississippi, we got through to Crosby, we got through to one or two other people, but the first thing we noticed was that nobody wanted to talk to us. We called the gentleman on whose place my Uncle Mose lived, and we asked him to take a message to Uncle Mose. He said he couldn't hear good over the telephone, he didn't have a pencil, he didn't have any paper in the house and besides he was old and couldn't see and he couldn't even hear. There was nobody else there to take the message. Well, I don't think much of people who go off and leave an old man in that condition.

We tried calling other people that we had known through the years, name families down in Mississippi. They too, had other business. They couldn't get a message to anybody. Their cars were out of fix. Pretty soon it got so that when we put a call through down there we would hear the person on the other end say that I have nothing to say, I don't want to talk to them. The cotton curtain in Mississippi is tougher than the Iron Curtain in Russia. It's that cotton curtain that we're going to have to penetrate.

We went on like that for several days, from Sunday until Wednesday. During that time I just really can't tell you what all didn't happen. I went out to take care of something, but most of the time I spent there at the telephone taking messages trying to put through calls and just trying my best to find my baby. But Tuesday I had to leave. I got back and the family was all in smiles. They had had three telephone calls. My mother had taken one of the calls, my cousin had taken one, and my stepfather had taken a call. And they met me at the door and said, "Emmett Till's on his way home." For some reason, my heart didn't skip a beat, I said, "How's he coming?" Nobody knew. I said, "Well, is somebody bringing him?"

Well, it was a pretty hard time around there for awhile. Everybody just seemingly gave up all sorts of hope. But I said to my mother, "We can't give up now, if we stop hoping, we'll stop living. We've got to keep going." I sat down again and started taking care of the telephone. I said, "If you will just let me, I'll answer the phone myself, and I'll write everything down," (because I didn't trust my memory, but I would be able to get the message perhaps as good as anybody else). And I had to be doing something; I couldn't just sit still.

When I would go and lie down it felt like I had no right to be in a bed when I didn't know where my baby was. I sent him away from me happy, cheerful, a normal boy, a boy that was excited about a vacation in

Mississippi. I got a letter from my aunt and from my son, one week from the day he left home. And she was just amazed at the job that I had done of bringing Emmett up. And, frankly I was a bit amazed myself, because he had turned out to be a very nice boy. At the age of thirteen, he took over the laundry for me. I guess I've been down to the laundry room six times since last Christmas. And when I went then, it was under protest, because when Emmett started doing the laundry, I found out I wasn't able to do it anymore. About two years ago, Emmett took over my housecleaning. I don't think there are many eleven-year-old boys that take over the mopping and the dusting and the waxing for their parents. But I found out after Emmett went on his vacation, that I couldn't even mop a floor anymore. I was going to leave the house really nice for him. I was supposed to leave the Tuesday after he left. I was going to leave it for him as nice as he had left it for me when he took his vacation. We depended on one another. He said, "Mother, if you go to work, and cook, I'll clean up and wash." And that was the way it was. And not only did he do those things, but if I had painting to be done, or a wall to be washed, that was Emmett's job. He didn't think I could wash the wall good anyway, and I was very happy for him to do it.

As we lived together, we grew up together and I'm sure that I learned just as much from Emmett as Emmett learned from me. One of the things that Emmett taught me, or that I know that he knew, was that he didn't realize that he was a Black boy and had to look up to a White boy. I was taught in school that I was as good as I wanted to be. If I excelled in something in spite of the fact that I was dark, that still made me hold the top spot. It didn't matter that a Colored person or a White person were vying for the same position. Whoever earned it was the one that got it. Consequently, it wasn't until I looked down, that I realized that I was dark. Out of a class of a 130 White children, there were only three Colored that graduated. I happened to have been at the head of that class. And nobody wanted to hold me back because I was dark. I earned my spot and I got it. I have never been race-conscious. I had White friends that I loved just as much as I did the Colored—perhaps even a little bit more. And I still have White friends that I love. And I wouldn't take anything in the world for them. Because they have stood by me, and I know that you can't judge a race by one or two people. Because I know some people in my race that I wouldn't want to be judged by.

I think that the only way that we're going to be able to be a nation, is to get ourselves together because divided we cannot stand. Anybody knows that when there's friction in a house, there's no peace there. Any outsider can walk in and tear everything up. That's just the position we have our country in today. It's the White man against the Black man, the Red man against the Green man, and everybody is against everybody. It's even the Black man against the Black man. All some of these other countries have to do is just walk in and take over because we are so stupid. We are arguing among ourselves until we can't see what we are doing to ourselves. As long as we keep those people down in Mississippi ignorant, we're going to have White men killing Colored boys. And we're going to have other people killing White boys. And we can't have that, because the other nations are looking at us.

I said that I sent Emmett Till down South. I sent him down there a happy boy. He usually went to Argo on the weekends to spend the weekend with my grandmother. And he came home one night, a little bit later than usual and I was waiting for him, I was pretty mad. When he came in he knew about the only way to get around me was to out-talk me. He said, "Mamma, I think the people pick on me when I ride the bus." I said, "What do you mean? Because I was ready and as soon as he got through, I was going to let him know just what I thought of him coming in late." He said, "Well, I think all the women stand over me because they'll know that I'll give them a seat." I said, "Uh huh, who would you give your seat to if a White lady and a Colored lady stood up by you?" He said, "I'd give the seat to the one who had the most packages or the one who was holding a baby." I thought that was a pretty good answer. I mean, I was mostly testing, I didn't know really how Emmett thought about the race problem. Except that I know he's brought many a little White boy to our house and he has always treated them nice. He has pushed them around as much as he pushed the little Colored boys around, and he's treated them as good as he did the little Colored boys. I just knew that he was a normal well-adjusted child, and that's why I thought that I could let him go to Mississippi. But I did warn him that he had a place down there that was a little bit different than Chicago. I told him that if anything happened, even though you think you're perfectly within your right, for goodness' sake take low. If necessary, get on your knees and beg apologies. Don't cross anybody down there because Mississippi is not like Chicago. What you can get away with here, you might not be able to do it there. I said no matter how much it seems that you have the right, just forget your rights while you're in Mississippi.

In time, I called the uncle that was going to take him down there, and I asked him, "When you let the boys go to town, please go with them. Take the car keys. If you get six teenagers together, anything can happen. I didn't really think all of these things, it just seemed that I had to say them. If I exaggerated a little bit, maybe I would make Emmett conscious that he was going to a different place and to be reasonably careful. But I, like everybody else, felt the conditions were changing in Mississippi. I certainly thought that everything was getting better. I couldn't really tell though because I was confining myself to my house and my job. I didn't go out and see what the city's problem was. I felt that I had done pretty good when the government gave me two hours off and I used a half hour of that time to vote. I really thought I was making a noble sacrifice. I didn't go to the different civic meetings and listen to what was happening all over the world. I depended on what I might happen to read as I was rushing through the morning paper just before leaving for work. Now I know that that was very wrong. If I had sat down, if I had made the problems of the nation my problems, maybe I would have had something to say, or maybe I could have done something about the situation before now. Maybe I could have done it without having to lose a son to find out that I had a part to play.

Even though I've lost my son, crying won't get him back. Nothing I can do will get him back. But now I realize that other people's sons are going to go that way. There's a great job that's going to have to be done. People are going to have to be awakened. I certainly was no more than an average citizen, perhaps even a little below average because, just a boy and his mother (and a government worker at that) he didn't have too much. There are many of you sitting here tonight that are in far better condition than my son and I were in. Everything we got we struggled for. So that's proof positive right there that race haters don't care, they don't have a particular group to pick on. If I had been rich, then it could be assumed that they wanted ransom or that they wanted any number of things. But I could have given them anything under the sun hardly if they had asked me for it in return for his life. I was just as average as any of you. And inasmuch as they walked up to my door, you might say, and took my son, and I know beyond a shadow of a doubt that he was not guilty as accused, then they can do the same thing to your sons and your daughters. But it's not for us to get up and hate one another. Rather we're going to have to stand together and love one another, share the problems, and try to work them out together. Because in the United States of America there can be nothing but Americans. We can't have Negroes, and White people, and Jews, and Indians, and Greeks, and what-not. We have to be one. Because only as one unit can we stand.

Finally, I got the news that Emmett Till was dead. The Chicago Tribune *called, but they didn't feel like they wanted to give me the message. They just didn't have the heart to do it. They called a girlfriend of mine and asked her to break it to the family as gently as possible. When she called I was on the phone. She didn't want to talk to me either. But it seemed like I just knew what had happened. So I told her, "For God's sake, whatever it is, let me have it, because I can probably take it better than anybody around here anyway." And that's when she told me that Emmett was found dead in the Tallahatchie River. That his skull was beaten in on the left-hand side, and that he had a chin fan around his neck tied with barbed wire. I wrote the message down on the paper and I turned around to my mother and my aunt (those were the only two I can remember being in the house). I read off what I had written. My aunt started to break down. I said, "Take her out, and don't let her start. For some reason, we don't have time to cry, there's something we've got to do. Maybe tomorrow, maybe the next day—" (and someone said, "Well, maybe you'll never get to cry.") "But right now it's just necessary to think." Well, I really didn't know what to think about because after the child was found dead, I had no doubts that I would get the body. Surely they would let me have that.*

By holding ourselves together, my aunt remembered to call the undertaker, my mother left the house to call Crosby again. She informed Crosby that Bo's body had been found. The potentates down in Mississippi said the minute they got any news of that boy they would notify my uncle. Instead, when Bo's body was found, it was in such horrible shape when the sheriff called an undertaker and ordered him to bury that body immediately. He didn't even have time to let that undertaker go and wash the mud off the body and prepare it for burial. The main thing to do was to get that body in the ground so nobody could see it.

As God would have it, we didn't stop and cry, we didn't cut ourselves off. Only by not wasting any time, were we able to get that body on the way out of Mississippi. We got hold of Crosby and Crosby went and got a sheriff and went down to where they were burying the body. There were twenty men that had dug a two foot grave. They were getting that body away as fast as they could. Believe me, if night had fallen, with that body in the ground, nobody would have ever seen it again. Because it wasn't going to stay there very long. Crosby went down and asked the undertaker if he would take the body and prepare it for shipment. The Colored undertaker said, "Well, Mrs. Smith, I'll tell you the truth, I'm afraid to let Nate catch that body in my undertaker's shop. But I will take it back there and you will get somebody to get it out of there before night. My orders are to bury it and bury it immediately."

They went on back to town and my uncle called a White undertaker in Charleston, Mississippi. That undertaker came over to look at that body and he said, "Yeah, I could embalm it. And I will do so. But you'll have to promise that this top will never come off of this box, otherwise I'll have nothing to do with it." Well, Crosby wasn't in a position to argue about anything. But he promised, and he intended to keep that promise. When Crosby called me, he said, "I'm coming. I'm bringing Bo with me. I'll be at the station at such-and-such a day." I said, "Okay, we'll meet you." But I didn't know how I was going to react when I saw that big box come off of that train. It just seemed terrible that I would send my boy down there happy and alive and he would come back to me in a pine box. And that's one of the times that I broke down. But that still was nothing, really.

They took that body to the undertaker shop. We went in there to see if we could see the body. The undertaker met us and he said, "For God's sake, Mrs. Bradley, don't look. I'm a friend of the family, and as a friend, I'm telling you don't look." I said, "Mr. Rayner, I have to see it if I have to break it open myself. I'm not asking you to, I'm telling you to." He shook his head and he turned around and he went back. I think Mr. Mooty went and looked first. When they came back to me, he said, "Well, if you insist, you come on."

I turned to my father and I turned to Mr. Mooty, and I said, "Will one of you get on each side?" because I just didn't know if I was going to be able to make it or not. I wanted to, but I didn't know how long my strength was going to last. They got on each side and we started walking. That was about the longest walk and the hardest walk I've ever had to make. When I stood up over that casket and looked down in that box, the thing that I saw down there, changed my mind completely. I started crying then. And as Mr. Mooty said, I got real mad. And I've been mad ever since.

What I saw in that box was not like anything I've ever seen before in my life. I had been reading funny books because Bo read them. I read them too. Not so much to see what he was reading, but because I liked to read them. We read the spooky kind until they were taken off the market. In these spooky books I have seen everything that I can imagine—things beyond the imagination. But what I saw in that casket hadn't been touched in a funny book. I looked down and I saw that there was a hole in my son's head that was big enough to stick your hands through. It looked like it had been made with an ax. I said, "Oh, my God!" And then I looked a little bit further and I saw that there was a hole in his jaw. You could see that every tooth in the back of his head had been knocked out. And he had twenty-eight real nice ones; I was very proud of them. I looked at his mouth and it was choked open and his tongue was bulged out of his mouth. His lips were pushed back and only a few teeth remained right in front there. I shook my head again. They even had the nerve to put a bullet hole right up over his ear. I do remember asking, "Was that bullet necessary, because surely he was dead before they did all of that." You just wondered what kind of a person, or what kind of people, or would they be human beings who would do a job like that. The more I looked, the more confused I became. Finally, I said, "Well I've got to look down here and really look good and see if I can find Emmett, because that's not the Emmett that I knew." After looking, and after searching, I found my boy. I tried not to, I didn't want to. But it had to be and it was. I asked Mr. Rayner if he would be good enough to take the body out of the casket and lay it on a board, because I wanted to look at it real good. I couldn't see it down in those satin covers. He looked at me again, as if to wonder what on earth in the world—is she crazy or what? But he just shook his head and went ahead and did as I asked him to do. When the body got here it didn't have any clothes on it. It was just covered up in a whole lot of white powder, because nobody was supposed to see it anyway. But I couldn't look through all of that steel and tell whether that was Emmett. I couldn't say that I was burying Emmett until I looked to see for myself. I worked around that body and that's when I ran into another shock, when I looked at the left side of Emmett's face. And I looked at that left side, it looked like somebody had taken a knife through, it was made in a crisscross shape. They had just sat down and had chop, chop on the side of his face. And the right eye had been picked out. It seemed like it had been picked out with a nut picker. And the right eye was almost out, it was just hanging. I had to examine that eye, examine those teeth. I started to examine the ear and that's when I found out that the entire back of the head had been knocked off. I said, "Roy, anybody that wants to look at this, can see it. I'm tired of stuff being covered up. If some of these lids had been pulled off of Mississippi a long time ago, then something like this wouldn't be happening today. So far as my personal feelings are concerned, they don't count. Because the thing that has happened to me now is more than I will ever have to face again. I can take it just a little bit longer. I have lost the only thing that I held really precious and dear beside my mother and father." And if my son had sacrificed his life like that, I didn't see why I should have to bear the burden of it alone. There was a lesson there for everybody. Because if it happened to him, it can happen again. And I've never been one to sit by and accept defeat anyway. Not if I could see a way out of it. And if I couldn't do anything else but raise a lot of sand, I would do that. So that temper, or whatever you want to call it, came in a little bit handy this time.

I know my mother has been trying to get me to shut up for about twenty-nine years. Every time I go to shut up it looks like that's about the best opportunity to go to talk and so I start all over again. Well, I'll tell you. As long as somebody wants to hear what's going on in our United States that's the land of the free and the home of the brave, as long as you're willing to try to get up and do something about it (and I don't think you would be here tonight unless you did want to do something about it), as long as that condition exists, then I will be before you. I will try to tell you, because I think that we all have children, and I think that we want to leave them a heritage a little bit greater than ours. We want to leave them a land that they can be proud of. Some of the letters that I have gotten have told me that we should go back where we came from. I don't know where I came from. My mother told me that I was born on the Tallahatchie River. Well, I don't want to go back there, that's for sure. And if they're talking about Africa, well I don't know anything at all about Africa. The climate might not agree with me. This is where I was born and this is where I was raised. This is where I intend to stay. But I'm not going to stay here backed up against the wall afraid to open my mouth. Because if I have to live in fear then I think that I'm a lot better off dead. That little baby sitting on that floor—she shouldn't ever have to know that she's Black and that she's inferior. If she grows up and she's smart enough to work a crossword puzzle, she should be given credit for working that puzzle. If she's able to sew a fine seam, then surely she shouldn't be denied a job because her face is black. I feel that we should stand up and be counted. I don't know how the men feel, but I know that when women die to bring a child into the world, we don't want anybody to bother that kid. We're going to discipline him or her the best that we can. But we don't want anybody kicking them around. You'll fight more for your children that you will for yourself. Because I know a lot of things I have taken on the chin. I've fought a little bit, I said that I wasn't going to take it, but I learned how to live with it. But when they picked on Emmett, they just did the wrong thing. And so help me God, until my dying day, I'm going to be fighting that thing. I'm not going to be fighting color, I'm not going to be fighting creed, I'm not going to be fighting anybody's belief, so long as it's a safe and sound one. So long as it doesn't reach out and destroy me or destroy somebody else. But I feel like we should stand up, we should make a stand once and for all, we should say that we're going to live as men and women, as long as we're paying these first-class taxes, we're going to demand this first-class citizenship that goes with it. I don't feel like going down to the Bureau of Internal Revenue on taxpaying day and they tell me, "Come on and pay your tax." And then I ask for just a little bit of freedom and I'm told, "You can't have it." If they were telling me, "You're Black, Mrs. Bradley, you'll only have to pay second-class taxes, then I would expect that second-class citizenship. But they're not making any allowances for me on income tax day. They're not making any concessions for me on any other things either. They're asking me to pay, they're asking me for the best that's in me, and I want the best in return. Oh, my God if our children have to come along, if we have to be afraid of the man next door or the woman over there, then we don't have very much to live.

We buried Emmett. The state of Mississippi said that that was not Emmett. They said that it was impossible for a body to deteriorate that much in that length of time. But what they didn't say, they didn't bring out that the body was badly beaten, that the river water had bursted the skin and it had pealed off the body. The water was hot, the beating was brutal. Then to beat him, they didn't hear his cries. They didn't touch them whatsoever. This one little Colored boy that did hear them said that he heard screams coming from that barn about an hour and a half. He cried for God, he cried for his mother, he pleaded with them. But they were having such a good time, so they didn't consider that he was a human being. I don't see myself how he stood the beating. But when they got good and through, when they got good and tired, then they took Emmett and put a canvas over the truck and dumped him in the Tallahatchie River with a [ginmill's] band around his neck. Oh, Emmett wasn't supposed to show up anymore. If they had thought he was going to show up, they never would admit they had gone to my uncle's house and taken him away.

But as God would have it, three days after he was dumped into that river, his feet came up and a little

White boy saw his feet sticking there. He called the people that he knew—his friend, his father, or somebody. They got a man with a boat, they went out there and they got Emmett, they took this band from around his neck and put it in another boat and got him to the shore. They called the sheriff. The sheriff already knew that a little Colored boy from Chicago was missing. But he didn't bother to report to anybody that he had found a body or that my Uncle Moses Wright had identified Emmett by the ring on his finger that said, "L. T." Louis Till was his father, who died overseas. As God would have it, they didn't get the body in the ground. But this sheriff stood up in the courtroom and said that when he saw this body he didn't know if it was a White man or a Colored man. They called a doctor to the scene. He signed the death certificate, that this was a Negro. His name was Emmett Louis Till, age fourteen, resident of Chicago, Illinois. He did all of that. But when he stood up on the witness stand, he too, didn't know if it was a White man or a Colored man. Still, the state of Mississippi sent me three death certificates, and it was on the basis of these three death certificates that I collected his Metropolitan Life Insurance (and they don't pay off unless they know they're paying on the right individual). They made so many mistakes, but God wouldn't let it be a perfect crime. In a way I feel that it had to be. Because if that hadn't happened, I wouldn't be standing up here tonight, I wouldn't be worried as to whether the NAACP had fifteen million Negroes and as many Whites as possible joining their forces to fight for democracy. I would be home perhaps arguing with Emmett about wearing out shoes so fast because that's the way I spent most of my time. I had never done any public speaking before.

People have asked me how I do it. And as I told you before, I don't know how I do it. But it's something I believe in, I feel that it's through the NAACP, and through we people who will get behind the NAACP, that's going to make the difference in our today and in our tomorrow. And I'm with them one hundred percent. It's not a job that they can do by themselves. I, too, have sat aside and criticized the way things were run, but it never had occurred to me to get in there and try to help run. Well I'm in here now and I'm willing to perform any services they ask of me. I feel like when my job is done, when there's a better place carved out of this democracy for us, when justice and freedom and democracy last until they get to you and me, then I will feel it is time for me to go home and try to make a new life for myself. I feel like I have fifteen million sisters and brothers that I'm partially responsible for and every child in this United States, part of him belongs to me. So with your help and with my help and with the help of the NAACP and mankind as a whole, we can make this United States the place that it was originally intended to be. We can make it what our forefathers and what the other people who came over here from the other countries, to carve out was a life where everybody could be free and equal. Well, we'll have to help them do it. There's a job for us to do too. And there's one thing that we'll have to remember. Nobody is going to walk out and hand you anything on a silver platter. Just because you're good, nobody walks up and hands you a Cadillac. You go out and work for it. You're going to have to work for your freedom and you're going to have to buy it. To me it's just as important to buy five hours' worth of freedom as it is to buy a fifth of Scotch, because you can do more with the freedom than you can with the Scotch. I want to thank you all for listening so attentively.

Bibliography

"100,000 Across Nation Protest Till Lynching." *The Chicago Defender*, 1 Oct. 1955: 2.

Adams, Olive Arnold. *Time Bomb*. New York: The Mississippi Regional Council of Negro Leadership, 1956.

Allen, Barbara, and William Lynwood Montell. *From Memory to History: Using Oral Sources in Local Historical Research*. Nashville, TN: The American Association for State and Local History, 1981.

Atkins, Joe. "Slain Chicago Youth Was a 'Sacrificial Lamb.'" *The Clarion-Ledger Daily News*, Jackson, MI, 25, Aug. 1985: 1.

Baldwin, James. *Blues for Mr. Charlie*. New York: Dell Publishing, 1964.

_____. *The Murder and the Movement*. Edited by Rich Samuels. Chicago: WMAQ TV, 1985.

Bates, Arthenia J. "Lost Note." *Seeds Beneath the Snow*. Washington, DC: Howard Univ. Press, 1969.

Bennett, Lerone, Jr. *Before the Mayflower: A History of the Negro in America, 1619-1964*. New York: Penguin Books Inc., 1961.

Bergman, Peter M. *The Chronological History of the Negro in America*. New York: The New American Library, 1969.

Berry, Mary Frances, and John W. Blassingame. *Long Memory: The Black Experience in America*. New York: Oxford Univ. Press, 1982.

Bethune, Mary McLeod. "My Secret Talks with FDR." In *The Negro in Depression and War*, edited by Bernard Sternsher. Chicago: Quadrangle Books, 1969.

Birchman, Robert L. "10,000 Jam Till Mass Meet Here." *Chicago Defender*, 1 Oct. 1955: 1.

Blaustein, Albert P., and Robert L. Zangrando. *Civil Rights and the American Negro: A Documentary History*. New York: Washington Square Press, Inc., 1968.

Booker, Simeon. In "The Murder and the Movement," by Rich Samuels, National Broadcasting Company, Inc., 1985.

_____. "30 Years Ago: How Emmett Till's Lynching Launched Civil Rights Drive." Jet, 17 June, 1985: 12-13.

Bradley, Mamie. "Mamie Bradley's Untold Story." *The Chicago Daily Defender*, 29 Feb. 1956: 5.

_____. Tape-recorded speech. South Bend, IN, 1955.

Bradley-Mobley, Mamie. Tape-recorded interview. Chicago, IL, 6 January 1988.

_____. Tape-recorded interview. Chicago, IL, 24 March 1988.

Branch, Taylor. *Parting the Waters: American in the King Years 1954-63*. New York: Simon and Schuster, 1988.

Brooks, Gwendolyn. "The Last Quatrain of the Ballad of Emmett Till." *Selected Poems.* New York: Harper & Row, 1963.

Brownmiller, Susan. *Against Our Will: Men, Women and Rape.* New York: Simon & Schuster, 1975.

Burtoun, Paul. "Mose Wright Prepares to Leave Home." *New York Times,* 1 October 1955: 2.

Carver, Theo. Telephone interview. November 1987.

Catarow, Ellen. *Moving the Mountain.* Old Westbury, New York: Feminist Press, 1980.

Chambliss, Alvin O. Telephone interview. November 1987.

Cleaver, Eldridge. *Soul on Ice.* New York: Dell Publishing, 1968.

Douglass, Mary. *Purity and Danger.* London: Routledge & Kegan Paul, 1966.

Duster, Alfreda M., ed. *Crusade for Justice: The Autobiography of Ida B. Wells.* Chicago: The Univ. of Chicago Press, 1970.

Evans, Walker. "South Street 1932," photograph.

Franklin, John Hope. *From Slavery to Freedom: A History of Negro Americans.* New York: Alfred A. Knopf, 1980.

Garfinkel, Herbert. *When Negroes March.* New York: Atheneum, 1973.

Giddings, Paula. *When I Where I Enter: The Impact of Black Women on Race and Sex in America*. New York: Bantam Books, 1984.

Hernton, Calvin C. *Sex and Racism in America*. New York: Doubleday & Company, 1965.

Higginbotham, A. Leon Jr. *In the Matter of Color: Race and the American Legal Process*. New York: Oxford Univ. Press, 1978.

Holland, Endesha Ida Mae. "From the Mississippi Delta." Unpublished, 1987.

_____. Telephone interview. November 1987.

Hudson-Weems, Clenora. *Emmett Till: The Impetus for the Modern Civil Rights Movement*. Doctoral dissertation, University of Iowa, Iowa City, May 1988.

_____. "The Unearthing of Emmett Till: A Compelling Process." *The Iowa Alumni Review*, October 1988: 18-23.

Huie, William Bradford. In *My Soul Is Rested,* edited by Howell Raines. New York: Viking Penguin Books, 1953.

Jacques-Garvey, Amy, ed. *Philosophy and Opinions of Marcus Garvey*. San Francisco, CA: Julian Richardson Associates, Publishers, 1967.

Jet Magazine. "GI Buddies Say Till's Dad Was 'Railroaded' in Italy." 3 Nov. 1955: 4-5.

Jones, Delmos J. "Towards a Native Anthropology." *Human Organization*, Vol. 29, No. 4, (1970): 251.

Jordan, David. "Land of the Till Murder Revisited." In *Ebony*, edited by Clotye Murdock Larsson. March 1986: 58.

_____. "Slain Chicago Young Was a 'Sacrificial Lamb.'" *The Clarion-Ledger Daily News*, edited by Joe Atkins, Jackson, MS, 25 Aug. 1985: 1-2.

Jordan, Winthrop D. *White Over Black*. Baltimore, MD: Penguin Books, Inc., 1968.

King, James S. Telephone interview. November 1987.

King, Martin Luther, Jr. *Stride Toward Freedom*. New York: Ballantine Books, 1958.

Logan, Rayford W. *The Negro in the United States*. Princeton, NJ: D. Van Nostrand Company, Inc., 1957.

"Looking for Justice." *Chicago Defender*, Chicago, IL, 22 Oct. 1955: 1.

Martin, Tony. *Race First*. Dover, Mass.: The Majority Press, 1976.

Matisse, Henri. Cited in *The History of Photography*. By Beaumont Newhall, New York: The Museum of Modern Art, 1964.

McGlaun, Clyde. Telephone interview. November 1987.

McLemore, Richard Aubrey. *A History of Mississippi, Volume II.* Hattiesburg: Univ. & College Press of Mississippi, 1973.

Meier, August, and Elliott Rudwick. *From Plantation to Ghetto.* New York: Hill and Wang, 1966.

Milligan, Arthenia B. Telephone interview. November 1987.

Moody, Anne. *The Coming of Age in Mississippi.* New York: Dell Publishing, 1968.

Mooty, Rayfield. Speech under the auspices of the NAACP. South Bend, Ind., Oct. 1955.

_____. Tape-recorded interview. Chicago, IL, April 1986.

_____. Tape-recorded interview. Chicago, IL, May 1986.

_____. Tape-recorded interview. Chicago, IL, 19 July 1986.

Murdock, Clotye. "Land of the Till Murder." *Ebony,* April 1956: 91.

Myrdal, Gunnar. *An American Dilemma.* New York: Harper & Brothers, 1944.

Newhall, Beaumont. *The History of Photography.* New York: The Museum of Modern Art, 1964.

Parker, Wheeler. In "The Murder and the Movement," by Rich Samuels, National Broadcasting Company, Inc., 1985.

_____. Tape-recorded interview, Chicago, IL, 19 July 1986.

Payne, Ethel L. "Army Gave Till Facts to Eastland." *Chicago Defender*, Chicago, IL, 22 Oct. 1955: 1.

Pitts, George. "Violence Continues to Fester." *The Pittsburgh Courier*, New Orleans, LA, 24 Sept. 1955: 4.

Popham, John N. "Kidnapping Case Revived in South." *The New York Times*, 30 Oct. 1955.

_____. "Mississippi Jury Frees 2 in Killing." *The New York Times*, 24 Sept. 1955: 38.

Quarles, Benjamin. *The Negro in the Making of America*. London: Collier-MacMillan Ltd., 1969.

Rayner, A. A., Jr. Tape-recorded interview. Chicago, IL, 19 July 1986.

Roberts, Bishop Isaiah. Tape-recorded interview. Chicago, IL, 20 July 1986.

Rose, Arnold. *The Negro in America*. Boston: The Beacon Press, 1948.

"Steelworkers Condemn Racial Slaying of Boy." *Steel Labor: The Voice of the United Steelworkers of America—C.I.O.* Indianapolis, Ind., Oct. 1955: 11.

Thompson, Paul. *The Voice of the Past: Oral History*. Oxford: Oxford Univ. Press, 1978.

Trelease, Allen W. *White Terror: The Ku Klux Klan Conspiracy and Southern Reconstruction*. New York: Harper & Row, 1971.

Turner, Darwin. *Black American Literature*. Columbus, OH: Charles E. Merrill Publishing Co., 1970.

Tuttle, William. *Race Riot: Chicago and the Red Summer of 1919*. New York: Atheneum Publisher, 1970.

Williams, Gladys. "The Ballads of Gwendolyn Brooks." In *A Life Distilled: Gwendolyn Brooks, Her Poetry and Fiction,* edited by Maria K. Mootry and Gary Smith. Urbana & Chicago: Univ. of Illinois Press, 1987.

Williams, Juan. *Eyes on the Prize: America's Civil Rights Years, 1954-1965*. New York: Viking Penguin Inc., 1987.

Woodward, C. Vann. *Origins of the New South, 1877-1913*. Baton Rouge, LA: Louisiana State Univ. Press, 1971.

_____. *The Strange Career of Jim Crow*. New York: Oxford Univ. Press, 1957.

Wright, Simeon. Tape-recorded interview. Chicago, IL, 19 July 1986.

_____. In "The Murder and the Movement," by Rich Samuels, National Broadcasting Company, Inc., 1985.

Index